DOROT

CALLED BY

DOROTHY KERIN

CALLED BY CHRIST TO HEAL

by

DOROTHY MUSGRAVE ARNOLD

First published 1965
Third impression 1969
Fourth impression 1972

ISBN 0 340 00625 0

Printed by K&SC (Printers) Ltd., 19/27 Grove Hill Road, Tunbridge Wells, Kent.

Author's Note

THE papers in which Dorothy Kerin's mystical experiences are recorded were given to the author by Dorothy to be made known to the world after her death. There was never any thought on her part of seeking glorification for herself. Throughout her life, everything she did in connection with her work was done solely for the glory of God, and for the healing and helping of His sick and suffering children. In common with the great mystics, she shrank from revealing these manifestations of the wonderful graces God bestowed upon her. But we live in an age when materialism is dominant, and rejection of the supernatural the normal attitude of most men and women, and it is right therefore that the full story of this dedicated life, lived so close to God, should stand before the world as a witness that He does intervene, as He has ever done, in the affairs of those whose belief in His willingness and ability to do so is the motive power of their day-to-day living.

"Ask and ye shall receive . . ." Jesus did not have in mind the 'doubting Thomases' of this world when He spoke these words, but those whose faith in Him is rooted in the very ground of their being, as was the case with His servant Dorothy Kerin.

D.M.A.

A Tribute to Dorothy Kerin

From The Lord Bishop of Coventry

SAINTS are rare phenomena. They do not make their appearance frequently, nor are they limited to any one Church or denomination. God raises His Saints in every part of the world and in every religious persuasion.

A Saint is usually, though not always, a person with a message peculiarly relevant to the generation in which he lives. Dorothy Kerin's message was simple but necessary. She believed with all her heart that God, Who heals normally through physicians, surgeons and nurses, can also heal through prayer and through the touch of a dedicated life.

That Dorothy Kerin was used by God to heal diseases apparently unresponsive to any other treatment, is undoubted and amply proven.

It was not my privilege to meet Dorothy Kerin until later in her life, but from that moment I met her frequently and always the impression she made on me was twofold – she radiated peace and faith.

I have seen her surrounded by milling crowds; I have seen her before and after making an important speech; I have seen her in the middle of a long night's journey by car – for she always motored home after every evening meeting – always and invariably there was about her a shining, radiant calm, a strange but healing poise. One could not worry or be tense in her presence for she was so filled with peace herself that it was communicated to others.

This inward peace was built upon her faith. Never in all my life have I met anybody with such a remarkable faith. She believed that God could, and on occasions (but not always) would, work along a certain direction, whether that direction was the healing of a diseased person or the provision of a sum of money, from that moment on she never gave it another thought. She knew that it would happen – and it did.

We ordinary mortals who worry and wonder and have doubts and fears, could not but marvel in the presence of a faith so sublime and effective.

Such faith did not come easily. It was the result of long years of sacrificial prayer and holiness. Day by day she would rise at 4.30 a.m and spend the next hours in prayer and in prayerful writing of letters Her intercessory prayer list and her correspondence were immense, and the more she travelled the longer that list became and the more numerous her letters.

For seventy years Dorothy Kerin lived as a shining light – beginning and ending her life as an ardent Anglican, living and serving His Church with devotion and zeal.

Now she has gone to her well-earned rest and reward, but she has left behind her a shining example which has been inherited by her valiant and dedicated staff at Burrswood, and she has left a challenge – the challenge to believe and trust in the supernatural, to put our whole confidence in a God who can do all things, "beyond all that we ask or think".

May the challenge of the life and work of Dorothy Kerin recall the Church to her first duty – to love and trust and obey our Lord and Saviour Jesus Christ and to believe that His miracle working power is still available today.

I commend this book, simply but movingly written by one who knew Miss Kerin well. I hope that it will bring comfort, healing and inspiration to many.

CUTHBERT COVENTRY

The Bishop's House,
Coventry,
Warwickshire.

March 1964

Contents

PART THREE

GATHERING OF THE SHEAVES

List of Illustrations

Acknowledgements

I SHOULD like to make grateful acknowledgement to all those friends of Burrswood who have kindly allowed me to publish their letters and personal narratives, and also Bishop Loyd's next of kin for giving me permission to publish some of his letters to Dorothy Kerin. I should also like to thank Desclee & Cie, S.A. for their permission to quote from *The Spiritual Life* by Father Tanquerey; likewise A. R. Mowbray & Co. Ltd. for permission to quote from R. P. Stacey Waddy's book, *Bishop Loyd: Missionary and Bishop*; the Bishop of Coventry for permission to include extracts from his addresses to the Fellowship; and lastly I am indebted to "G. R-M." for permission to quote part of an article that appeared under his signature in the French Protestant weekly *Reforme* on the occasion of Dorothy Kerin's visit to Paris in May, 1961.

I should particularly like to thank G. P. W. Earle, B.A.(Oxon.), to whom I am deeply indebted for his unfailing encouragement and help in reading the book in typescript, and also for reading the proofs.

D.M.A.

Introduction: The Charismatic Gift

by Eric Abbott, Dean of Westminster

I NEVER met Dorothy Kerin. Once, a few months before her death, I saw her in a television programme which set out to describe the life and work of Burrswood.

It is obvious that Dorothy Kerin had a special divine gift of healing, a 'charisma'. Charismatic gifts are bestowed of God through the Holy Spirit upon lay, no less than upon ordained members of Christ's mystical Body, upon women and upon men.

Some need, some crisis, and, we may add, some neglected aspect of the Church's ministry, evokes the use of this gift and discovers it to the possessor, often to his or her own surprise, but at some key moment of his or her life.

The recognition of the gift is accompanied by awe, which is followed by long and deep consideration, and by a sense of being an instrument in the hands of Another, despite personal unworthiness and inadequacy. The spirit of personal dedication increases, and as a result of a measure of reverent experimentation the 'signs' of the charisma are repeated and the gift and calling become unmistakable. This is not the same thing as 'total success', for total success is not given in this fallen world, but it means 'sufficient success', and real 'signs of the Kingdom of God', and a vocation offered to God for His glory and to the Church for its edification and to mankind for its help in need.

Such charismatic gifts are always a responsibility to their possessor, for the charismatic person is responsible to God for the true use of the gift. Unless rightly accepted and used, the gift could be a temptation or a burden. The gift defines the vocation of the person who has it; there will be joy in it, but there will also be pain; there will be power in it, but also limitation; there will be an irreducible measure of publicity, and that never deliberately sought, but the greater part of the vocation of the person will be a hidden and interior life, in which our Lord confers upon His servant the fellowship of His sufferings as well as the power of His resurrection; and there will be some matters of moral and mystical union between the disciple and the Lord, both of joy and of pain, which are of such intimacy that they can never be spoken of.

The charismatic person is not only responsible to God but also to the Church, and this relationship is not always easy, nor is it always perfectly achieved. The ideal is that the charisma should be exercised within the Church, under its authority, with its glad and discerning approval, discerning because we are bidden to "test every spirit", glad because we are to see the Lord working with us "with signs following". Often there is some tension, for the gift, being of the Holy Spirit, cannot be quenched, but the Church is cautious, and, in the matter of the healing ministry, still somewhat uncertain, hesitant and afraid. But when we are given a charismatic person with great holiness of life (likewise a divine gift) and unmistakable ministry, evidenced by signs and acknowledged by the Church, then we can indeed give thanks.

The power of healing is the power of the risen Christ and this power resides in the whole Church. The whole Church is a healing agency in a world of sin and suffering. Charismatic persons incarnate and concentrate in themselves the power that is spread abroad in the Church at large. Charismatic persons are always rare.

Therefore when such a person is taken away from us by death, a testing time follows. The institution may be well founded, its spirit true, its intention clear, its policy defined. There may be a legacy of personal power and inspiration bequeathed by the founder around whom the institution grew. We may ask God that a double portion of the founder's spirit may rest upon us who seek to continue the work. But nothing alters the fact that the head has been taken from us, and in terms of 'charisma' there may well be no direct succession. For around the charismatic person there may have been gathered friends, intercessors, priests, doctors, nurses, helpers of many sorts, all of whom share in the spirit which informs the healing work. But it is very possible, and in no way culpable, that to none of these has the same particular charisma be given.

What then do we do in such a case? We do not grieve as men without hope. We do not think that the great work begun has come to an end. We remember the founder thankfully, but not slavishly. We have a sense of the way she would have done things and the spirit in which she would have acted, but we know also that she would have bidden us go forward and judge and decide for ourselves. We know that she would have prayed that her departure, so far from diminishing the grace and power of the Spirit in our midst, would rather increase that grace and power. We shall therefore give prayerful and careful attention to the very real spiritual problem, how God would have us treat the memory of our founder. For if a Saint of God has passed by, how can we both keep her *and* let her go, retain the secret and the grace that were hers and yet in our own particular way go beyond them, and advance into the vocation which is now ours through her legacy?

Those with a special charisma are rare, but the Church of God continues. The Church of God is a Spirit-filled Body. Thus those of us who are left, bereaved though we may be, will go forward, using those gifts of the Spirit which God bestows, "dividing to every man severally as He will". The work which Dorothy Kerin began enters now into its second phase, and it is a phase which will ask for great wisdom and skill, in the power of prayer and faith working through love in the group who, as a group, succeed to her unique leadership.

All of us who thank God on the remembrance of Dorothy Kerin and know sympathetically and intuitively what her friends and helpers at Burrswood are experiencing, will pray that this wisdom will not be withdrawn from them.

"God buries His workmen but continues His work."

PART ONE

The Years of Preparation

CHAPTER I

Foreshadowings

FOR half a century, from 1912 until her death in January, 1963, a saint moved among us to exercise in all the beauty and compulsion of holiness her healing and redemptive ministry. This she did in obedience to God's command laid upon her at the time of her miraculous healing "to comfort the sorrowing, heal the sick and give faith to the faithless".

The story begins with the raising by our Lord Jesus Christ of Dorothy Kerin, in her early girlhood, from a bed of sickness, when she could be said to have already crossed the threshold of death, a story which is unparalleled in its moving similarity to the Gospel stories of miraculous healings. She has testified in her writings; in pulpits up and down this country and abroad; in the course of interviews, and in conversations, that many years ago at the time of her healing, she had a personal encounter with the Living Lord, adding with emphasis, "by this, I mean that I met Him face to face".

From this momentous encounter have proceeded all the events recorded in this book. It is the record of years of selfless ministry which in a world darkened by disease, suffering and fear has shone as a beacon of light and hope to countless numbers.

Dorothy Kerin has told the story of her miraculous healing with great simplicity and beauty in her book *The Living Touch*. "My healing", she wrote, "came from God alone; to Him be the glory. God is the same yesterday, today and forever. There was no earthly intermediary. What our Lord did in Galilee and along the banks of the Jordan 2000 years ago, He can and does do now."

This is the glorious Truth she fearlessly proclaimed to an unbelieving and materialistic world; this is the Reality abundantly demonstrated in her beautiful Home of Healing at Burrswood, at Services of Divine Healing held in her Church of Christ the Healer and in churches of all denominations in this and other countries; this is the Gospel of Good Tidings our Lord Jesus Christ laid upon His sanctified servant to bring back to the very centre of His Church's sacramental activities.

Ireland, land of faith in a faithless age, claims Dorothy Kerin as one of her children. Her father's family came from County Clare, and the Catholic tradition was strong in her. Ireland has produced many saints and saintly men and women. She remains today what she has always been: a storehouse of holy souls from which religious houses everywhere draw their recruits to lead lives of contemplative and intercessory prayer, or to spend themselves in selfless service in every field of Christian endeavour. Among Dorothy's ancestors figures Saint Keiran who legend says was the first man in Ireland to lay down his life for Christ's sake.

She was born on November 28th, 1889. Three brothers and a younger sister shared in the family life. She tells in her book *The Living Touch* of her deep devotion to her father. Her mother, a woman of great gentleness and sweetness of character, was a gifted singer and early inculcated in her children a love of music and all things good and beautiful. The question is sometimes asked, "Was Dorothy Kerin an ordinary child? Did she in her earliest years show signs of her remarkable destiny?" She has often said, when referring to her miraculous healing with the humility so characteristic of her, "Why, you may ask, did this thing happen to Dorothy Kerin? Certainly not because she had any virtue or merit; she was just an ordinary person like yourselves."

It is improbable that Dorothy could ever have been described as an ordinary person. She certainly was not so at the time of her healing, nor subsequently. If the veil that conceals her childhood from us could be lifted, the truth of the ancient adage that the child is the father to the man would at once become apparent. This is borne out by a story which she told a large gathering of the Burrswood International Fellowship in the Church of Christ the Healer on the occasion of the forty-ninth anniversary of her miraculous healing. This is what she then said:

"I would like to tell you a story, if I may. It is a story full of spiritual significance to me, and I want to share it with you, because there was a wonderful indication this morning that it was in God's pattern that I should do so. How many of you have wondered why you see such evidences of acorns and oak leaves at Burrswood? You see them in every conceivable place; you'll find them on the foundation stone; you'll find them in the decorations of the ceiling of this church, and everywhere they hang. It is because to me they have this special significance. One day, when I was a child, our Lord Jesus came to me, and in His Hand He held a little brown object, and He said: 'Tend this with obedience, and I will water it with the dew of my love, and one day you shall behold a mighty oak.' That little brown object was an acorn, and those acorns have pursued me through my life. They come in the most unexpected way from various sources. And today that little acorn is represented in a mighty oak in this Church of Christ the Healer. Now, as this Church extends its branches, and drops its acorns, I pray that there will be many who will gather up those acorns, and tend them with obedience, and that our Lord will water them with the dew of His love, and that they may be planted in His Kingdom."

Ordinary children are not visited from on high to be shown visions of this nature. Rather is Dorothy to be seen as one with whom our Lord Jesus walked in her childhood, to whom "He showed His Kingdom and His work complete"; to whom Eternity was manifest in the Light of Day; a child who felt at home with the heavenly mysteries and the sun and the moon and the stars; to whom all things created by God were spotless and pure and glorious.* A child to whom it was early given:

"*To see a world in a grain of sand,*
And heaven in a wild flower,
To hold infinity in her hand
And Eternity in an hour."

A child conversant with the heavenly places where Angels dwell; a child beloved of God even as was the young Samuel of old.

We read in *The Living Touch* that up to the age of 12 Dorothy's life was uneventful and full of happiness. In the year 1902 her father died and her health began to deteriorate rapidly. The family doctor was consulted, and pronounced the child to be very delicate and in need of constant watching and care, and so for the next four years she was under the close supervision of her physicians. When she was 15, she had diphtheria and was sent to the Grove Isolation Hospital, Tooting. This illness made great inroads upon her health and she went to a Sanatorium to recuperate. Here she stayed nine months.

On her return home, she was medically examined and found to be far from well, and was ordered to spend much of her time resting in bed or lying out-of-doors. A chill resulted in pneumonia and pleurisy. Her life was despaired of and for two weeks she hovered on the brink

* Traherne: *Centuries of Meditation.*

of death. This illness marked the beginning of long years of confinement to her bed after a bacterial examination revealed that she was stricken with a general tuberculosis.

On December 26th, 1911, the two doctors who were attending her noted new and critical developments in her condition. After an examination had revealed her chief ailment to be tubercular peritonitis, her condition was considered to be quite hopeless from the medical viewpoint, and for the last fortnight of her illness she was unconscious and blind, this being due, the doctors said, to tubercular meningitis. On February 17th, 1912, the doctor warned her mother that death might occur at any moment and expressed his doubts whether she could live through another day. This period of unconsciousness Dorothy has called her "Beautiful Day" during which she entered into the great mystical experiences that are described in her book.

What follows is taken from a tape recording made by her at Burrswood not long before her death.

"Many years ago, the Living Lord laid His Hand upon my life and restored me to perfect health and wholeness in the twinkling of an eye. My healing was instantaneous and complete; there was no moment of weakness or convalescence. This after five years of so-called 'hopeless invalidism'. All efforts to maintain life had been abandoned and the inevitable end was expected at any moment. A little company of friends and relations were gathered around my bed waiting for the last flicker of life to depart, when some of them saw a great light over the bed. They at first thought it was Jesus taking this little spirit to Himself, and as they watched, they saw the emaciated little form raised to a sitting position by unseen hands. She opened her eyes and began to speak, and this is what she said, 'Do you not hear? I am well, I must get up and walk.' As they watched, they saw her who was dying get out of bed and stand before them every whit whole, this in the twinkling of an eye. Jesus had touched her; she was healed. There are two significant things concerning this miraculous healing. The first is that had it been any voice other than the Voice of the Living Lord nothing would or could have happened. Secondly, the servant to whom the Lord spoke *knew* it was the Lord and obeyed without hesitation or question, and so the miracle happened."

At the time of her miraculous healing, Dorothy Kerin was a young girl as yet untried by the vicissitudes and stresses of life in the outer world. By the grace of God, during the long years of illness that held her a prisoner within the four walls of the little bedroom in her mother's house at Herne Hill, she had, nevertheless, mastered the supremely important lesson of subordinating her will to that of God. Many good and pious people pay lip service to this important virtue of obedience, but few there be who make of it the corner-stone of their lives. Obedience, Dorothy constantly taught, is the key that unlocks the door to every true spiritual experience. No matter, she would say, how insignificant and trivial a thing may be, if it is done in a spirit of obedience it is more profitable in God's sight than any other conceivable activity. Absolute obedience to God's will, as it is revealed to us, implies an unconditional renunciation of all that belongs to self. The prayer transcending all others, which was constantly on Dorothy's lips and in her heart, "Lord, do with me as Thou wilt in any and every way", resulted in such a degree of sensitivity on her part to the least promptings within her soul of the Holy Spirit that she was able instantly to obey God's guidance as He unfolded to her His pattern for her life and work. This little poem composed by her illustrates better than volumes could do how completely the necessity for this supreme virtue of obedience had become engraven in her heart in letters of fire fanned by the Living Flame of Love that burnt within her, and was reflected in all she undertook to do for the glory of God and the helping of souls.

"*Laid on Thine Altar, Oh! Lord Divine,*
Accept my gift this day for Jesus' sake.

I have no jewels to adorn Thy shrine
Nor any world-famed sacrifice to make.

But here I bring within my trembling hand
This will of mine.

A thing that seemeth small
Only Thou, dear Lord, canst understand.

Hidden therein Thy searching eye can see
The struggles of passion, visions of delight,
Fond hopes and longings infinite.

It has been wet with tears and dimmed with sighs
Clenched in my grasp till beauty it hath none.

Now from Thy footstool where it vanquished lies
The prayer ascendeth "May Thy will be done."
Take it, oh! Father, ere my courage fail

And I ask back my gift.
May it have been so cleansed, so purified,

So fair have grown
That in gaining back my will, I may find it Thine."

CHAPTER 2

London's Modern Miracle

A BOOKLET has recently come to light in which the Rev. J. L. Thompson – who ministered to Dorothy's spiritual needs during the five years of her illness – narrates the circumstances of what he calls "London's Modern Miracle". This account contains matter of great interest, and in it is included a message from Dorothy to the world, which appeared in a weekly journal of the period.

LONDON'S MODERN MIRACLI

"I know of no better way in which I can bring glory to God, and good to man, than by rehearsing here the wonderful story of Dorothy Kerin. The word has been given me, a necessity is upon me that I must tell it to others. Perhaps no one knows the case better than myself. I have known it from the beginning; and Miss Kerin has stayed at my home as one of my family for six weeks; so that all the facts here given are first hand – from Dorothy herself.

"Dorothy Kerin and all within the walls of 204 Milkwood Road, Herne Hill, London, will never forget Sunday eve, February 18th. Friends and neighbours were then gathered together to see the last of Dorothy. The doctor had said she could not live until the morning. He had kept her alive for six weeks by means of brandy and opium and starch. During the last fortnight she had lain like a log of wood, and never moved her position in the bed, and was now *blind* and *deaf*, and for the most part unconscious. She had been attended by eight and twenty doctors, and had been sent home from an Incurable Home in an ambulance with only a week to live. She had been five years confined to her bed, and had been turned out of five hospitals – incurable.

"Such was her condition, and now the end had come. About half-past nine on Sunday evening, as mother and friends stood watching, she seemed to breathe her last. Anyhow, for eight minutes her lungs ceased to breathe, and her heart ceased to beat, and they deemed her dead. But just at this juncture, Dorothy tells us SOMEONE called her by name, three times distinctly, and she replied, "Yes, I am listening, who is it?"

And He said, "Listen!", and she felt two warm hands take hold of hers. A beautiful Light then flashed over the screen and came right over the bed. In the midst of the Light stood the Angel of the Lord, who, still holding her hands in His and lifting them up to her eyes and touching her ears, said "Dorothy, YOUR SUFFERINGS ARE OVER. GET UP AND WALK."

"She then opened her eyes and sat up, greatly wondering to see so many friends around her bed, to whom she said, 'I am well now! I want my dressing-gown. I want to walk.' Of course her request was unheeded, and she began to get up without it, when her mother came and held her down, saying, 'No, Dorothy, you will fall, you must not get up!' While thus held, the Angel again the second time said, "Get up and walk!" Dorothy then appealed to her mother asking her if she did not hear, on which she then relaxed her hold on her, and someone suggested that the dressing-gown should be given her just to gratify her and convince her that she could not walk.

"Just then a part of the beautiful Light, seen only by Dorothy, came and stood at the right-hand side of her bed. Then, with eyes and ears opened, and strength imparted to every limb, she threw off the bed-clothes from her, and stepped on to the floor, placing her hand upon the Light that was to lead her.

"The Light then moved forward, and she followed saying to her friends, 'I am following the Light.' It led her straight out of the room, through a passage into a room where she expected to find her step-father, who, however, was not there. The Light then led her into another room, where she found him, and in the joy of her restoration she threw her arms around his neck and kissed him.

"The Light then led her back again to her own room, where she found the whole company shaking and trembling with fear! Her step-father, who was following her, then fell upon the floor, and began to cry – in the attitude of prayer.

"In the midst of this fear and amazement, Dorothy seated herself saying, 'I cannot understand why you are all so FRIGHTENED! I AM QUITE WELL. Indeed, I feel as though I should like some supper!' And presently they brought her some invalids' food, which she refused, saying, 'I have had enough of that. I am well now, and want well people's food.' Then after much gainsaying on the part of the company, she sat down to her choice – cold beef and pickled walnuts and coffee; her mother saying, 'Well, it will be her last meal!' And she ate it before them all. She who had not tasted any solid food for six months, and had been kept alive for the last six weeks on an injection of opium and starch, etc. And all were amazed and ASTONISHED BEYOND SPEECH!

"When most of her friends had gone to their homes, she was persuaded by her mother to go back to bed at 12 o'clock, and while her mother and another watched her all night, she slept the sleep of a child, both sound and sweet, till 8 o'clock next day.

"Early next morning, as she further testifies, a message was sent to Dr. Norman, saying, 'Dorothy is better', and naturally on seeing the messenger, the doctor thought he had come for the Death Certificate; but when he said, 'Dorothy is better and up,' he thought for the moment he was dealing with a madman! Thus confounded, he set off in post haste, and on reaching the house, instead of finding his patient in bed where he had left her, she ran to the door to meet him with smiles of joy, and when he saw her so plump and well and smiling, he lifted up his hands in astonishment, saying, 'Can it be possible that this is the girl which I LEFT DYING!' Recovering somewhat from the shock, he then examined her and pronounced her well and healthy: and just to test her muscles, he asked her to walk up a rather steep stairway, and when he saw her *run* up the staircase he could find no expression for his amazement, saying 'WHAT DOES IT ALL MEAN?'

"The news spread over London in a very short time, and visitors began to pour in from all sides, increasing day after day until the road became literally blocked with people.

"The first day she interviewed sixty people, and the day after one hundred, and *huge crowds* came just to see the house, without the least hope of seeing Dorothy.

"Then came the reporters of the various London papers, through whom the facts, stranger than fiction, were carried to the ends of the earth.

"Several local doctors also came in to see and examine her at the request of her own doctor, but all were equally outwitted and amazed. On the fourth day Dr. Ash, who is a specialist, motored from Portman Square to examine the case, and when he had done so, he persuaded her mother to allow Dorothy to go and stay with him at his home, saying he would like to look into the case and watch it. She stayed six weeks with Dr. Ash, and while there, they applied the X-rays to her lungs (for she had been in the last stage of consumption) and saw, not the old lungs which were wasted away, but quite new lungs in their stead!

"Not content with this, other experiments followed – the testing of her blood, with this result that not a trace of disease could be found anywhere. She had been made whole every whit, in an instant, and immediately she was commanded, she got up and walked, and ate at midnight a meat-meal which amazed all present. Long illness and fasting had reduced her body to a mere shadow, and one of the most extraordinary things connected with her healing was the suddenness with which the flesh came up on her bones. Her doctor, as well as her mother and friends, could not get over the shock of this for a long time – they being like the prophet in the vision of the dry bones – eye-witnesses of the fact. She had been reduced to four and a half stones, and during that night her doctor declared that she must have put on two stones of flesh. Now she is nine stones.

"So tender and bruised was her body, that overnight several parts had to be wrapped in cotton wool, but on the following morning every part was strong and all discolourations gone! So astonished was her doctor at all this, that he came again and again that first day to see and examine her, and her mother, on this account, could scarcely realize her to be her own child, she looked so plump and bonny. 'Dorothy, you look now just as you did before you became ill,' said her mother."

This ends the witness of the Rev. J. L. Thompson.

Included in the booklet is this testimony of Mrs. Amy Newark, signed by her and six other witnesses who were all present on the evening of the miraculous healing, February 18th, 1912.

ATTESTATION BY MRS. AMY NEWARK

"Dear Mr. Thompson, It was about 8 p.m. when I went into the room. Dorothy was lying on her back, eyes closed, head slightly turned to the left, her arms were raised towards the ceiling. She was breathing very slowly. She remained in that position for some minutes, then her arms dropped and crossed on her breast. I thought she had passed away as her breathing had stopped, and we could not feel any heart beats. She remained like that for eight minutes, then gave a deep sigh and her heart started beating slowly, her breath came with a peculiar rattling sound which I thought was the end. Then she started speaking very slowly and softly, 'I am listening,' and 'Yes, yes,' she said. We then gave her a very little weak brandy and water, which she had great difficulty in swallowing. It was then turned half-past eight. At this time I left the room for a few minutes. When I returned, my daughter Nellie came with me. Dorothy was lying in the same position as when I left her, with her hands folded over her breast, breathing with difficulty, and I prayed God to take her and end her suffering. But she did not seem or look as if she were in pain, as she had such a beautiful, happy smile on her face. About nine o'clock I sent for my husband. He came up at once with my daughter's fiancé. Dear Dorothy was hardly breathing at all then, and both the men thought she had passed away, when she suddenly said, 'I am listening', and then she extended her left arm upwards. She still had her face turned towards the left, as if Whom she was speaking to was there. After a few minutes, her right arm went up, her fingers had been slightly closed, but in a few minutes her hands opened right out; she stretched her arms out still further, and gradually sat right up in bed, bending forward, as if she wanted to reach someone. Her eyes were still closed, as they had been for a fortnight, but she brought her hands to her eyes, and passed her fingers downwards over the lids, dropped her hands on the bed, and her eyes slowly opened. At first the eyes were right down in the corners, looking towards the nose, but in less than a minute they righted themselves and our darling was looking round at us all and smiling. We were all too frightened to speak for a minute or two, and thought it was a final spurt before the end, and that she would fall back on her pillow dead. But she still sat there smiling, and looked surprised to see us all there. At last her mother said, 'Dorothy, do you know me, dear?' 'Why, of course I do, mum,' she said, and then she knew us all, even my husband, whom she had not seen for three years. She kissed and hugged us all, but she appeared to be listening, and suddenly said, 'Isn't it wonderful! I haven't got any pain anywhere; I am quite well. I want to get out of bed.' Of course, we all tried to persuade her to lie down again, but she said, 'No, I am quite well; I want my dressing-gown. I am going to get up; can't you hear what the Angel says? Well, He says, "Dorothy, your sufferings are at an end; *get up and walk.*" ' And then she said, 'Can't you see the beautiful Light?' She insisted on having her dressing-gown, and her sister brought it from upstairs. She would hardly wait for it to be warmed, but took it, and slipped her arms in, and buttoned it up as quickly as anyone in full health. All the time, she was still listening and answering an unseen Presence, and kept repeating she must get up. We told her she could not stand, and her mother tried to persuade her to lie down, but she said, 'I can stand; I am quite well.' So her mother asked the two gentlemen to leave the room. They were hardly out of the door, when Dorothy threw off the bedclothes, as if she were in a hurry, and to our surprise stood upright and started walking towards the door. Her mother and my daughter put their arms round her, thinking she would fall, but she said, 'Don't hold me. I am quite all right', and when she got to the door, we said 'Don't go out, dear'. But she said, 'I must follow the Light. Can't you see it?' All the time she was walking quite strongly with her right arm up and her hand as if she were carrying a lamp. It was impossible for me to follow her along the passage, for my legs seemed suddenly to have turned to jelly, and were knocking against each other. She came back into the room, right over to the bed, and then turned without speaking, and started walking out into the kitchen again. Her mother said, 'Whom do you want out there, dear?' and she said, 'Dad; I want Dad'. She walked into the kitchen the second time, calling, 'Dad, where are you?' By that time, I had managed to pull myself together a bit, and stood in front of the fire. I was afraid she would fall in. I was quite sure she would collapse, but instead of that she walked into the room quite firmly, and sat down on the chair and asked us why we were all there. She seemed surprised we could not see the Light or hear the Voice that told her she was well, as she said 'He spoke so loudly'. I think Dorothy herself can teli us best all that has happened since then. I was with her all day and every day until Dr. Ash took her away on the 22nd, and all the time she ate well, slept well, and was quite calm and collected, and nothing seemed to tire or excite her."

The Rev. J. L. Thompson states in his booklet that perhaps the most remarkable thing connected with this healing is the Message she gave to the Church and to the world on 30th June, four months after she was made whole by the Living Touch of the Living Lord. This Message occupied the whole first page of one of our national newspapers. This is what she wrote under the guidance, she said, of the Holy Spirit:

DOROTHY'S MESSAGE

"In my restoration to health, I have been entrusted with a message to the whole world, a promise of healing to the sick, comfort to the sorrowing and faith to the faithless. This message is for everybody as soon as they are ready to accept it and have the desire.

"How these things are going to be brought into practice has not been revealed to me yet. I only know that it will depend largely upon Prayer and Faith. I do know there is a beautiful truth for us as soon as we are ready for it.

"I am confident that as soon as people are brought to open their spiritual eyes, these great and beautiful manifestations wil! be for them also. The vast multitude build up a barrier between the seen and the unseen – between spiritual beauty and themselves – by worldly lives and by foolishness, but as soon as this barrier is broken down there will be a great inrush of spiritual beauty and glory. I have seen it and I know.

"People do not realize that the spiritual part is much the greater portion. It is the true inheritance of all, but we do not claim it. Sometimes when I see people who have not this beautiful outlook upon things that are eternal, I wonder how they can exist; it is puzzling to me.

"I believe we are on the threshold of a great revelation from the Spirit that is Infinite. I feel that man is about to have a great awakening. What strengthens me in my belief? PRAYER. I am confident that Prayer is the only tonic that will create an appetite for the things of the spirit. Through Prayer we shall receive the Great Benediction. Prayer is the desire of the soul for spiritual things. There is a form of Prayer without words, a voiceless prayer in the heart, that God and God only understands.

"People ask me how the Divine Presence, or God, appears to me. God appears to me as an inexpressibly beautiful BEING – an Infinite Power impossible to describe. I know that with God all things are possible.

"I am asked if I feel that there will come another revelation to me. I answer that in God's own time all will come right. In the kingdom of the unseen one cannot presume to make plans for oneself. People say to me, 'What are you going to do with your life?' If you ask me what God is going to do with my life, I answer, 'I do not know.' It will come from God. One life lifted from the shadow of death and brought into the sunshine of happiness should be enough to convince the world. I am asked whether when the revelation, which I await in faith and trust, comes to me, pointing the way for ministration, I will announce it, and I say I will, of course. I know that it is by prayer, faith and obedience that it will come. *It will belong to the world.*

"I know that it was not for me alone, but that there is a divine purpose in my being singled out to manifest the healing power of the spirit. God knows the way. I do not know. I know that whereas I was prostrate, now I am well. I am an instrument in God's Hands. I know that He closed my human eyes and ears so that I might receive His Message. He took my conscious self away for a time, so that I might know spiritual realities. And the harmony and health and happiness that have come to me are so complete, that of the pain and suffering of those years I remember nothing.

"People ask me if I attribute my recovery to any of the established systems of healing, such as healing by hypnotism, suggestion, the help of 'friendly spirits', 'faith healing', Christian Science, suggestive therapeutics, etc. My restoration did not come through any of these or any other systems, nor did I pray for my recovery. I prayed that I might be happy in doing what God might will. I wondered sometimes why God ordained that I should suffer, but I was confident that it was for a purpose. I had no one attempting to heal me by any means, except the regular physicians, but many people knowing that the doctors had pronounced me incurable, and that I had been given up to die, think that my restoration was due in some way to some form of suggestion without my knowledge that that power was being invoked. There was no one at my bedside to make suggestions, no one attempting it – and had there been, how could an unconscious person have grasped them? No one can claim my restoration but God. My healing came direct from Him alone. There was no intermediate agent or agency.

"Christ is as much alive today as He was when upon earth, and is sending His message to those who will receive it. I feel no weight of care. Life is radiant when it is rightly lived, but there is swift retribution for those who are prodigal regarding the heritage which God gives. The Spirit of the Infinite lives in the truth, and the truth should make us not only free but joyous. Religion should be like the song of the birds.

"The glories of existence are all about us. The ineffable Power of Infinite Life is ours for the taking. There is nothing to hinder us except our own blindness. The Master in His day said they did not need to go to the mountain or to Jerusalem to worship, for God was Spirit. It is possible for every door to open into Paradise. It is possible for every life to come into communion with the Infinite.

"People say to me, 'Come out into the world and live,' but I say, 'Come out from the world and live,' and by that I do not mean come out and live your life away from your fellows. The old idea that people should go into the mountain or into the deserts and serve God by shunning society has been proved a fallacy. To be of help to your fellows; to share their joys and have them share yours; to smile with them; and if possible to banish their tears, are efforts worth while. What I mean by coming out from the world is to put aside the worldly things that pamper for a moment and perish – things that leave the soul empty and seared. It is not a denial, not a renunciation, but the embracing of things that are supernal, things that are spiritual and do not die. The world has repeated for centuries, but without realizing the full significance of the thought, that God is everywhere, and that the Kingdom of Heaven is within us. I believe that the world is ready today for a complete revelation of the literal and beautiful truth of these sayings that have largely come to be formal in their endless repetition.

"The great truth is that POWER unlimited, sublime and free, is within reach of us all.

"Yesterday, I was thinking much of my mission and message to the world, and wondered how I was going to bring it into execution. I prayed, 'How is this to be done?', and I heard a voice say distinctly, 'By prayer and faith.'

"Sometimes people in London come up to me in the street and speak to me. The other day a man came to me in the street and said, 'Excuse me, Miss, but may I touch you, perhaps the Spirit of the Master may pass through you into me.'

"You must break down the barrier before the inrush of glory can come in. The Spirit of God cannot come into the soul that is not receptive. Wealth could not buy my experience. It could not have effected my cure. It is the Spirit, the Spirit of Jesus, the Living God, that has given me this NEW LIFE.

DOROTHY KERIN"

CHAPTER 3

Bush Hill Park, Enfield

THE stir made in the medical and journalistic worlds by the miraculous healing of Dorothy Kerin was widespread. Doctors came from all over the world to investigate the authenticity of this twentieth-century miracle, and crowds of reporters and visitors invaded the privacy of the little house in Herne Hill where she lived with her mother, brothers and sister.

The following letter gives a portrait of her, as she appeared at the time of her healing to the first reporter who interviewed her on February 19th, 1912.

"I have just read with interest the narrative by Mr. Ross of your wonderful work at Burrswood. I was the more interested in it because for twenty-nine years I was on the staff of the *Daily Chronicle*, now the *News Chronicle*, and it was I who interviewed you on the morning after your miraculous cure.

"I well remember your telling me of your heavenly vision, and of the voice saying, 'Dorothy, your sufferings are over. Get up and walk.'

"When you told me of your wonderful experience, you were sitting by the fireside wrapped up in two blankets. The only dresses of your own that your mother possessed were some you had worn before you were bedridden. That was several years before. Then you were a child, now you were a young woman. And in those days there were no such places as Marks and Spencers where you could buy a ready-made dress. A dressmaker had to be sent for to take measurements, buy material and make it up. It took a week or a fortnight. So there you were wrapped up in blankets. I remember telling my parents you looked exactly like some pictures of the Virgin Mary. There was the same type of feature and your face bore such a lovely expression of divine beauty and peace. I remember it as well as if I had only seen you yesterday."

It was judged necessary to withdraw the young girl from the disturbing influence of the constant stream of enquirers. After residing with a friend of the family for a time, she eventually found a permanent home with Dr. and Mrs. Langford-James at Bush Hill Park, Enfield, where, at the time, Dr. Langford-James was the Vicar of St. Mark's Church. For the next fourteen years Dorothy lived with him and his wife, moving with them from Enfield to Thruxton, and finally to Edgbaston, Birmingham, where she received her call to go out into the world and fearlessly proclaim the message our Lord had entrusted to her.

Deeply versed in mystical theology at a time when the subject was largely ignored by his brother clergy, Dr. Langford-James was a scholar and a theologian learned in church doctrine and intimately acquainted with the lives and writings of the great saints who are the glory of the Catholic Church. To this erudite priest, God, in pursuance of His mysterious designs, entrusted the privilege of directing the early footsteps along the Mystic Way of this pure and spiritually gifted soul, for whom in the fulness of time He was to make known His purpose. We shall see that the design of God's pattern for Dorothy Kerin followed the familiar lines of the lives of all God's great servants who have left their mark upon the religious life of their day, and influenced man's spiritual thinking down the ages.

The great Saints have left us in no doubt as to the arduous nature of their ascent up the Mount of Purification. There are three essential qualities of the soul that characterize all true mystics, as opposed to the spurious variety. These are love, humility and obedience. Without them no aspirant to the higher reaches of the spiritual life can hope to proceed far in their search for God, a search which has as its aim the Transforming Union or Spiritual Marriage that consists in the perfect union of the will with God, so that the two wills become one. Those who were privileged to come close to Dorothy in whatsoever capacity would say without hesitation that she possessed to an unusual degree these all-important virtues of love, humility and obedience.

The mystic life is a life of love. To be a mystic is to participate to a greater or lesser degree in the Eternal Life, and because the Eternal Life manifests Itself in the universe It created as Love, this Flame of Love burns for ever within the hearts of these great lovers of God.

No one whose path in life, by the Grace of God, crossed that of Dorothy Kerin failed to be struck by the transforming and healing power of love that emanated from her. Because of this indwelling Christ-like love that poured itself out in tender understanding upon those who opened to her the innermost recesses of their hearts, the greatest sinners found no difficulty in unveiling to her compassionate gaze the dark regions in which their souls were accustomed to dwell, only to find by the time their interview was over that darkness had given place to light. She possessed to a supreme degree the ability to bring Christ the Healer to souls, and in the light of that healing Presence fear and darkness have no place.

The love that inspired Dorothy Kerin to fulfil her divinely ordained ministry of healing was, in the words of Dame Gertrude More, "an ardent love, a charitable love, a humble love, a constant love, never worn thin with labours nor daunted by any difficulties". We can almost hear the accents of her prayer in the silent watches of the night as she implores her beloved Master, "O Lord, give this love into my soul, that I may never more love nor breathe but out of a most pure love of Thee, my all and only Good."* This gentle, retiring woman whose days were filled with the exacting tasks of an arduous spiritual ministry, and whose nights were often given to communion with God, or in waiting upon His guidance, was supremely susceptible to that "rippling tide of love that flows secretly from God" into the souls of those who have surrendered themselves totally to His will.

St. John of the Cross tells us that "the touch of God upon the soul is most real for it is the substance of God that touches the substance of the soul. The sweetness of delight which this touch occasions baffles all description". *The Living Flame of Love*, that burning treatise of the great Spanish Saint, is an exposition in language of great lyric beauty of the play upon the soul of the Fire of the Holy Spirit through the media of these divine "touches". The ecstasy normally accompanying this mystical experience was as familiar to Dorothy Kerin as to St. Teresa of Avila, St. Catherine of Siena, St. Mechtild, St. Gertrude, St. Brigit, St. Angela of Foligno, to mention a few of those who were her forerunners on the Mystic Way, a path that leads to union with God only after it has traversed the dark shadows of Gethsemane and the abysmal darkness of Golgotha.

For many years, Dorothy's spiritual director nourished the soul of his gifted pupil upon the writings of the giants of the spiritual life. If, in the early stages of her schooling, the guiding hand of the teacher was needed to direct and sustain her soul's endeavour to pierce through the Dark Cloud of Unknowing to the Light Supreme of Dante's unsurpassed Vision, a time came when the pupil gave evidence of graduation from further need for tuition, as the following incident will show.

One day Father Langford-James called his ward into his study, and

* Fr. Baker: *Life of Dame Gertrude More.*

taking down a book from the well-lined shelves of his library, he opened it at random to read a few sentences. Presently, staying his reading, he told Dorothy to continue from where he had left off. To his satisfaction and amazement, she accomplished the incredible feat of reciting page after page to the end of *The Living Flame of Love* without faltering for a single instant. She could have done this only because the very essence of St. John of the Cross's teachings had entered into the substance of her being and so become for her a matter of experiential knowing. The pupil had joined the ranks of the privileged few to whom it is given to *know* the mysteries of God, and faith, that priceless handmaiden to the life of the spirit, had given way to knowledge which in the course of the years spent in her God-given ministry deepened into the wisdom that is of the very breath of the Power of God. It was by the light of this transcendent wisdom that Dorothy was able to unravel the tangled minds and to mend the broken lives of those who through personal interviews or by means of a vast correspondence sought from her the help and guidance they stood in need of.

God's chosen servants whom He calls to knowledge of Himself in the Transforming Union of the Spiritual Marriage are all endowed with tremendous vitality, great sensitivity of mind and heart, and indomitable will-power rooted in obedience. The whole aim of the self-discipline to which they are subjected is to ensure the maximum amount of responsiveness to the divine promptings and guidance which in one form or another constantly attend their path through life. They lead lives of creative and fertile activity; they are channels for renewed rebirths in the world of the creative and regenerating Power of God; their lives are lives of superhuman activity and inexhaustible industry; they affect the destinies of innumerable souls who come under their influence; they leave the imprint of their personalities upon the religious life of their time and for centuries after.*

Souls such as these, to whom it has been given to tread the Transcendental Way of the Unitive Life, no longer live and work of themselves, but God lives and works in and through them. The Divine Energy which burns as the Living Flame of Love in their hearts drives them with unrelenting pressure, in the fulness of God's timing for them, into the world of men to lead lives of creative, fertile and active participation in Christ's redemptive sacrifice for creation. The arduous travail of their contemplative years brings forth spiritual fruits which they feel constrained to use in the service of mankind.

* Evelyn Underhill: *Mysticism.*

Their dual capacity for suffering and a fulness of joy beyond the normal is the hallmark of their attainment. To them is granted to gather up in the crucible of their souls, the pain, the sorrows, the cruel strains and stresses of those whom life has crucified. Through the transforming alchemy of their Christ-like love, God often releases in men and women who come within the influence of their ministry the hidden springs of the Divine Life in which we all live, move and have our being. This inflow of grace enables them to accept with patience God's will for them and in that humble acceptance to find the peace that surpasses all understanding.

At some moment in God's pattern for them, a St. Paul, a St. Augustine, a St. Gregory, a Catherine of Siena, a St. Francis of Assisi, a Teresa of Avila, a St. Ignatius, and in our own time, within the Anglican communion, a Dorothy Kerin, are all torn from their contemplative lives of solitude and prayer to become immersed in the discordant clamour of the world of mankind. Architects of the Faith like St. Paul and St. Augustine, great administrators of the Church like St. Gregory the Great, founders of religious orders like St. Francis, or those called to a far-reaching public ministry as was Catherine of Siena, every one of these great captains in God's army of Saints have felt within themselves the conflict between the call of their contemplative natures and their lives of ceaseless activities. Some have left on record their lament that their immersion into the world of activity has entailed the sacrifice of their lives of contemplative prayer. A sacrifice freely assented to in obedience to God's will and call, but carrying with it a far greater depth of frustration of spirit than those who are not contemplatives by nature can ever hope to understand.

And so it was with that 20th-century servant of God, Dorothy Kerin, whose life followed the spiritual pattern of the great men and women who were her forerunners in the service and love of God and humanity. Clothed in the armour of light, forged during the years of preparation, imbued with that sense of obedience to God's will and purpose for her which was the genius of her life's work, she was ready when the call came to her in 1929 to go forth as God's messenger to proclaim to our disease-ridden and fear-stricken world that our Lord Jesus Christ is the same yesterday, today and for ever, and that He has not gone back upon His eternal promise to remain with us until the end of time. The tiny acorn placed in the hand of the child Dorothy by our Lord Jesus Christ yielded over the years its creative fruit in the shape of a great spiritual movement which is profoundly influencing the religious thinking of men and women everywhere, and therefore changing their daily living.

It may be objected that other workers have also been called to labour in God's vineyard of Divine Healing, and that I unduly emphasize the part played by Dorothy Kerin. To this I would reply that when, through the operation of the Holy Spirit, a fresh spiritual impulse to meet the needs of an age is given to mankind's spiritual evolution, we find this particular manifestation of the Spirit of God coincides with a receptive climate of thought expressing itself in little spiritual currents at work everywhere with their promise of a new departure for humanity. This is another way of saying that when mankind is ready to accept the revelation of God's Power and Love as expressed in His pattern for His children at some given moment in the history of the race, He reveals Himself through many channels. None the less, every great spiritual movement can be traced at its inception to the use by God of some one human instrument through whom He gives to the world the revelation of Himself it needs, and the importance of that revelation is to be measured by the potential dangers that beset the path of mankind in the critical epoch in which it is given. The great mystical flowering which was the direct result of the endeavours of St. Francis was not an isolated factor at work for the renewal of the springs of Christendom's inner life. Before ever the Poverello came upon the scene of his day, little centres of the spiritual life were in being, but historians point to St. Francis and the Portiuncula as the starting-point which gave the impetus to the flowering of spirit alluded to above, and in like manner, in years to come, students of Religion will point to Dorothy Kerin and her Home of Healing at Burrswood as being the focal point for the great spiritual movement of our time, which we know as the Ministry of Divine Healing.

CHAPTER 4

Mystical Experiences

FOR some years, Dr. Langford-James kept records of his personal relations with his ward, Dorothy Kerin, during the years she spent under his roof. In his Foreword to *The Living Touch,* he wrote: "Marvellous as is the story she had here to tell, yet my wife and I have been witnesses of wonders almost as great which happened to her during her long stay with us. The story of them has been carefully recorded, and when it is God's Will, it will be given to the world at large, as this one has been." It is to these records that we are indebted for information in regard to this period about which little has transpired.

The corner-stone of the spiritual life is prayer, and the end of all prayer is communion with God and conformity to His will. In her book *Fulfilling*, Dorothy has told how greatly indebted she was to her spiritual director for the long spells of quiet and prayer which he made possible for her to have. The fruits of these years of communion are still with us today, visible to our sight and mightily used of God.

The design of the Divine Pattern for Dorothy Kerin's spiritual unfolding follows the familiar lines of all God's Saints. The Cross, with all it represents stood rooted in the very ground of her soul. A mystic has said the Cross is an abyss of wonders, the school of virtues, the place of sorrows.* In *The Living Touch,* Dorothy has told us that the Blessed Virgin Mary came to her bearing in her hands a large shining Cross which she placed on her knees and said, pointing to it, ". . . this must come first".

On the night before she passed to the Eternal Life she said to those by her bed, "Mine is the Way of the Cross." The Via Dolorosa has run through her entire life, interspersed with periods of radiant joy and sunshine, but always casting in the background its divine shadow. All through every phase of her dedicated life she consciously linked herself with our Lord's own intercession on the Cross, and offered up to Him

* Thomas Traherne: *Centuries of Meditation.*

on the altar of her heart the pain and suffering with which at times her Cup was filled to overflowing to be used by Him in His redemptive sacrifice for mankind.

This prayer of hers reflects the constant and conscious offering of her body, mind and soul in vicarious sacrifice for the salvation of those countless numbers to whom she ministered during her life-time.

> "By the bruising of my whole life, strengthen me with sympathy for every wounded soul, and let my prayers be a balm for the wounds of Thy children, that they may be healed."

God granted this request of His servant to a degree that will never be fully revealed.

Miraculously healed on February 18th, 1912, Dorothy was made by our Lord Jesus Christ "every whit whole in the twinkling of an eye", as she has often stated in her writings and public utterances. The condition of tuberculosis from which she suffered at the time of her healing showed no traces of activity during the various so-called 'illnesses' which from time to time beset her before she began her public ministry. The records state explicitly that the fear of the tuberculosis once more becoming active proved groundless, whenever, at repeated intervals, her doctors made the requisite tests, bacterial and other, to see if this disease was again attacking her. Nevertheless, during this period, she experienced the same physical and psychological disorders, resulting from the tremendous tensions to which her psycho-physical organism was subjected by her mystical states, as did St. Catherine of Genoa, St. Teresa of Avila, St. Catherine of Siena, St. Margaret Mary Alacoque, to name only a few. Like these, she suffered severely at times from heart troubles, fever heats, headaches, strange hemorrhages from the stomach or lung, mental depressions* and other complications, all of which she bore with heroic fortitude and patience. Truly could she say with St. Paul, "I am crucified with Christ; nevertheless I live; yet not I, but Christ liveth in me" (Gal. 2. 20).

If Dorothy never mentioned, even to her intimates, that like many of her fellow Saints she had had to endure these psycho-physical disharmonies, it was because she knew they were the inescapable accompaniment of her great mystical experiences about which she remained to the end of her life consistently reticent. Had they been disclosed, their disclosure must inevitably have led to the revelation of the many

* Fr. Von Hugel: *The Mystical Element of Religion.*

extraordinary marks of divine favour granted to her, which she so humbly and jealously guarded in her life-time from the curiosity of the outer world.

Dr. Langford-James first met Dorothy in London at the house of his cousin, Mrs. Wynne-Ffoulkes, in January, 1915. Mrs. Wynne-Ffoulkes was anxious for her cousin to meet her friend because she felt she was in danger of being spoilt through speaking at too many theosophical and spiritualist meetings. He had read *The Living Touch*, and although deeply impressed by its spirituality and the mystical experiences it portrays, did not feel sure whether the author of this little book, which he recognized to be a veritable treasure house of the spirit, was in fact a real Catholic or not. A conversation of two hours over the tea-cups convinced him that Dorothy was in everything touching doctrine and faith a loyal and devoted daughter of the Catholic Church. As she lived at Highgate, he walked back with her as far as Finsbury Park Tube. On the way there he referred to Confession and asked her if she had made her Christmas Confession. She replied that she knew she ought not to delay further in making her Confession, but added, "What would you do, Father, if you had been to a priest and he had refused to give you counsel?" He answered, "It all depends upon what grounds." To which she replied, "I have been refused counsel because the priest said he did not wish to stand in the way of the Holy Spirit." He then said, "I should go to another." She told him she had been to three priests who had all acted more or less in the same way. Dr. Langford-James assured her that he would give the matter his earnest thought and would write to her. He felt it must be on account of her special gift of prayer that these priests had hesitated to give her spiritual counsel.

For some days, Dr. Langford-James gave much thought and prayer to the matter, but could not think of any priest in London who understood mystical theology sufficiently to be able to help her. He had himself made a close study of this subject for some years, and finally suggested she come to him, stressing that it was not his intention to propose himself as her regular Confessor, but that he felt strongly the necessity to deal with the immediate need of her not leaving the tribunal of penance any longer unvisited. By return came a letter saying, "I know I ought to come to you. Don't *you* know? Have you not seen?" He replied that he neither knew nor had he seen. Dorothy then told him that she had twice seen a vision of our Lady and himself, and that our Lady had led her to him. He put to her a number of searching questions to test the reality of her vision, and was completely convinced by her answers. He asked her about her way of prayer, basing his queries upon Poulain's *Graces of Interior Prayer*, and was satisfied that her prayer life showed all the characteristics of a true contemplative who possessed to a marked degree the required virtues of great purity of heart and mind joined to an ardent and generous love.

Dr. and Mrs. Langford-James invited Dorothy to stay with them for a few days so that they could better get to know each other. This short visit, during which she spent long hours in conversation with Dr. Langford-James, led to her being invited to make her permanent home with them at Bush Hill Park. Among the difficulties with which her life was at that time beset, the priest felt that the most dangerous threat to her physical and spiritual well-being was the fact that she was trying to lead a dual life. In order not to distress her family, she was making every effort by day to fit herself into the pattern of their way of life with its ordinary mundane demands, while the nights were given to prayer and to dealing with a correspondence amounting to some fifty or more letters a week, the inevitable outcome of the publication of her book. The result of these two-fold demands upon her physical and nervous energies was that she was getting insufficient rest, and this was reflecting itself in her general state of health which was showing symptoms of a breakdown.

At this period of his life, his portraits show Father Langford-James as having a sensitive, ascetic type of face, in which the most arresting features were his piercing blue eyes. The general impression is that of a man of a somewhat fanatical temperament endowed with exceptionally strong will-power. A brilliant conversationalist, he had a large fund of witty stories and an irrepressible sense of humour of the kind that finds an outlet in humorous limericks, at the spontaneous composition of which he was adept. Dorothy had a similar gift, and on occasions they would cap each other with rhymes that were a source of immense amusement to their entourage. His intellectual endowments were considerable. A past master of the rubrics of the liturgical services of the Catholic Church, he was an impeccable Latin scholar, an accomplished musician, a fine linguist, and a delightful companion, who, by reason of his study of mystical theology, as well as his grasp of theology in general, was fitted to instruct and guide this rare soul entrusted to his care by God. He effectively taught her to appreciate all that was finest in religious and secular literature, enabling her thus to detect what was shoddy and spurious from that which embodied the enduring qualities of the Good, the True and the Beautiful. It was from her spiritual director that Dorothy acquired her knowledge of all that pertained to correct Catholic procedure in Church Services. This was later to be a constant source of wonder and admiration to the less initiated, and explains why the Services held in her various Chapels, and towards the end of her life in her beautiful Church of Christ the Healer at Burrswood, were conducted with that exquisite attention to order, rhythm and harmony handed down to us through centuries of liturgical tradition, but all too frequently ignored in our Anglican worship.

The other members of the Vicarage household consisted of Mrs. Langford-James, a first-class musician of German extraction, who had in her day been summoned to Windsor Castle to play before the King and Queen; also a Mrs. Cave and a Miss Buckley, two delightful old sisters who were deeply religious and became devoted to Dorothy. They were privileged to witness many of the miraculous happenings of this period.

It was not without a considerable struggle that Dorothy consented to become part of the Langford-James household. She was burdened with the thought that it would be too much for her to receive from them, seeing they were very busy people and not well off. She prayed much about it. After she had come to live permanently at the Vicarage, her spiritual director told her she must learn to accept sacrifices from others, even as our Lord had done in His earthly life. Dr. Langford-James had placed in her room a beautiful Crucifix that he had got many years ago at Oberammergau. Dorothy became much attached to it. The night after he had told her to imitate her Lord in His acceptance from other people of the necessities of life, she saw the Crucifix shining with light. She asked him the next day what he thought it meant, and he reminded her of their conversation of the day before, pointing out to her that the Crucifix was *the* Symbol of Sacrifice, and that he believed it to be an indication of the Divine Will that she should accept the sacrifice he wished to make on her behalf.

After her visit to Bush Hill Park, Dorothy went to Sandgate at the request of a sick friend. While she was there, her beloved little dog Mab was run over by a motor-car. Dorothy sat up with her for two nights, and Mab completely recovered, although the vet had said she could not possibly live. She had a vivid dream that she was in a garden full of lovely lilies which she much wished to pick. The next morning, she found four of these lilies on her pillow, all wet and fresh with dew. She put them in water, where they remained for a time and then disappeared. On another occasion, she found her bed strewn with violets. She went all round Sandgate but there were no violets to be seen in the shops. The lilies played their part in helping to heal Mab, as this letter she wrote to Dr. Langford-James shows:

"When Mab was in great pain, I put the lilies on her, and prayed at the same time that she might recover. After a few moments, she licked my hand and became quite quiet, and has improved rapidly since then. What do you make of this story? Is it all right? Or does it savour of spiritualism? I am not sure about it. All I know is that the flowers were real and very beautiful.

"I will not make any definite plans for coming to you just now, for I think it will be better to wait until you tell me it is quite convenient for me to come, and I can stay here two weeks longer, if necessary, or go to Cambridge. It is probably not intended that the 'healing touch' should be started at once in the C.L.* I am sorry though, for you had, I know, hoped great things from it. It will come one day, and until it does there will be lots of other things to do – will there not?

"Needless to say, I am disappointed about the past, but of course you are right. You really do mean what you say about keeping me when I come to you, don't you? I hope this will be soon, for I know I am slipping back again. For two Sundays it has been impossible to get to Mass, and I have not made more than seven Communions all the time I have been here. This news will I fear hurt you – but I must tell you for I know you think I have done as much as I could, but I have not. Every day, I mean to do that which I know to be God's Will, and some one gets ill, or something happens to take up my time, and I say my prayers very late, and consequently get up in the morning tired out, and things get put off. I am very wicked and hate myself. I marvel often at my badness and the patience dear Holy Jesus has with me. I must feed Mab now, so goodbye. Please don't rush up against another batch of microbes."

In October, final arrangements were made for her to live at St. Mark's Vicarage, Bush Hill Park, Enfield. With the exception of occasional visits to her family and friends, she was to remain a part of the household for the next fourteen years.

Soon after Dorothy's arrival at the Vicarage, Dr. Langford-James was given the opportunity to see his ward lost in contemplative prayer. She had been in the Church for a Catholic League Service from 8.30 to 9.30 p.m., and then went up to the Blessed Sacrament Chapel at the

* Catholic League.

top of the house. A little winding staircase led to this Chapel where she was to spend many long hours in prayer. He found her there deep in prayer at 10 o'clock. Knowing it was wrong and useless to disturb her, he left a candle with a note to say he would wait up for her. When he again went up an hour later, she was still in her prayer. Miss Iris Moody, who was staying at the Vicarage, waited up with him; at 1 a.m. they entered the Chapel to find her still kneeling with a rapt face, motionless and her senses oblivious to the outer world. They stayed to pray with her for an hour, and her spiritual director prayed earnestly that she might be taken out of her prayer, for he feared the consequences for her health of an all-night vigil. His prayer was granted, and Dorothy came out of her prayer and consented to go down with them. Before leaving the Chapel, she looked long at the Tabernacle, and said, "How can I leave Him here all alone?" to which he answered, "He is not alone. His Angels are guarding Him."

Volumes have been written about the various stages of prayer comprised within the term 'contemplation'. Briefly summarized, contemplation can best be defined as a "simple, loving, protracted gaze on God and things divine under the influence of the Holy Spirit and a special actual grace which takes possession of us and causes us to act in a passive rather than in an active manner."* So far as we can tell, Dorothy Kerin was led by the Spirit through the stages of mental prayer to contemplation and to a unitive prayer of such intimacy that we can only believe that she *knew* what the Saints have described as the Spiritual Marriage.

Not long after Dorothy came to live at the Vicarage, she had an encounter with the Arch Enemy. She was brushing her hair before going to bed, and on turning round saw the Devil sitting in a chair behind her in the form of a beautiful Angel but with baleful eyes that held in them all the powers of evil. She had been thinking of a prediction of our Lord relative to her death. The Devil told her it was utter presumption on her part to think she would have so much honour done to her, and that he intended to kill her there and then. He tried his best to shake her faith. This encounter was followed by a severe heart attack and hemorrhage from the lungs which left her very exhausted. Dorothy told Father Langton-James that she had prayed very hard to be allowed to learn something of the sufferings of the Passion.

About this time, she began a period of desolation greater than she had ever known. Dr. Langford-James explained to her that this distress-

* Father A. Tanquery: *The Spiritual Life.*

ing experience was the normal accompaniment of her way of prayer, and was necessary to deepen and strengthen her spiritual life. Without it she could know nothing of the disciplinary work of the prayer of the soul. This thought helped her to bear with patience the sufferings of this painful state.

There was a sequel to the encounter with the Evil One. She went one morning into the Church to prepare for her Confession, and became aware that the Devil was standing behind her; he said to her in an indescribably jeering tone of voice, "I will never leave thee nor forsake thee" – the words our Blessed Lord had used to her in her healing. He then leered into her face. At that moment, Father Langford-James came into the Church, and instantly felt something was wrong. He beckoned Dorothy into the Sacristy and the Devil followed her. He tried to drive him away with Holy Water but Dorothy said he would not go. She then told her Confessor, "He fears the Crucifix." He turned to the Sacristy Crucifix and bade him depart, and then suggested they should go to the Blessed Sacrament Chapel. She told him afterwards that the Devil had gone out of the Sacristy when he was shown the Crucifix, but had followed her down the Church. In the Chapel she managed to make a sufficient Confession.

On the Vigil of the Feast of the Immaculate Conception, Dorothy suffered a greater pain in her heart than she had ever known before. The next day she was no better, the pain increasing in intensity. In the afternoon of the Feast, she again took to her bed, and when her spiritual director went up to give her the laying-on-of-hands, he found her to be suffering from the most terrible attack of pain he had ever witnessed. He began to feel it was a supernatural pain. He noticed she appeared to have great pain in her left hand which she opened and shut constantly, while plucking the bedclothes with it. He saw a red spot gradually appearing on the back of it.

Later that same evening, he found her in a great state of distress. She said to him, showing him the palm of her left hand in which a wound was clearly visible, "Do you think the Devil could have done this?" He replied, "No, certainly not." "But," she said, "I am so wicked, God could not have done it. And if He had, surely He would have done it in both my hands. Do pray that it may go; not the pain, but the mark. I could not bear anyone to see it." He replied he was sure it was the doing of our Lord, and that she must be thankful, and that we had no right to say to our Lord what He must or must not do. This comforted her, and she eventually went into a deep sleep. He questioned her as to whether she had any idea of what it might be, and found that she had not and thought the Stigmata were always invisible. Before she fell asleep, she asked him to pray that the Stigmata might be removed in the night, not because she wanted to be rid of the pain, for she said she never wanted to lose that, but because she could not bear it to be seen. He prayed as she had asked him to do, but he also prayed that if it were God's Will the Stigmata might be given also in the right hand, so as to reassure her.

The next afternoon, December 9th, Dorothy received the Wound in her side. Dr. Langford-James had to go up to London and so was away when this happened. She told him she was kneeling in front of the Crucifix kissing its Feet, when, preceded by a pain worse than on the previous occasion, she felt two stabs, as if a knife were being driven into her side. She collapsed in an agony of suffering, and when she came to herself she found the Wound in her right hand had also appeared.

On the following day, Saturday, December 10th, she was given the Wounds in her feet. In both her feet there appeared a round red mark on the instep. Dr. Langford-James inadvertently touched one of the feet, and the pain was so great that it was not possible for him to see the inside of the foot. Her hand when she woke on the first occasion was full of blood, which vanished though she did not wash it. There remained a mark on the back of the hand like the head of a flat triangular nail; and on the palm a round wound that was bloodless.

There are two things to be signalled in regard to this momentous happening. First, Dorothy had no idea that our Lord would fulfil His promise that she would share the pain of His Passion in this particular way. Secondly, that the Stigmata have usually been given during an ecstasy. From October until the end of February, Dorothy experienced utter desolation and the Stigmata were given during this time of desolation.

Dorothy was most reluctant to let anyone except her director see the Wounds. He finally persuaded her that she ought to let him call in witnesses. He urged this all the more because by Sunday the Wound in her left hand, the first to appear, was beginning to heal. They all healed by the Saturday week after they began to appear. But the marks still remained quite clear. The Wounds partially opened up on more than one occasion during the next six years.

ATTESTATIONS TO THE STIGMATA

Among the witnesses whose attestations have survived are the Bishop of South Tokyo, Archdeacon Cross, Father Fynes-Clinton,

Father Adams, Father Taylor, Mrs. Cave and Miss Buckley, Father Nugent, Mrs. Langford-James and her maid Edith White; also Miss Iris Moody, Secretary to the Bishop of South Tokyo's Mission in Devon.

c/o Church House,
Westminster, S.W.
August 5th, 1916.

"Dear Mr. Langford-James,

You asked me (for your own reasons) to put on paper for you that yesterday I was allowed to see those sacred marks (though now only scars, but quite unmistakable) of the Stigmata on the hands (and palms) and feet of Miss Dorothy Kerin.

"I feel sure this thing has been granted for the glory of God in more than her own spiritual joy and comfort. Yet, except for your request, I shrink from putting the fact on paper. It would somehow shock me to hear anyone make such a statement in public or to see it in print. For myself I feel that I may some time mention in sympathetic privacy that I *know* of such a fact but without clue or identity. This is only *instinct*. I don't mean by saying it to dictate to you. Will you tell her again for me that she has blessed and helped a 'heathen bishop' just as he is going back to where faith has to do without some of the unconscious props of Home atmosphere (though certainly it gets some other experiences of its own); and also what a real pleasure it has been to see one whom Miss Iris Moody loves and to hear her laugh – as GOD's dear children can afford to do on sick beds and in war time. Whether we can meet again or not, there is no fear of my forgetting. For all your own trouble and personal escort, I beg to thank you: and I have written as you desired to the Archdeacon of London (Holmes). I shall ask Miss Moody to tell me if there is ever anything *special* for me to know (or try to pray about) as regards yourself or Miss Kerin.

Yours most truly,
CECIL, BISHOP IN SOUTH TOKYO."

From the Rev. H. J. Fynes-Clinton, 27, Finsbury Square, London, E.C. November 28th, 1916:

"IN THE NAME OF THE FATHER, THE SON AND THE HOLY GHOST. AMEN.

"I depose that on Thursday, December 16th, 1915, I having previously been informed by my friend, Father R. L. Langford-James, of the reception of the Stigmata by Dorothy Kerin, and that the Stigmata in one hand came visibly to him as he watched, went to Bush Hill Park, Enfield, and visited Dorothy Kerin in St. Mark's Vicarage.

"I saw the Stigmata in both hands and feet. They appeared as distinct wounds, apparently passing right through, being visible both on the backs and on the palms, of a size as though made by an instrument of the thickness of a pencil. There was discoloration as of a half-healed wound, and in one hand at least there still appeared some exudation. There was also in one wound a small projection of flesh, more darkly coloured, as though caused by something projecting from the wound.

"I remarked especially, as Father Langford-James asked her to show me the Stigmata, that this appeared to cause great shrinking. I then had a long conversation with her, for nearly an hour, and noted especially the following.

"She appeared to be endowed with a deep humility; and told me that she shrank very much from the showing of the marks to others: but that she obeyed in the matter, and said that after all, it was 'He, not me.' She was evidently still suffering, and spoke of having prayed that she might suffer, if it were God's will, on behalf of others. She said that previously to this event, after which Father James had explained it to her, she had not known that the Stigmata of St. Francis had been visible to ordinary eyes, but thought that they were only 'spiritually discerned'. She spoke of her great pain, and above all of the awful pain of entering into the Sacred Dereliction, yet she felt perfectly happy, she said, as it was His Will and for Him. After she realized that the Stigmata were visible, she had prayed that if it were God's will, 'she might have the suffering, and others the marks'. She felt the pain of showing them so much.

"She then told me that when the pain in her feet began she had 'felt impelled, quite apart from my own will' to offer the wounds in her feet for the Catholic League.

"I was much impressed, indeed more deeply than I have ever been in speaking to any other person, with her simplicity, humility, her patience and spirituality. The whole atmosphere seemed full of the spirit of prayer and Divine Love.

"She was lying down, appearing very weak, and suffering, but radiant, though tranquil, and quite calm and entirely natural.

"I have written this from notes that I put down at the time; and quote in marks from her words noted down soon afterwards.

"I am absolutely convinced that the Stigmata are supernatural, and the visit was a profound spiritual experience to me.

Signed: H. J. FYNES-CLINTON.
Nov. 28th, 1916. Priest"

1, St. Mark's Road,
Bush Hill Park,
Enfield.
December 13th, 1915.

"On Sunday, December 12th, 1915, I was told by Dr. Langford-James that Miss Dorothy Kerin had received the Stigmata. Dr. Langford-James asked me to come and see Miss Kerin, that I might see for myself the truth of what he told me. I did so, and saw distinctly the marks of the Wounds in both her hands and feet.

CYRIL F. S. ADAMS, Priest."

George Hotel,
Enfield.
December 15th, 1915.

"For the strengthening of faith in all who shall read, we desire to place on record what it has been our unexpected privilege to behold this day. It was our intention to spend the night at Tunbridge Wells, but owing to the illness of a relative this arrangement was altered at the last moment. We felt then a great wish to spend the time at Bush Hill Park as we had arranged to call at the Vicarage on the day following. On our arrival about 5.30 p.m. Dr. Langford-James stated that Miss Kerin had in the week previous received the Stigmata and he explained to us the manner in which the marks had come. About 5.50 p.m. my wife and I were taken to Miss Kerin's room and there saw for ourselves the marks on both sides of each hand and foot. We were told that she had also received the mark in her side, but this of course we did not see. We stayed with Miss Kerin until 6.35 and when leaving we again noted clear definition of the marks in her hands.

GEORGE H. WIDDOWS
Fellow Royal Inst. Brit. Archts.
MARY WIDDOWS."

St. Oswald's Presbytery,
Coppermill Lane,
Walthamstow.

"I, Austen Robert Taylor, clerk in Holy Orders, and priest in charge of the church and district of St. Oswald, Walthamstow, in the county of Essex, Master of Arts, and member of Jesus College in the University of Oxford, make the following statement: On Wednesday, December 15th, being the Octave of the Feast of the Immaculate Conception of our Blessed Lady, I was summoned by telegram to St. Mark's Vicarage, Bush Hill Park, where Miss Kerin is residing. When I arrived there, I was taken to Miss Kerin's room. She told me that Our Blessed Lord had particularly told her to send for me, that I might see with my own eyes the Most Holy Stigmata of His Passion with which He had been pleased to mark her; that it had been borne in upon her very plainly that I was in trouble; and that it was His Will that I should take courage from this signal favour.

"She then allowed me to see and examine her hands. In both there was a Wound right through the palm. In one the colour was a much deeper black-red (the colour of clotted blood) than in the other; in the darker one something like a nail head seemed to be coming away. Dr. Langford-James, who was present, then obtained permission to uncover the feet. There, also, in both feet showing through from the upper side to the sole, were the Wounds, in that part of the foot which is flexible just below the arch. The Piercing of the Feet seemed to have been in a slanting direction towards the toes and not just through the shortest way. I particularly noted this, which surprised me. I was not shown the Wound in the side that I was told had bled somewhat, and had been extremely painful, until our Lady Herself came and placing Her Hand upon it had removed It; on Sunday, December 12th, I think I was told this had occurred. I talked some time privately with Miss Kerin, was allowed to touch and kiss the Sacred Stigmata, and then withdrew.

AUSTEN R. TAYLOR."

15th day of December, 1915.

Rosemount,
Bovey Tracey.
April 4th, 1916.

"Dorothy Kerin came to stay with us on Monday, January 24th. On Tuesday evening she showed me the Wound in her side. It was on the left side, lower than her heart, and in the form of a Latin Cross about five inches long, with the arms in proportion. It was perfectly healed up, but the scar was standing out, perhaps a third of an inch, like a weal. It was pale in colour, and the flesh round it was slightly flushed.

"A few days later I saw the Wound again. The scar had then subsided to the level of the surrounding flesh, and was red in colour. It remained during the rest of the time she was here. I saw it last on Monday, January 31st, and it had then the same appearance.

"Dorothy told me that the condition of the Wound the first time I saw it was due to the effect of a trying interview she had had that day with some people of spiritualistic beliefs and practices. They had said many things that had hurt her, and she had felt great pain in the Wound while she was with them.

IRIS MOODY."

The Abbey,
Pershore, Worcs.
28th May, 1917.

"On the 26th May, 1917, I was granted the great privilege of witnessing the Sacred Stigmata of Miss Dorothy Kerin in the presence of her director, the Rev. Father R. L. Langford-James, D.D. The marks in Miss Kerin's hands and feet are distinct and as though pierced by the Holy Nails, bearing the impress of the head of same in the palms of her hands and the instep of her feet and the sharp point on the backs of her hands and the soles of her feet. On her left side over the heart is a large deep red cross, and one knelt in thanskgiving that God had granted one more stigmatic to His Holy Church.

BROTHER WILLIAM."

Account of an interview with Father Fynes-Clinton made at Miss Kerin's request a few months before his death:

"For some time Miss Kerin had urged me to have a talk with Father Fynes-Clinton as he was one of the very few people still alive who had known her in her early years, and who had, moreover, been an eye-witness to the Stigmata received by her in 1915. On August 5th, 1959, I secured an interview with him, and this is what he told me.

"One day in December, 1915, I was rung up by my friend, Dr. Langford-James, who asked me to come and see him, because a very remarkable and momentous event had happened shortly before to his ward Dorothy Kerin. I went, as requested, and Langford-James met me and told me briefly what had happened, and said he wanted to take me to see Dorothy, and be an eye-witness to the Stigmata she had received. He took me to Dorothy's room where she was lying down. The room was filled with an indescribable atmosphere, very beautiful and very moving, and I have never forgotten the expression on Dorothy's face. I was struck by the great purity and humility that emanated from her. I was told all five Wounds were present, and I was shown four of them – those on feet and hands. The blood was still welling up and staining the linen. I could see how much it distressed Dorothy to be asked to show these Wounds. She visibly shrank from doing so, and only consented in obedience to Langford-James who was her spiritual director, and to whom she considered herself to be under a vow of obedience. I was not shown the fifth Wound, that on the side. Dr. Langford-James told me afterwards that this had caused Dorothy such excruciating pain that he had prayed it might be healed; his prayer had been answered and the Wound did heal.

"I remember I was struck at the time by Dorothy telling me she had always believed the Stigmata received by St. Francis were not physically visible. I did not after that see her except upon a few occasions. Later, I heard that she had left Dr. Langford-James to take up her life work.

DOROTHY M. ARNOLD."

Burrswood, Groombridge,
Kent.

CHAPTER 5

Interior Progress

IN the weeks following the appearance of the Stigmata, Dorothy gradually recovered her health. Her strength had been tried by this great spiritual experience with its accompaniment of excruciating physical pain, and for a while she had a succession of hemorrhages from the lungs and stomach. She was herself by Christmas, and had much joy in being allowed to arrange the Crib, and in decorating the Church with flowers, for which art she had an unrivalled gift. She was also given charge of the Altar linen and church vestments.

In the small hours of the night, on St. Stephen's Day, while she was kneeling in prayer, she was vouchsafed a vision of the Holy Family at Bethlehem. A description of this vision exists in her own handwriting, just as she wrote it down at her spiritual director's request:

"On this night my soul was moved by the Holy Spirit to pray. In my prayer, I beheld the Holy Family at Bethlehem: the Divine Infant lying in a manger, watched over by St. Joseph and His Blessed Mother. She bade me 'draw nigh and behold THE LAMB OF GOD'. As I gazed, adoring my little Saviour, our Lady lifted Him out of His nest and put Him into my arms saying 'Share also my joy.' O unspeakable rapture of delight! The Holy little Head pillowed Itself against my breast, and the tiny baby hands caressed me. He lay in my arms cooing with glee as babies are wont to do. As I held Him, He grew heavier and heavier, until His weight became too much for me. Then our Blessed Lady took Him back and the vision passed. The King asked in my soul then: 'Little Beloved, lackest thou anything?' And I answered, No, Lord."

Father Langford-James felt the time had come to draw his ward into some of the parish activities. He asked her to look after the Mothers' Union and to organize their meetings. He also asked her if she would hold a Bible Class for youngsters on Sunday. Children have always instinctively loved and trusted Dorothy, and she was always immensely popular with them, so that her classes became a much appreciated feature of the religious life of the parish. She later conducted a similar class for adults that was equally successful.

In the early part of 1916, Dorothy suffered greatly from malicious stories spread about her by one of the parish workers, a spinster of a narrow and suspicious disposition, who became intensely jealous of her. She endured this cruel persecution with great patience and humility, virtues which she possessed to an extraordinary degree, and told her spiritual director that she was glad to be given the opportunity to offer up to our Lord the pain this woman had caused her. She also confided to him that whenever she meditated on the Passion, and at the Consecration at the Mass, she felt intense pain in all five places where the marks of the Wounds showed themselves. The woman eventually left the parish, but not until she had inflicted much suffering upon her innocent victim.

Early in Lent, Dorothy had a vision of our Lady, who showed her a blue rope dependent from her hands and doubled, having at one end three large knots, one white at the top, one blue, and one black. Father Fynes-Clinton had spoken to Dr. Langford-James about the advisability of his ward taking private vows. He approached her on the subject and found her very reluctant to commit herself to such a course of action.

That summer, Dorothy went to stay with her old friends, the Macauleys, at Paignton, and while there saw Dr. George who had attended her during the illness that followed the attack made upon her by the unknown ruffian, which she has described in *The Living Touch*. He thoroughly overhauled her, and said there was nothing organically wrong with her, but that she was suffering from collapse, and must be very careful to do all that was possible to build up her strength.

She wrote from Devon to her director:

"Your letter has just come and cheered me up immensely. I had not written before because I knew you had all the news from Iris and Josey. The joy at seeing the former was great, as you can imagine. Josey loved her and hopes to see her again. The 'King' has not come yet, Padre. I had a feeling deep down in me that *perhaps* He would, but now I feel that He cannot come until I have done what He has asked. I long to do it, and am so sorry to keep Him away by my rebuffs. It sounds presumptuous to say that He is longing to come back, but I believe this is so, therefore I am eager to get back for I have not been able to do much here in the way of preparation for my Confession. It is impossible to be recollected with dear Josey about, so I must possess my soul in patience until Saturday next. By the way, Dr. George has thoroughly overhauled me every inch. I will not bother you with his diagnosis until my return, but then I fear I must. The weather has kept fine and we have enjoyed lots of drives. If only you were here. Please give my love to everybody, but please keep all my best love for yourself."

On her return from Paignton, it was evident to her spiritual director that the long period of desolation was over. She told him that she had been able to resume her way of prayer, and had been given the ecstasy of full Union. She had had a Vision in which she felt herself united to our Lord. She said she seemed to enter right into His Sacred Heart and His Wounds, so that she did not seem any longer to have her own body, but that His and hers became one. Previously she had felt Him coming into her, but now she felt herself lost in Him. At Dr. Langford-James's insistence, she likewise recorded this vision:

"I cannot put into words the utter desolation, the indescribable ache, and longing, for the *realization* of the King dwelling in my heart. There can be no desolation like it, hell itself cannot be blacker than these past months in which my divine Jesus has hidden Himself, and taken away all spiritual consolation. I have failed Him so badly, in hopelessness, grumblings, and despair, and have indeed deserved that He should never more reveal His divine nearness to me, His faithless servant. But He has not rewarded me as I deserved, with hell. He has come out of His House, and ravished my soul with delights, embracing me in His love until I ceased to be and there remained nothing save JESUS in His Majesty reigning and possessing *all*. The 'little house' shook and the King burst out of it and seized me to His Heart, saying 'little beloved'. I asked Him: 'My Jesus, why have you left me?' And He said, 'I have never left thee, I have hidden in the secret of thy heart. Reproach me not that I have given thee the darkness of Gethsemane. I was there with thee. For thy comfort, know that every tear and cry wrung from thy heart for me, I have counted as drops of blood from MY heart. Come, little beloved, into the garden.' And from the shelter of His Sacred Heart (for I was *in* His Heart) I saw a Cross, firmly planted in the ground, the top of it I could not see for it reached up into heaven. The Cross was marked with spots of blood, out of each spot – I saw a soul reposing, then, the spots became steps, up which the souls mounted. The King showed me much more which I cannot write."

To the spiritually discerning, this Vision foreshadows the redemptive nature of Dorothy's ministry in the years to come. The Cross – always the Cross – marked with spots of blood; in each spot a soul reposing; the ascent up the steps leading to the Heaven hidden from view; here we have symbolized that impressive cloud of witnesses, redeemed and brought to knowledge of the Living Touch of the Living Lord through the compelling power of the Christlike love of His servant. Who can measure in human terms the costly nature of these spiritual labours? The sleepless nights spent in intercessory prayer; the pain of the 're-buffs' promised her by her Master, blows often inflicted by those nearest and dearest to her; the Cup spilling over with the red wine of suffering that she for ever lifted up in a spirit of at-one-ment with her Crucified Lord to Whom her whole life was one constant hymn of love and dedicated service.

Nor must be omitted that "Joy of the Lord" which at times welled up within her from the hidden springs of the Eternal Life, in which she so consciously had her being, to find expression in outbursts of joyous songs of praise and thanksgiving for His bountiful mercies in so richly blessing her ministry. This "Joy of the Lord", known to all God's saints, can be likened to a silver lining to the over-all mantle of pain and suffering in which He so often enfolds the chosen vessels of His grace.

During this period of renewed power of prayer, Dorothy saw the Crucified Figure on the Oberammergau Cross come to life and stand out every night. It hung just opposite her bed. This miraculous Cross now stands in the Oratory of the Reserved Sacrament at Burrswood.

Dorothy was professed about this time; that is to say she took the Simple Vows of Holy Poverty, Chastity and Obedience. The *Forma Receptionis Votorum Simplicium Privatorum* reads as follows:

"Priest: Dost thou wholly and of thine own free will and assent take before God and me His priest the Vows of Holy Poverty, Chastity and Obedience, according to what thou shalt now profess, and to the laws of Holy Church?

"R. I do so desire, God being my helper.

"Priest: Thanks be to God. Read your Vows and sign them."

Priest countersigns, and offers them on the Altar.

Written on a sheet of paper torn from a notebook are these words constituting the Simple Vows of Holy Chastity, Poverty and Obedience, made by Dorothy Kerin on the Feast of the Epiphany, 1917, signed by herself and witnessed by Father Langford-James:

"In the Name of the Father and of the Son and of the Holy Ghost.

"And under the invocation of Blessed Mary, Mother of God, and of Blessed Raphael, Angel of Healing, and of St. Teresa, and looking for their assistance, I DOROTHY KERIN, believing myself evidently called by God to do so, do wholly and of my own free will, undertake and promise to Almighty God and to my spiritual father who now receives these vows, from this day forward to observe the Rule of Holy Chastity, thereby abstaining from any act or purpose with the end of marriage, and keeping the spirit of the same in all that I think, say, or do, endeavour to consecrate my whole being to God, my heart with all its affections and my body with all its powers and desires.

"I do undertake and promise to observe the Rule of Holy Poverty, thereby binding myself to use all my moneys under obedience to my Director, making necessity and charity the rule of my expenditure and consulting him as to all amounts over £1.

"I will endeavour to keep the spirit of this counsel, retaining in my possession nothing as 'my own' and using all that is given to me as lent by God for His greater glory.

"I do undertake and promise to observe the Rule of Holy Obedience, thereby to obey my Director in all things lawful, and consecrating my will wholly to God, place myself in entire dependence upon Him.

"These things I undertake and promise to do for the rest of my life. I pray Almighty God to accept these my Vows and to grant me grace to fulfil them in all perseverance, and I do now in token of my oblation and promise sign my name trusting to His mercy.

(*Signed*) DOROTHY KERIN

(*Countersigned*) RICHARD LL. LANGFORD-JAMES."

From Hindhead, where she had gone to recuperate from a setback in health due to a bad chill, Dorothy wrote this letter to her spiritual director:

"My dear Father. I am so sad at the news your letter brings this morning. We have prayed so hard for you and had hoped to hear that the headache had passed off. Today when your letter came we went off and lit candles for you and felt later on that you were better. I do hope this is so.

"Of course, I want to rush back, but perhaps we can help more by staying here and praying. I do not think that our Lord will let you get worse, and shall trust and hope to hear that you are better. You *must* rest. It is good to hear that you are in bed, and hope you will stay there until quite rested. It is all my fault and I am so unhappy about it. I ought not to have let you give out so much to me. It was selfish; I always knew it was wrong, but you would go on, and this is the result. You have to suffer and I cannot bear it. Please do give in to it and rest it out, I will pray my poor prayers of course, but I long also to give you some strength back. I shall ask Jesus tonight to let me come to you whilst you are asleep. You remember, it did make you feel better before, you told me so! Mrs. Cave is so sorry too, and sends her love; she is praying all the time for you. Dear, dear Padre, there is some muddle over these letters. She redirected them and cannot remember whether she posted them in the Hall or took them out, however you do not seem to have received them, we hope they were not important. Today, we have been for a long walk. It was delightful, but we wished you were here. Mrs. Cave thinks we had better come back on Monday, unless you tell us not to. It will be good to get back. This air has done much for me, and I have gained two and a half pounds, which is a good beginning. I'm not quite up to sample, this throat has taken it out of me rather, but it is nearly gone now."

We have in this letter a passing reference to Dorothy's ability consciously to leave her physical body when in her prayer at night to minister to the suffering for whom she was praying. Many people have told of their awareness of her healing ministrations despite the separation in space.

As December 8th once more drew near, her director wondered whether this first anniversary would be marked by a renewal of the Stigmata. He purposely refrained from alluding to the event as he did not wish any element of suggestion to be associated with it. The day passed quietly without a supernatural manifestation of any kind. On December 12th, Dorothy had an ecstasy that lasted all night, and found herself at the foot of the Crucifix at 5.45 a.m. with no recollection of how she went there. She woke up with an extraordinarily happy feeling, but apparently without seeing anything this time.

Christmas Day was preceded by a period of acute depression which Father Langford-James attributed to anxiety about her two brothers who were serving with the Forces at the Front, and of whom nothing had been heard for two weeks.

On Christmas Eve this depression went. Dorothy wished to spend the night in a vigil of prayer in the church, but was not allowed to do so because it was feared she would become too exhausted. She was made very happy by being permitted to clean the Sacred Vessels in preparation for Christmas Day. She went to stay with her mother after celebration of High Mass on Christmas Day, and did not return to Bush Hill Park until December 27th, looking tired but happy. She told Dr.

Langford-James the cause of her happiness. On Christmas Day she had to go down from the Blessed Sacrament Chapel when she made her Communion, just before the 10 o'clock Mass, to fetch a taper to light the candles. She had to pass the Crib on her way. She said she felt a very strong desire to seize the image of the Holy Child and bear it away with her. All Christmas Day she felt a longing to get away to her prayers. This could not be satisfied till night, except for a few minutes in a Church near her mother's home where there was a large Crib. That night she heard footsteps and saw our Lady bearing the Holy Child, which she placed in Dorothy's arms. It nestled its little head on her breast, and our Lady looked adoringly happy. The Child remained with her quite a long time. Dorothy told her director that she had hoped that our Lord would come to her on Christmas night. She said the Devil had been very busy telling her all day (the 27th) that this COULD not be a real experience because our Lord is now a man and could not become again a baby. Father Langford-James reminded her that He *became* the Sacred Heart, and she said, "I never thought of that." He notes in his diary that Dorothy always had a very great love for babies and a delight in holding them; that she possessed a strong maternal instinct. When he once told her of a woman who did not desire to have children, she was horrified and said, "If I ever married I should want fifty of them!"

The experience of having been privileged, in Vision, to hold the Holy Baby twice in her arms took away from her (her director says) any desire for a child of her own. Before she took her vows, the vow of chastity had been a difficulty for some time because of this desire. Now she felt that our Lord Himself had satisfied that desire with Himself.

Father Langford-James begins his diary for 1917 with a partial examination of the spiritual progress made by his ward since she came in 1915 under his direction.

Masters of the spiritual life tell us that God permits imperfections in His chosen ones to keep them humble, to leave them something to struggle with so that they may be safeguarded from the danger of spiritual pride.

Dorothy possessed an unusually strong will allied to very real intellectual gifts, which made obedience to her director a difficulty to her, but, he remarks, she had made considerable progress in this respect. He also notes that she had learnt to be more discerning and less obliging in the sense of putting herself at the mercy of the sentimentalism of her friends. Since she was endowed with great natural gifts in the way of personal beauty and charm; possessed a sparkling wit and a naturally happy disposition; a gentle and attractive manner combined with a voice whose lovely cadences expressed her varying moods, she was in every respect a magnetic and fascinating personality. All her friends of either sex had a tendency to fall in love with her. When Father Langford-James first knew her she was so anxious not to hurt feelings, that she used to allow the display of a great deal of natural affection Interiorly she was averse to it by instinct, and this instinct he sought to strengthen by instruction. In the process of acquiring discrimination, there had been a certain amount of excess on the other side, viz. in the way of critical judgement. Dorothy was, thank God, a very human person, and remained so to the end of her days. It could be said of her, as was said by an ancient chronicler of Catherine of Siena, with whose temperament she had many affinities (as also with that of St. Teresa of Avila), "Everybody loves Catherine Benincasa because she was always and everywhere a woman in every fibre of her being." It was a measure of Dorothy's spiritual greatness, that the frequent 'letting down' of herself by many of her friends, which had taken place over the past two years, did not make her bitter or cynical. She may sometimes have been a little severe in her judgement, but this, Father Langford-James thought, was better than being sloppy. Sloppiness, he remarks, was a fault she had been only too prone to fall into two years ago (and to some extent had done so) out of mistake for Charity. He ends his brief disquisition by saying, "She has really learnt very well, and will do better."

Bush Hill Park was a centre for the making of munitions of all kinds. The Small Arms Factory was a vital part of this war industry, and therefore a constant target for air-raids, which during 1917 became increasingly frequent and caused much damage to property as well as taking its toll of human lives.

A particularly bad air-raid took place in July on a Saturday at about 10.30 a.m. Dorothy was as frightened as were the other inmates of the Vicarage. She had no fear of death, but a great shrinking from the physical effects of such a raid and the suffering caused to so many of its innocent victims, especially to the children and the old and helpless. The household assembled in her room, and at their request Dorothy prayed aloud, kneeling before the Crucifix towards which they all faced. Shrapnel began to hit the house and Dorothy asked the priest to give them absolution. As he did so, she saw a great light shoot out from the Crucifix, and this was likewise seen and attested to by the Vicarage maid, Beatrice. Others in the room said afterwards that the Figure on the

Cross appeared larger than it normally was. They all felt a supernatural power present, with assurance of divine protection.

The strain of these air-raids affected Dorothy's health considerably. The nights spent in prayer for the many killed and wounded at this time at the Front, where her brothers were serving, added to the ill effect, and she became alarmingly weak physically. Her doctor urged an immediate change to more peaceful surroundings. Dr. Langford-James decided to hasten his annual holiday, and early in August he took his wife and his ward to Wales. Their destination was the village of Beddgelert where they stayed for a week. Dorothy bore the journey well although it had necessitated all night travelling in a crowded train.

The next day, Dr. Langford-James took her up a little hill near the village to see how she would stand it, and she pointed to Aran (some 2300 feet), one of the highest mountains around there, and asked why they could not go up that. He told her they could at any rate try. They did try and got right to the top where they were met by a squall of rain and wind which affected Dorothy's heart. The Cross in her side was inflamed and painful on the third night she stayed at Beddgelert. They moved to Llyndu and from there climbed Snowdon a fortnight later, going very slowly by the Aran Gap route and coming down into Cwm Dyli and by the Glasllyn waterfall. Dorothy was very tired and stiff, but otherwise suffered no ill effects from the unaccustomed and strenuous exercise. She did not sleep well at Llyndu on account of rats which made a great noise in the rafters over her head at night.

Owing to the noise of the rats, they moved to Nant Efrancon on September 28th. They drove over because of a high wind and heavy clouds on the Glyders. They stopped at the foot of Tryfan and did the Milestone Buttress roped, Dr. Langford-James leading, Dorothy second and Mrs. Langford-James last. While climbing in the district Dorothy had an alarming experience. Following the practised mountaineer that Father Langford-James was after years of mountain climbing, she nearly came to grief as the result of disobeying his instructions. She often told the story to stress the importance of obedience. He had told her to do in all respects as he did, putting her feet where he put his, holding on to the same handholds as he did. At one point, it seemed to her that were she to follow a route promising a quicker ascent, she would arrive at the crest ahead of him. She started her climb, but before long got hold of a loose bit of rock which came away in her hand, and she began rolling down the steep slope at a pace which made it appear as though nothing could prevent her from being dashed to pieces on the rocks below. Just as she reached a narrow ledge from whence there was a sheer drop of several hundreds of feet, she felt strong and compelling hands preventing her further progress. The Angels were busy upholding her on the very brink of disaster. She looked up and saw the ashen face of her director gazing down at her. Shouting to her not to move, he scrambled down and roped her to himself. To enforce the lesson of obedience, he made her go up the ascent once more; this time she was careful to obey in every movement his instructions. His insistence that she should continue the climb may sound rather heartless, but had he not done so, she would probably have lost her nerve permanently and never climbed again.

There is no record of what the doctor had to say about this strenuous and exhausting holiday! Dorothy was not well on her return from Wales. She had a succession of hemorrhages from the lungs and constant headaches. Her nights were devoid of sleep and her prayer became again desolate and arid. She felt very restless and had a vision of our Lady beckoning her away from Bush Hill Park.

Dr. Langford-James had occasion to reproach her more than once for laxity in the observance of her Rule. He says that during this time of difficulty, he got much help and comfort from reading Father Baker's *Life of Gertrude More.* He found her to resemble Dorothy in many ways. Their dispositions were similar and so were their temptations. He reminds himself that he has had always to keep in view that Dorothy was progressing towards perfection, and that she had still faults to amend. Her temptations were just as fierce, in their way, as those of more ordinary people. There had been times when she had been really wilful and 'touchy', but she had at all times the desire and wish to overcome faults. Dr. Langford-James was grateful to Father Baker for the reminder that it was necessary for a director to exercise great patience, and that he must not expect perfection to be achieved all at once, or even that great strides should be made, and must not be discouraged when progress seemed slow. In reality, Dorothy had made considerable advance in the past three years. Her former manner of life, which suited in many ways her quick interest in people and things, had dissipated her and left a good deal to be done. By affection, she was now rooted in the Langford-James household. She had borne more than could ever be assessed in giving up her freedom, and it was not to be wondered at if at times she felt restless.

Our Lady appeared to Dorothy and comforted her much, giving her a grip over herself again, so that her life once more resumed the even tenor of its way. For some time, Father Langford-James had urged her to write down her experiences in prayer, and it is thanks to his insistence that we have the following beautiful description of a 'showing' of her soul to Dorothy by our Lord Jesus Christ.

"This will be the third attempt I have made of trying to tell you about my last visit to the garden. It is so very difficult, nay, almost impossible to tell you in words what happened there, for in the kingdom of the garden there is no language, save that of the Divine Heart, which you know so well does not consist in words. I have asked the Holy Spirit to help me and if He wills it so, then I shall be able to share with you in some degree the unspeakable joy and pain that came to my soul in those moments of seeing. You know, Father, how unhappy I have been for some time, knowing in my heart that I have done so badly with the difficulties that have come lately, and how ill I have used the graces that the King has given me! Well, I was in my prayer (which was taken up with these thoughts) when I found myself in the garden (I have not been there for some time). There was a difference there. It looked fuller, and there was more scent, but something felt quite new. I could not understand. Then I saw our Lady in it (she has not been before), and knew she had been working there. She came to me, and you remember I told you about that wonderful smile when she gave me the baby Jesus to hold? Well, it was the same, but it passed and she looked sad. I think she knew how bewildered I was about things for she took my hand and led me to the different plants. Her tears were still wet on some of them, and her caress was on others. When they had all been visited, I was alone. In the corner of the garden, I saw a little heap of weeds, the ones our Lady had pulled up, but there were others, some quite near the plants, and as I looked at them, it was given to me to see my life since the King made the garden. He showed me every sin and imperfection which had produced these weeds, the small ones came out and were added to the heap, but the others would not yield; bit by bit they were creeping towards three of the King's best loved plants, and one little tendril had started to clutch the stem of the HOPE plant and the weed was *fear*. The same with the CHARITY plant, only the weed had not quite reached it. That weed was *judging*. Then the FAITH plant, the weed was not so near this, but was creeping on. That weed was *despair*. As I saw these things, the Holy Spirit showed me everything that had been done by me to produce weeds, which have pierced the Heart of Jesus. I was so truly sorry that I knelt down and confessed it all to the King, and oh! Father, it is impossible to tell you the joy and the peace which came into my soul after I had received absolution. Then the King opened the door of His little House, and came out. He took me to the other side of the door, and showed me the other plants. He *had* been pleased with them. The OBEDIENCE plant had got some new flowers (there were no weeds by it!!) and two were big ones. Then the 'Lily' plant, that had also some new blooms, and how do you think they got there? It was through Beatrice, and now I am so thankful for that time. Then I saw a new plant. It had blooms on it. It was the tree of pain borne for His sake. The flowers were red like rubies and hung down like great red hearts.

"Then He showed me about the last one, and clasped me in that unspeakable love embrace and drew me into the little house. I dare not try to tell you in words of those transcendental moments for it would be impossible. But I can tell you this: that in that space there was nothing but GOD, and, oh! Father, in that divine embrace I was God, for I was *in* God, nothing else existed. You will not be afraid of my saying this, for you will know that I dared to say it, because there was no 'me'. When the King put me from Him, I saw that all the weeds had gone from the garden and my heart was breaking with thankfulness. I have promised the King that I will be more watchful over that garden in future, for He loves it and means it to be so fair a place. I must tell you now, dear Father, how sorry I am for my lack of obedience, and all the difficulties I have made for you. You have been ever gentle and patient with my wilfulness and sinning, and the little progress I have made. I am indeed ashamed of it all, and was horrified to see what sad havoc it had made, as I know how it will pain you, but I had to tell you. It is almost too much to bear alone, and you will also share the joy of knowing that the King has renewed it all. I am very, very happy; so happy that I almost dread the possibility of forgetting those moments of real sorrow. Help me to remember them always, dear Father, *for that sorrow is the remedy against weeds.*"

The hall-mark of the experience known as the Transforming Union or Spiritual Marriage is this sense of utter transmutation of the self in God, a transcendental experience which those who have undergone it find impossible to express in terms of human language, hence their use of the word 'deify'. 'Deification' is a term familiar to both the Eastern and Western Fathers of the Church.

"The body of God deifies me and feeds me," says Simon Metaphrastes (10th century). "It deifies my spirit and it feeds my soul in an incomprehensible manner."

St. Athanasius declares, "He became man that we might become God." St. Augustine, in one of the most beautiful passages in his *Confessions* says: "I heard Thee saying to me from on high: 'I am the food of those grown up; grow, and you shall feed on me; neither shalt thou, like bodily food, change Me into thee; but thou shalt be changed into Me!"

Richard of St. Victor, 12th-century Prior of the Abbey of St. Victor in Paris, who has been called the 'spiritual Master of the Middle Ages', taught that "The third grade of love is when the mind of man is rapt into the abyss of the Divine Light, so that utterly oblivious of all exterior things, *it knows not itself* and passes wholly into God. While it is on all sides encircled by the conflagration of Divine Love and is intimately penetrated and set on fire through and through, it strips off self and puts on a certain divine condition, and being configured to the Beauty gazed upon, it passes into a new kind of glory."

Louis of Blois (Blosius), a Benedictine Abbot who died in 1566, has this to say of the soul's sublime union with God: "It is a great thing, an exceeding great thing, in the time of this exile to be joined to God in the divine light by a mystical and denuded union. This takes place where a pure, humble, and resigned soul, burning with ardent love, is carried above itself by the grace of God, and through the brilliancy of the divine light shining on the mind, it loses all consideration and distinction of things, and lays aside all, even the most excellent images, and all liquefied by love, and, as it were, reduced to nothing, it melts away into God. It is then united to God without any medium, and becomes one spirit with Him, and is transformed and changed into Him, as iron placed in the fire is changed into fire, without ceasing to be iron."

The great mystics are unanimous in their conformity to the teaching of the Catholic Church that the state of Union with God in no way implies annihilation of their individuality, or absorption into the Godhead, but that always the self, although divinely penetrated, remains intact and retains its full personality. This experience of *deification* is in fact the consummation towards which their lives of contemplative prayer with its costly demands have led them. Their hitherto limited lives are henceforth enhanced by the Absolute Life, and therefore they become spiritually fertile and creative, for ever seeking their outlet in the service of mankind.

CHAPTER 6

Apostolate of Prayer

DR. LANGFORD-JAMES felt the time had come for him to seek another parish with a more salubrious climate than that of Bush Hill Park. The place was not favourable to Dorothy's health, nor was it to his own, as it was very damp and the Vicarage stood on clayey soil. Dorothy had been eager for a change since the day she had seen St. Mark's with a wall around it, and himself and herself standing on the opposite side of the wall. She told her director she believed this 'showing' meant they were to leave Bush Hill Park. He wrote to the Archdeacon of London to enquire if there was any likelihood of his being given a City living. He wanted a smaller parish where he would have more time to devote to the Ministry of Divine Healing. Nothing came of his enquiry, and he continued his search. Among the many parishes he made an unsuccessful bid for was that of St. Barnabas at Tunbridge Wells.

In February, Dorothy caught a chill which resulted in severe nausea accompanied by hemorrhage, and on the following day she had pain in her cross. Someone was falsely accusing her, or, rather, not believing in the validity of her experiences, and this she felt acutely. All she told her director was that someone was offending our Lord, and she prayed to offer the pain in her cross for this person. He told her she was to pray to have it removed. She had difficulty in accepting this direction, but did so. The Devil tempted her to disobey, telling her the direction was contrary to the Divine Will. The pain ceased for a while, and then the wound burst and Dorothy had great pain and discomfort from its sticking to her clothes and to a handkerchief she had placed over it. After two days, she decided she should try to remove the handkerchief which had got pressed right into the wound. She knew this would cause agony, and shrank from it. She prayed before the Crucifix for strength. She was just on the point of taking hold of the handkerchief when she felt her hand held, and the handkerchief fell out and off the wound of its own accord on to the floor. The next day the wound was quite healed.

Easter was a time during which Dorothy was blessed with transcendental and experiential knowledge of God's Being and Presence. She woke one night at midnight and remained in prayer, kneeling in front of the Crucifix, until 6 a.m. The next day, she asked Father Langford-James whether the Incarnation was still a mystery to him. He replied, "Of course." She then said, "What if it ceased to be?" He answered, "The Incarnation can never cease to be a mystery. Our Lord is always man till all eternity." "But," she said, "supposing one knows about the Incarnation?" She refused to tell him more except that she had been shown the Mystery of the Incarnation, and that before this had been revealed to her in an ecstasy, she had been led for some time to meditate upon this great Mystery. She also told her director that she had seen her Angel with a gold pen in his hand, and had seen the same thing before writing *The Living Touch*. He asked her to write down what she had seen about the Incarnation, but she said she could not. He told her that if it were in God's Will she would be enabled to do so, and that perhaps she would be led to do this in her prayer, as St. Teresa had.

On Maundy Thursday, Dorothy went up to the Blessed Sacrament Chapel and was in her prayer for many hours. She told Father Langford-James afterwards that our Lord had told her to watch with Him until His hour came. The next day, Good Friday, she spent in the Chapel. Her director found her there in the early hours of Saturday morning. She had just come out of her prayer. She told him that she had seen the whole of the Passion; that our Lord had kept her close to the Cross all the time. He had not spoken to her. She had seen optically the Divine Desolation and also the piercing of the heart of our Lady. She said, "When they killed Him, I felt I could have died myself." She experienced the pain in her wounds but they did not open, and the pain only lasted for the time of the ecstasy.

Father Langford-James asked her to write down what she had seen as far as she could, and she said she would try to do so.

On Friday in Easter Week all her wounds opened, but only for a day. She was staying at Bovey Tracey with the Moodys, and during the time she was there she was frequently in her prayer at night. She said she had prayed that if she loved our Lord well enough He would allow her to bear the pain in her side (in the cross). She had been afraid her love was growing cold, and had said so to her director a short time previously. He then explained to her that love did not consist in feeling but in the direction of the will. On her return, she had a severe pain in her side. It increased, and at 10 p.m. Father Langford-James went to her room to see how she was, and stayed with her for she was obviously in great pain. At midnight she opened her eyes and said with a wonderful smile and a ring in her voice, "Father, I DO love Him!" He replied that he knew she did. Then the pain suddenly left her, and she went into a deep sleep.

In April, Dorothy went to stay with friends at Worthing. While there, she had an acute attack of appendicitis and had to be moved to a Nursing Home. Dr. Langford-James received an urgent call from the Hospital asking him to get in touch with the doctor. This he did, and the doctor told him that in his view the operation should be performed without further delay, as he felt every hour was of consequence. Dr. Langford-James said he would come at once to see him. He arrived at Worthing at 9 p.m. and went straight to the Hospital. That night he sat by Dorothy's bed, and they both prayed that if it was in God's Will that the operation should not take place He would give them a sign. In the morning, the doctor found Dorothy's pulse was racing, and he said she was in danger. An eminent Brighton surgeon was called in consultation, and he decided to perform the operation upon her immediately. The surgeon found a bad septic state with a quantity of fluid. Later, her doctor told Dorothy all about the operation and said they had been terrified because the appendix had been so very septic. The morning after the operation, Dorothy noticed that the cross in her side had disappeared, except for an almost imperceptible white scar. She was so grateful to have thus been able to keep it from the notice of the doctors and nurses. She made a quick recovery and left the Nursing Home in record time.

She asked the King for a sign as to whether they had been right in consenting to this operation, and told her director that He had taken her for a whole night into her prayer, and the cross in her side had been restored to her. She returned to Bush Hill Park at the end of May, and stood the journey very well. She insisted upon taking her place again in the Vicarage household and doing all she could, in every way she was allowed to help domestically. Dr. Langford-James remarks that he never met anyone with such extraordinary thought for others, and that she was really excessive in her desire not to be a burden and give trouble.

The Enfield doctor said the 'air' at Bush Hill Park was 'suicidal' for Dorothy, and in consequence of his urging him to do so, Dr. Langford-James renewed his efforts to obtain another parish, preferably in the country. He had had hopes of being given one near Dorking which would have done very well, as it stood on high ground, was very healthy and was also promising from the parish point of view. But again he was disappointed, as the living was given to someone else.

They all went to stay at Sidley near Bexhill for a month, and her director noticed Dorothy seemed strained and unlike herself most of the time they were there. As they consisted of a party of three, it was difficult for him to have a private talk with her, but on their return she told him that soon after their arrival at Sidley an 'Angel' had come to her and suggested that her spiritual director was neglecting her, therefore he had been sent to comfort her. This pleased her. She welcomed the visits of this Angel, until he began to sow doubts in her mind, notably about her lack of faith in submitting to the operation. The dubious 'Angel' also told her she must leave the Langford-James household as her soul was in danger. Father Langford-James reminded her that they had both prayed that if it were not in God's Will that the operation be performed, He would give them a sign to guide them. No sign had been given and the operation had taken place with beneficial results. He said he did not think her 'angelic' visitor was one who belonged to the army of light but rather to that of darkness, and that he was a messenger of the Evil One. The fact that he had threatened to show her something of an impure nature confirmed him in this belief. He impressed upon her that she was never to show fright at such a threat, as that was to play into the Devil's hands, because God would never allow it to happen.

There came at last the day when the Armistice was signed on the Feast of St. Martin, November 11th. St. Martin is the patron saint of all soldiers.

With the passing of winter, the news from the Front had improved. This improvement coincided with a marked amelioration in Dorothy's health. Two years before, when the war was at its blackest, she had told her director that while praying for the soldiers at night, she would often find herself, out of her body, on the blood-stained battlefields of Flanders, kneeling by those left to their fate in the barbed wire entanglements and waterlogged pot-holes of the devasted no-man's-land between the contending armies. Many of those dying under the cold, wind-swept skies must have felt sustained and comforted by the appearance of an angelic presence who helped to make their transition to the life beyond an easier and happier one than otherwise it would have been. Her director was convinced that much of her ill-health was caused by spiritual sympathy and at-one-ment with the suffering of the war years.

Dorothy was immensely cheered that year by a steady succession of miraculous healings of patients whose lives had been despaired of by their doctors. She was frequently vouchsafed a sight of her patients when praying for them, and the vision would often be followed by news of their recovery. All through these years of withdrawal and preparation, she never ceased to exercise her God-given ministry of healing. By means of a correspondence which, although not comparable in size with that which reached her in her later years, was nevertheless considerable, she helped many whose lives had been shattered by problems arising out of the unnatural conditions of home life that prevailed during the war years. By no means the least part of her ministry consisted in renewing the faith of those whose belief in a God of Love had been destroyed by their war experiences, and among these were not a few priests. Interviews were rarely granted (though they sometimes took place), owing to her spiritual director's conviction that such interviews had a disturbing effect upon the prayer life of his ward. Occasionally he allowed her to speak in public, but only at meetings held in the drawing-rooms of friends. He appears to have felt impelled to keep the 'light' entrusted to his care within the four walls of his home. Nevertheless, that 'light' shone with increasing brilliance, and its fame gradually spread abroad to reach the homes of many whose darkened lives were lit by the beauty and radiance of its holiness.

On the night of December 8th, anniversary of the Stigmata, our Lord came to her and showed her His Sacred Wounds again. She felt the pain in herself, but no marks showed the next day. She remembered the anniversary for the first time when she saw our Lord's Wounds, and felt very happy all day.

In 1919, Dr. Langford-James was offered the living of Thruxton, near Andover. They all went down on May 26th to see the place and were delighted with it. The offer came unexpectedly, and everything seemed to point to its being the Divine Will that he should accept it, which he did. Dorothy had always said she thought an unexpected offer would come and would prove to be the right one. They were very thankful the period of waiting was over.

In June, Dorothy went to stay at Dartmouth. She had trouble with her heart while there, as she had strained it walking up the steep hills around the town. She was also unfortunate enough to put her hand on a viper, which stung her middle finger. She put it into boiling water and treated it with iodine, but did not send for a doctor. The next day her friend took her to see one, and he ordered her straight to bed as she had a temperature. This is how she described the accident in a letter to Dr. Langford-James:

"It is good to hear from you, for I had begun to wonder whether you were all dead. It is good to hear what the Bishop has said. [This alludes to a very nice letter from the Bishop of Winchester, in which he states his willingness to accept Dr. Langford-James.] And I am so thankful that it is all plain sailing for you now. Let us hope the great trek may take place before the autumn. What can have happened to my other letters? I don't understand it.

"Iris has told you of a misfortune I suffered. It was a snake. I fell into the stream and in clutching on to the bank must have barged into the viper and it bit my middle finger. We put on iodine and steeped it well in boiling water, and it seemed to go down, but in the night it got bad again, and the next day Iris carried me off to see the doctor. He found me with a temperature, and promptly sent me off to bed again, where I have been ever since. He has half promised to carry me out on to the verandah today when he comes. He will not allow me to move out of bed, so there is very little chance of my coming home on Tuesday. Josey came up and has sat up for a night, and the doctor is getting a nurse or someone today. He says I am getting on well, but *must* be still. We had a dreadful time on Thursday night, but he was so kind and helpful, and stayed till nearly 11 o'clock. It has been very trying, but the kindness of everyone here has been colossal. You'll not worry, will you, because it is really going to be all right."

Dorothy returned to the Vicarage on July 1st. She told Father Langford-James that the friend she had stayed with had delayed in sending for a doctor when the viper bit her. She had felt great pain the night it had happened. She got out of bed to get some brandy, and felt our Lady behind her. She squeezed some black stuff out of her finger, and slept well afterwards. She believed our Lady had saved her life.

On Wednesday, September 17th, the Vicarage household left Bush Hill Park. The parish was sad at losing Dorothy, for she had won a secure place for herself in their trust and affection, and their expressions of sorrow at her departure were both numerous and touching. This was especially the case with the children, many of whom wept bitterly when told their beloved teacher would no longer conduct their Bible Classes. It was a wrench on all sides, and the emotion and fatigue of the uprooting were a strain on Dorothy's frail health.

Thruxton was an old-fashioned village of a type now fast becoming extinct, the focal point of a genuine rural population interspersed with local gentry. The church was a typical country church, small in dimensions, with a mediaeval foundation dating from the 12th century. The present dedication is to St. Peter and St. Paul, though there is known to be an earlier one. When Dr. Langford-James went there, Thruxton enjoyed its full quota of services; now these are shared with two neighbouring parishes. Thruxton Rectory is a mid-Victorian house, in those days without electricity, water on the mains or telephone, in fact the essence of discomfort judged by modern standards, though redeemed to some extent by a pleasant garden. In the early days, the Rectory family entirely accepted the simplicity of their mundane equipment and used to drive to Andover in a pony cart (a distance of some five miles) to do their household shopping.

The parish took warmly to Dorothy from the day of her arrival, and she was readily accepted as a friend by people of all classes in the neighbourhood, even by those unable to understand the significance of her religious mission. She was given charge of the Sunday School and commissioned to take the magazine around and had care of the Altar. She took part with evident enjoyment in such 'social' pleasures as came her way, while with the humbler folk she endeared herself with deeds of genuine service, such as taking great interest in the Women's Institute on its inception in the village. It was from friends at Thruxton that Dorothy acquired her dog Bruno – the "brown verger" of later years.

Three new outdoor activities entered into Dorothy's life at Thruxton. Friends presented her with a bicycle. She quickly became proficient at riding it, and this enabled her to get about the parish with ease, and also to enjoy delightful excursions in the surrounding countryside. She also took keenly to gardening and undertook to grow flowers for the church. This she was very successful in doing, and her artistic arrangement of the altar flowers was a joy to behold. She had a passion for weeding, a task gardeners accept as a necessity but not usually as a pleasure. This dislike of seeing a garden invaded by weeds remained with her always. Often when walking through the gardens at Burrswood, she could be seen to stoop and firmly extract by the roots some obnoxious weed which her quick eye had detected among the flowers. "I cannot abide weeds," she would say emphatically. Could it be that our Lord's 'showing' to her of the mystical garden of her soul, earlier recorded, was at the root of her instinctive abhorrence of weeds?

She was asked to start a group of Brownies in connection with the company of local Girl Guides, and became Brown Owl for Thruxton after passing her tests. Later, her Brownies were reviewed and pronounced very good and efficient.

A friend who knew her well in those days has written the following appreciation of the significance to Dorothy of the Thruxton period:

"This was essentially a period when Dorothy was developing rapidly and striving to find her level mentally and spiritually, and, like all such periods in people's lives, it appeared mainly to be one of strains and contradictions. Looking back at that time, it would seem that two contrasting 'urges' in her make-up were waging war one with the other – the one (rarely allowed free expression in those days) a craving for 'normal' experience, and the other a sense of obligation towards a religious mission on which excessively rigorous demands were obviously being made. It was only during the constructive work of later years that these two aspects in Dorothy's nature were able to achieve their separate fulfilment. Nevertheless, during this period, as also later, there was a genuine capacity for enjoyment, also a sense of humour, coupled with a deep sympathy with, and understanding of, other people, reinforced by a highly developed intuition and mystical vision. In physical appearance, she was pale and ethereal-looking, and curiously young-looking for her years. Life at the Rectory, with its mental and spiritual tensions, added in Dorothy's case to physical ill-health and discomfort, constituted a state of affairs which, even if salutory as a transient experience, was mercifully not destined to continue indefinitely."

Shortly before Christmas, Dorothy went to stay in London, and while there she visited one of the Benedictines of Pershore Abbey, a man of great spirituality who helped her very much. She wrote to Father Langford-James: "After I went in to have tea, he handed me something and asked me if I could smell anything, as it was a little relic of St. Teresa of the Child Jesus, the 'Little Flower'. I could not and neither could he, but later on, just as I was going away, a great burst of roses came all about us, and was so strong on me that I might have been sprayed by a secret spray."

In 1922, Dorothy had a relapse. She went to stay in a convent at Ditchingham. There, Sister Althea (a sister of Mrs. Moody) and the Reverend Mother were a great help to her, but she unfortunately caught cold, and her doctor, on finding that her temperature was constantly oscillating between a high temperature and a sub-normal one, sent her for a time to a sanatorium. Later she was examined by a famous specialist of Harley Street who had an X-ray taken of her lungs. He told Father Langford-James that he felt certain her lungs were affected by T.B.

However, *when the plates were examined, they showed no trace whatsoever of T.B. in either lung*. This showed that the mischief had in reality never returned to her lungs since her miraculous healing in 1912, in spite of the verdict of the doctor who put her in a sanatorium. The specialist himself was very surprised.

While at Thruxton, Dorothy again entered into a period of desolation during which the marks of the wounds disappeared. When in her prayer, she had no experience of joy, only of utter blackness and pain. She had known many dreary stretches of spiritual aridity but none equal to this, and she told her spiritual director that the first week she entered into this particular experience of the Dark Night of the Soul, she thought she would go mad.

Much has been written in mystical literature about the Dark Night of the Spirit, the Great Desolation of Father Baker's Sancta Sophia. St. John of the Cross has traced for our help and understanding the various stages of dereliction through which the soul passes before entering into the pure and lasting joys of the Spiritual Marriage.

In his Treatise, *The Spiritual Life*, Father Tanquerey explains the purpose of the Dark Night of the Soul to be "the achieving of the final purification of the self, the emptying of the self of all that is not of God. The soul is cleansed of the remnants of imperfections and habits; of the least promptings of pride; of vain self-complacency, resulting from the abundance of spiritual favours received, an attitude which if persisted in carries with it the danger of falling prey to illusions such as the mistaking of false visions and prophecies for true ones; also the succumbing to over-confidence, causing loss of the reverent fear of God which is the soul's great safeguard. In order to achieve the purification of the soul, God leaves the mind in darkness, the will in aridity, the memory in forgetfulness, and the affections immersed in pain and anguish. The sufferings of the soul subjected to this process of purification are beyond description. It is a state that is a sort of hell by reason of the torture experienced; a sort of purgatory by reason of the purification achieved. In order to sustain the soul in this trial, God sends intervals of relief during which it again experiences a sweet peace in the enjoyment of divine love and consolations. These moments of respite are quickly followed by renewed anguish and darkness when the soul is filled with conviction that it is no longer loved by God and that it is *justly forsaken* by Him."* This is the very core of the anguish of spiritual dereliction.

* By kind permission of Desclee & Cie Editeurs S.A.

What are the fruits of this painful process of purification? St. John of the Cross says the effects of what he calls "this blessed night" are to darken the mind in order to give it light in everything; to humble the soul and make it miserable in order to raise it up and set it free; to impoverish it and empty it of all the natural self and affections in order to enable it to reach forward divinely to the possession and fruition of what are termed the heroic virtues. The duration and frequency of these periods of desolation depend upon how much imperfection there is to destroy, and the *degree of union with Himself to which God means to raise the soul.*

They had not long been settled at Thruxton before Dr. Langford-James began to encounter opposition from some sections of the parish owing to his extreme Catholic views and practices. He followed after a period of Protestant tradition, a fact which gave rise to considerable friction where the more bigoted section of the parish was concerned. This opposition increased with the passing of time, and its repercussions upon Dorothy's sensitive and loving nature were very hurtful. She had a deep affection for her spiritual director, as well as a sense of great loyalty towards him, and in consequence of this growing friction she suffered much for and with him.

In 1921, while Dorothy was still experiencing utter desolation, she received back the wounds in her hands and feet. Her director notes that the marks were smaller than they used to be, but that nevertheless she had had to use no less than four handkerchiefs in an effort to staunch the blood that flowed from them, and that she could only walk with great difficulty. She continued to be conscious of intense pain and of a darkness through which "no ray of light came". She felt that surely she had now reached the very depths of the darkness and that there could be no greater depth. The chief terror for her of this Dark Night was that she had not been able to feel she belonged to Christ as she was accustomed to do.

The epidemic of influenza that was then raging in Europe claimed its victims in England, and among these were the Rector of Thruxton and his delicate ward. They recovered, but both fully experienced its aftermath of depression and lassitude, and this, coupled with the sense of her abandonment by God, resulted in the treading by Dorothy of a veritable *Via Dolorosa* that was her ascent to Calvary.

In the course of the summer, the terrible darkness lifted. Dr. Langford-James was attending an Anglo-Catholic Congress in London when this happened. He received a brief note from Dorothy to say that our Lord had come to her and had said, "Arise, my love, and come away, for lo! the winter is passed and the rain is over and gone, . . ." When he got back, he asked her about it, and she told him that the 'little house' had seemed to burst and our Lord had come to her with such power of love that she could hardly bear it. He had told her that He had never really been away from her; she had, all this time, been securely held in his Sacred Heart, but that it had been necessary for her to experience the uttermost sense of desolation and dereliction. She could now say to her beloved Lord and Saviour in the fullness of union with Him:

"In my Saviour's Wounds is perfect and enduring rest. There I dwell securely. His Heart lies open through His Wounds. Whatever I lack, I draw for myself from the Heart of my Lord, for it overflows with mercy; nor does the Wound fail whence it flows. Through the Wounds of His Body, He opens to me the secret place of His Heart. The Wounds of Jesus Christ are full of mercy, full of tender love, full of sweetness and charity."*

* Hugo of St. Victor: *De Anima* (Mediaeval Mystical Tradition and St. John of the Cross by a Benedictine of Stanbrook) (Burns & Oates, London).

CHAPTER 7

Call to Public Ministry

IN 1923, Dr. Langford-James was offered a living at Edgbaston, Birmingham, which he accepted. From then onward he practically ceased his diary, which contains no matters of further interest concerning the mystical prayer life of his ward. It seems by then the pupil had outstripped her teacher, and that she looked for her guidance directly to her Lord, who reigned in her heart as supreme King and Ruler. During the years she remained with Dr. Langford-James, she helped with the many-sided activities of a large and busy parish; attended to her ever-growing correspondence; occasionally visited her family and friends; and spent long hours of intercessory prayer for the increasing number of sick and unhappy people who were turning to her for help and guidance.

In the summer of 1929 an American priest interested in healing, with whom Dorothy had for some time corresponded, came to England in the hope of inducing her to marry him. He knew of her vows but made little of them, considering them to be merely private vows. Shortly after his arrival a crisis developed at the Vicarage which was undoubtedly used by God to detach the chosen vessel of His grace from the Langford-James household in order that she should give to the world the great message entrusted to her by our Lord Jesus Christ at the time of her miraculous healing. The fruitful years of preparation came to an end with the abruptness that was often to mark the momentous happenings which from time to time occurred in the course of her God-guided life of active ministry.

Early one summer morning in July, when Dorothy came out of her bedroom, she found herself facing a small alcove in the passage opposite her room, which was banked high and deep with roses. Roses red, roses white, roses pink, crimson and yellow, their fragrance and beauty enveloped and caressed her on all sides. Dorothy, who loved roses above all flowers, was enchanted and stood rooted in speechless admiration of their loveliness, wondering who it was who had contrived to delight her with such an abundance of her favourite flower. Presently, her fascinated gaze alighted upon a card on which was written, "Meet me in the garden as soon as you can." She recognized the handwriting to be that of her American friend. Murmuring to herself, "How very kind of him," considerably mystified, but totally unsuspecting, she made her way to the garden, where he was awaiting her. He asked her to marry him, portraying to her in glowing terms a life of mutual dedication to the ministry of divine healing so dear to them both; dwelling also with insistence upon the far greater measure of freedom that would be hers in which to exercise her great charismatic gift in the peace and security of a home of her own.

Dorothy listened to him with that tender and sympathetic attention she gave to all who opened their hearts to her with earnestness and sincerity. When he had finished speaking, she shook her head and said with a sweet smile to alleviate the pain which she knew her refusal would cause him, "I am sorry, but it cannot be, because I have vowed to live my life in God's service in holy chastity, poverty and obedience." Realizing how final was her rejection of his proposal, he turned and strode across the lawn to tap at Dr. Langford-James' study window. Soon the sound of a heated argument rent the air, an argument that lasted for a considerable time, during which the American priest told his Anglican brother how wrongly he thought he had acted in allowing his young ward to make such vows for life, and that for his part he felt convinced that it was to do the work of the Devil to continue to keep hidden between the four walls of his Vicarage such a rare and precious soul whom God had endowed with so great a charismatic gift.

The disappointed suitor from the other side of the Atlantic returned to America, having done, beyond doubt, what he had been sent by God to do. Not long after his departure, Dorothy parted from Dr. and Mrs. Langford-James, deeply grateful for all that they had done for her, but making it quite plain to them that she knew God was calling her to serve Him in the outer world. She went to live with her mother in Ealing where, almost immediately, she began to exercise her public ministry. This part of the story of her life belongs to the second half of this book, but before closing this section, it would be well to try to assess the spiritual significance of these long years of patient and obedient preparation for the great work of healing in Christ's Name and for His glory which was to occupy the remainder of her life, and for which she became known and loved all the world over.

Dr. Langford-James closes his diary with these words:

"I have just read through consciously, for the first time, all the notes

I have made about Dorothy. In the light of experience, it now seems to me I expected too much of her vitality when she first came under my care. Her vitality is so wonderful, and she is so utterly unselfish in concealing so far as possible the fact that she is ill, that one is easily deceived. I had the fear of letting her give in too much to the physical. And, also, there was the fear – that she shared always – of her being regarded as an invalid, an idea against which she always protested vigorously. It is quite certain that some mistakes have been made by me. One can only plead that one has tried one's best to avoid them. At the beginning, of course, one had to go by what one read in books of possibly similar cases. As one has gone fourteen years now – and one's relations with Dorothy have really been that of father and daughter from constant association with her – one has gained invaluable experience which has helped me, I think, to avoid mistakes." He ends with this all-important testimony: "The acid test, of course, is the fruits of good living. *Dorothy's power has not diminished, in fact it has increased.*"

What were the fruits acquired during the years outlined in the preceding chapters, fruits harvested at the cost of so much suffering of body, mind and spirit? They were the gifts bestowed by the Holy Spirit upon this fervent soul, who, imbued with an ardent, generous and burning love, attained to a state of habitual communion with God, a state achieved as a result of constant endeavour and self-purification, a state in which she was able to persevere through God's bestowal upon her of His sanctifying grace.

What does such a flowering of the spirit signify? It means that the human personality who underwent this process of sanctification in preparation for her great mission, acquired the faculty of living constantly in God's presence, even in the midst of her many absorbing and exacting occupations. It enabled her to withdraw at all times into the innermost shrine of her heart to receive God's guidance. "I will hear what the Lord God will say concerning me" became the master-motive of her day-to-day living, which she applied to all matters affecting her ministry.

"The progressive steps by which God takes hold of a soul that He is moulding to His purposes are to some extent experienced simultaneously, and should not be viewed as a ladder with its well-defined rungs, a simile that lends itself to any attempt to express in human terms these transcendent states. One state imperceptibly merges into another. Nevertheless, if such be God's will for any particular soul, He sometimes omits one or other of these states and takes the soul directly into the experience of the Transforming Union with Himself. Broadly viewed, however, when God calls a soul to a high measure of sanctity, He first seizes the will, with the soul's free consent, in the Prayer of Quiet; next, He lays hold on the interior faculties in the Prayer of full Union; He then takes complete possession of both the interior faculties and the exterior senses in ecstasy; finally, in the Transforming Union, He binds the whole soul to Himself in an abiding Union."*

St. Teresa of Avila tells us what are the effects of this Transforming Union. She stresses the disappearance of ecstasies: "The raptures cease in the manner I have mentioned, and there are no more flights of the spirit; if they come at all, it is very seldom and almost never in public." The soul is so transformed that it forgets itself and thinks only of God and His glory: "All her thoughts and study will be how to please her Lord, and by what means she will be able to express the love she has for Him. In all that belongs to the service of God, she is more alert than before; and when not otherwise occupied, she rests in that happy companionship."†

As a result of this close companionship with God, the soul becomes filled with an ardent desire to win souls to Him, and to "give faith to the faithless". She no longer aspires to abide in the innermost shrine (St. Teresa's VIIth Mansion) and in sweet repose and stillness to enjoy her Creator in the profound silence characteristic of this Mansion. She is impelled to go forth into the world of humanity in order to "comfort the sorrowing and bring hope to the hopeless".

"Mortification of the senses that plays such a part in the early stages is no longer a necessity. Mortification is not an end in itself. It is a means to facilitate liberation from the shackles of our physical senses. Its purpose served, compulsion to its practice often abruptly ceases."‡

St. Catherine of Genoa, after many years of constant mortification of her senses, found that "in an instant, all thought of such mortification was taken from her mind in such a manner that had she even wished to continue such mortifications, she would have been unable to do so . . . The sight of her sins was now taken from her mind, so that henceforth she did not catch a glimpse of them; it was as though they had all been cast into the depths of the sea."§

So also with Blessed Henry Suso, Servitor of the Eternal Wisdom, who was led to discard all bodily mortifications. "On a certain Whitsun Day, a heavenly messenger appeared to the Servitor and ordered him in

* Fr. Tanquerey: *The Spiritual Life.*
† *Interior Castle.* VIIth Mansion CIII.
‡ Evelyn Underhill: *Mysticism.*
§ *Ibid.*

God's Name to continue it no more. He at once ceased and threw all the instruments of his sufferings into a river."*

Such instances of the compulsory cessation of the mortification of the exterior senses can be multiplied; in contrast, mortification of the interior faculties is a continuous process, bestowing upon the soul an ever greater measure of sanctifying grace to conform in all things to God's Will. The death of selfhood in its possessive, acquisitive sense is the object of mortification. "I live; yet not I; but Christ liveth in me" is the goal to be achieved.†

At the close of these fourteen years of withdrawal from the world, during which she lived in complete obedience to her spiritual director, subordinating her will to his in all matters relating to her spiritual welfare, we find that an instrument, tried and perfected to His purposes, has been forged by God in the person of His servant Dorothy Kerin. From this time onward, Martha is to walk side by side with Mary in a perfect blending of their two natures. The busy, active worker in God's Vineyard, the loving reaper of souls for Christ, the capable, far-seeing administrator, God's steward immersed in her Master's business and alert at all times to His guidance, is sustained in her arduous labours by the long hours of communion with Him in the silent watches of the night. Mary and Martha, these two sides of Dorothy's rich nature, henceforward find their respective outlets in manifesting the amazing diversity of gifts that adorned her unique personality. Having experienced the creative impact of the Transforming Union, she is driven to act, to labour, to suffer, to become the willing instrument of God, and the slave of mankind. She knows that, above all, her work must be inspired by LOVE, and it was the possession by Dorothy Kerin, called by Christ to heal, of this upwelling, outflowing Christ Love that enabled God to use her for those miracles of whole-making for which people in all lands hallow and bless her memory.

* *Life of Blessed Henry Suso by Himself.*
† Evelyn Underhill: *Mysticms.*

PART TWO

The Scattering of the Seed

CHAPTER 8

Chapel House, Ealing

AFTER leaving the home of Dr. and Mrs. Langford-James, Dorothy went to live in Ealing, accompanied by her mother and her younger brother. The separation from her spiritual director, to whom she was deeply attached, and who had done so much to help her, was a great test of her obedience to God's Will. The moment she became convinced that this was what He required of her, she obeyed without hesitation. This virtue of unquestioning obedience to the Divine Will marked each of the ventures in the dark, which at different epochs in her life she was led to make under divine guidance. In every instance these proved to be glorious milestones in the unfolding of God's pattern for her work. Dorothy was wont to say when referring to these events and their sequel, "I leapt over the precipice into His Arms." Securely held in the Everlasting Arms, she invariably found that the frustrations and obstacles confronting her gave place to tangible assurances that God was providing, where He was guiding. The venture at Ealing was the first of many similar evidences, after she began her public ministry, of God's providence in removing difficulties from the path of His obedient servant.

Dorothy has told in her book *Fulfilling** how the possibility came to her of renting a modest house of ten rooms that stood in a row of similar suburban homes in Culmington Road, a quiet locality in West Ealing. There was no money available, for she had no income of her own; yet, somehow, money had to be found to meet the costs of repairs, alterations and furnishings, if she was to realize her heart's desire to open a Home of Healing that was to be a place "to strengthen the weak hands and confirm the feeble knees" of some among the many suffering souls who were constantly appealing to her for counsel and help. It was not intended for cases of acute illness requiring the care of a trained nurse; its aim was to harbour the weary in spirit; to shelter the sheep that had temporarily lost their way from the fold of faith; and to be a place of rest for those convalescing, but who were as yet unable to take

* Dorothy Kerin: *Fulfilling*.

up the burden of life. In a surprisingly short space of time offers of help came from many quarters: gifts and loans of money, furniture and necessary equipment of all kinds flowed into the Home in a steady stream, until the day dawned when St. Raphael, as the Home was christened, was ready to receive its first guest.

In all Dorothy's Homes of Healing, the Chapel has always been the centre, the core, the heart of her work. The minute Chapel in St. Raphael was situated at the top of the house, and here, as at Bush Hill Park, Dorothy would kneel in prayer for long hours at night, after the rest of the household had retired to rest. It was blessed by the Bishop of Southampton* and licensed by the Bishop of London†, and in it, visiting priests celebrated the Holy Mysteries. The following little poem is an expression of Dorothy's fervent communion with her Beloved Master in the silence of her nightly vigils, during which she poured out her heart in intercessory prayer for those whom God had committed to her care:

"*A little Room up a winding stair,*
Blue walls, white altar, flowers are there.

Kneel and pray – wait and pray,
In stillness listen. Hear Him say:

Ye are my Friends. Feed my sheep;
Feed my lambs. O, mystery deep,

In the silence, I whisper, I love Thee, Lord,
Accept my service, my Friend adored."

Beauty, we too often forget, is an attribute of the Eternal Godhead, of no less importance than are Goodness and Truth. God created the universe and clothed it with beauty. His beauty, in the world He created, can be enjoyed by rich and poor alike. Those whose means are limited may not be able to roam as far afield as their more wealthy neighbours, but an excursion into any of the fields and woods of the countryside will quickly bring them face to face with beauty.

Dorothy was a firm believer in the healing agency of beauty. Beauty resided in her touch; beauty of spirit looked out of her compassionate eyes; beauty radiated from her personality. "Nothing is too beautiful for Him," she would say, and she was vigilant that in God's Home of

* Bishop Boutflower.
† Dr. Winnington-Ingram.

Healing beauty should surround His guests. She tolerated nothing that was slipshod or ugly. She once said to a friend who remonstrated with her for buying something beautiful and expensive for Chapel House, "People give our Lord such shoddy, cheap things, and 'left overs' for which they have no use. I am going to give Him all the best and most beautiful things I can." The attractive chintzes and materials that adorned the rooms were personally chosen by her. Harmony, rhythm, colour – each room was the creation of purpose and imagination inspired by love; each had its individual message to convey to its sick, bewildered or fear-ridden occupant. Every room was blessed by the Chaplain, and designed to be, as far as possible, a worthy sanctuary in which to receive the Lord of Life who ministered to the sick in spirit, mind or body through the channel of His humble servant. On the day of arrival, every guest was gladdened by the sight of flowers placed by Dorothy's own hands and arranged by her with the artistry that was her distinguishing feature. Some of her patients came from drab and unhappy homes; others from the bare, impersonal rooms of hospitals and kindred institutions; many from a middle-class environment; a few from stately homes, but no matter whence their origin, they found in Dorothy Kerin's Homes of Healing the distinctive imprint of beauty, harmony, peace and above all of LOVE, the love that is instinct with selflessness, compassion and understanding.

The first guest to be received into Dorothy's first Home of Healing arrived at St. Raphael in the autumn of 1929. Gwen Williams, now Secretary to the Burrswood Fellowship, has recorded her memories of those far-off days when she was rescued, under God, through Dorothy's ministry, from a life of chronic invalidism.

"I first met Dorothy in 1929, at Culmington Road, Ealing, sent by a priest. I was in great spiritual turmoil which was affecting my health. I had seen many doctors. One eminent Harley Street specialist, famed for his ability to diagnose, said I was very ill, but could not discover the nature of the illness. Verdict of the next Harley Street specialist, also a famed diagnostician, was that the cause was not organic. His prescription was 'rest in the care of a doctor for six months; you must have anything in the world you wish for, and you must be crossed in no way whatsoever!'

"When the six months was over, I was allowed to take a part-time post, and it was thought I would never be able to take up full-time work again. I was in this post for two years, having to have treatment in the holidays, and it was towards the end of two years that a priest suggested I went to stay for ten days with a very kind, helpful person called Dorothy Kerin, but told me nothing further about her. A few months after meeting Dorothy, I was able to take a full-time post, doing social work in the slums of London.

"The first night I was there, Dorothy began to tell me about her healing, but although I thought myself to be a Christian, and had had two years' training to be a missionary before my illness, I thought she must be mad and asked her not to tell me any more, as I did not believe her! I thought that night that I must get away the next morning from the house of such a strange person, but at breakfast everything was so normal, and her mother and brother such kindly and happy people, that I decided to stay on but to keep off the subject of divine healing, because that seemed to me to be the one point where Dorothy's madness showed itself. From that day Dorothy never again mentioned her healing to me.

"She was so radiantly happy and so kind, that by the end of my visit I was convinced there was something 'other' about her, and I longed for her to talk to me about herself, but I never had the courage to ask, because somehow I sensed I must not. It was not until some years later when I read *The Living Touch* that I knew the reason for her silence, for our Lord had told her to 'speak of these things in the secret places, and if they listen not, tell them not again'. Her obedience, though it was to my hurt, has always been to me clear evidence of her Divine experience and calling, and increased my faith in a way which perhaps nothing else could have done. Because of her obedience and love and gentleness, our Lord turned my unbelief into a breastplate of faith.

"In those early days, Dorothy was full of irresistible fun and laughter. She herself did not give the laying-on-of-hands, and did not even drop a hint that she was a great woman of prayer – she just seemed to radiate renewed strength and spiritual wholeness, and drew one to our Lord. In appearance, she was small, slender and ethereal looking. Her complexion was creamy with no colour except for her lips. She had very beautiful blue-grey eyes which were most striking. They shone with a spiritual light that seemed fathomless, and their expression varied according to the moods and needs of those she was with. Sometimes they sparkled with light-hearted mirth and joy; at other times they glowed with the tenderness of compassionate love; occasionally their expression was sad as if weighted with the sorrows of the world; and on occasion, they could blaze with righteous indignation. Her eyes were the genuine windows of her soul. She had masses of very dark brown hair, almost verging on black, that framed her sensitive face with attractive curls.

"Always I have felt the love of our Lord through Dorothy. Since 1929 I have had times of illness, and whenever I have had need there was always a bed for me at Chapel House, Ealing, and at Burrswood. I have been physically and spiritually exhausted on arrival, but returned to work with renewed energy and spirit. Once, when I was more seriously ill than I realized, I remember Dorothy writing to me saying, 'When you receive this note, pack your bag at once and come. Your room is ready for you. Our Lord wants you here; don't worry about the money.' My illness suddenly took a much more distressing turn, and if I had been alone in my flat I should not have known what to do, but at Chapel House I had the care and nursing I needed. Once, after delayed concussion through falling off a bus, I thought I would never be able to drive a car in traffic again, but after the laying-on-of-hands by Dorothy I completely recovered.

"One of my most treasured possessions is a most beautiful old silver cross, with a crucifix on one side, and our Lady and the Child on the other, in a blue case lined with white, which Dorothy gave me before I left. She told me she had worn it next her heart for some time until it rubbed too much, and she could bear it no longer. One day, she had taken it with her when she went to visit a mental patient, and a light shone around it and the patient was healed.

"Sometimes in the afternoons, Dorothy would take me for a walk across Walpole Park with Bruno, her dog. Bruno was a mixture, mostly red setter, large with a golden brown coat, and had one of the nicest natures I've ever known in any dog. It was on one of these walks that Dorothy pointed out Chapel House, Mattock Lane, whose garden at the back abutted on to Walpole Park, and told me she was going to buy it for her work. I was much astonished, for it looked large and expensive, and said, 'Don't be silly! How can you possibly have enough money?' Her very calm reply was, 'I shall have it, because our Lord has told me I shall.' On my next visit it was hers, and we collected the apples in the orchard. On a subsequent visit, she was in it, and I was at the blessing by the Bishop of Woolwich."

Once it became known that Dorothy had opened a Home of Healing she was inundated with requests for accommodation, and St. Raphael rapidly became inadequate to meet the demands of patients who longed to be ministered to by her, under her own roof.

It was during a walk with Bruno, her red setter, that she felt herself curiously drawn to a house that they passed on their daily visits to Walpole Park. She had passed the house many times without giving it special notice, but on that particular day it had been borne in upon her that our Lord had a much bigger work for her to do and that He wanted her to get possession of this derelict old house, once the property of the Walpole family. She pushed open the gate and stepped into the drive, and as she did so, at once there came to her the conviction that it was God's house, planned and prepared by Him, for some work He meant her to do there. It came quite unmistakably to her that our Lord intended it for an enlarged St. Raphael. As she left the grounds, she heard distinctly, "The Lord is King." With these words ringing in her ears the whole way home, she went into the little Chapel and prayed that God would show her what was His Will in the matter. The answer came clearly and unmistakably, and she then and there resolved that come what may, she would, by the grace of God, obey His command, "Get it for Me."*

Dorothy had no money. There was still a small debt to be paid off on St. Raphael, and enquiries elicited that the purchase price of the house was in the neighbourhood of £5000! She prayed to our Lord that He would give her a sign that He wished her to embark upon this venture, and asked Him that He would make it possible for her to pay off the debt that still remained on St. Raphael. She waited with growing conviction that God would grant her this sign. It came on the third day She has told in her book *Fulfilling* how a friend wrote to her: "I have received some unexpected dividends, and feel God asks me to send it to you. I have no doubt you will find some good use for it." The sign she asked for had been vouchsafed her, and Dorothy felt she could safely proceed with the enterprise. She consulted two of her closest friends, Mrs. Horace Porter, subsequently a generous benefactress to Chapel House, and the Bishop of Nasik, and asked them to give her their views on the project. Each, in turn, went over the house with her, and each had in mind to do their utmost to dissuade her from so heavy a commitment. Mrs. Porter has left a record of her visit to the future Chapel House:

"It seemed an almost wild venture, and when Miss Kerin invited me

* Dorothy Kerin: *Fulfilling*.

to come with her to see the house, I went in the mood of clear common sense, resolved to point out the rashness of undertaking so heavy a financial burden, to say nothing of the personal responsibilities involved. But as we went through the empty rooms, and looked out upon the sunlit garden with its tangled luxuriance of untended flowers, I could no longer resist the impression that it was all *waiting*. Waiting to be cared for and filled and used for such service as our Father should make known by His Holy Spirit, to be carried out in the Name and in the strength of His Beloved Son.

"The need for guidance in the matter was obviously very great, yet when we knelt together in the East Room – where the chapel of old had been – the *Gloria in Excelsis* seemed more appropriate than any direct petition. The empty room was filled with the unseen 'company of heaven', and Angels' wings seemed gently to brush us, as, in the golden evening light, we made our offering of the single desire that the glorious will of God for the house should be done in every part of it, by everyone concerned."

Bishop Loyd, at that time Bishop of Nasik in India, happened to be in England, and Dorothy asked him to visit the house with her, for she utterly trusted his wise advice and counsel, and knew that he would help her to see and do God's Will. The Bishop afterwards told her that he had come prepared to bring his common sense to bear upon her and save her from committing herself to so rash an undertaking. Instead, he felt, as they wandered through the silent old house, that our Divine Lord Himself was speaking, claiming the house for His own. As they went through the house each room seemed to be, not so much empty, as waiting to be filled with all the people and things that would bring back life to them. The Bishop knelt with Dorothy, as she had done with Mrs. Porter, in the former chapel, and again it was the exultant words of the *Gloria in Excelsis* that spontaneously rose to their lips in an outpouring of thanksgiving for the evidence that God's guiding Hand was upon the life of His servant.

There were plenty of advisers, at every step of the way, to urge the abandonment of the venture. On the other side, there was only the faith, to which Dorothy held fast, that if the use of the house as a Home of Healing was indeed what God willed, He would provide all things needful. Although dark hours had to be lived through, heavy anxieties faced, and discouragement endured, God's power to over-rule man-made obstacles and to honour the faith and the obedience of His servant was made manifest in a wonderful way during the ensuing weeks.

On July 29th, 1930, Dorothy made a definite offer to buy the house. The owner, who was sympathetic towards her work, consented to accept £3,700 in the place of the £5000 originally required. In addition to the purchase money for the house, a large sum would be needed to pay for the necessary repairs, alterations, and furnishings. There was nothing in hand towards meeting these heavy commitments: there was only the certain knowledge based upon His command, that God wanted her to buy the house for Him. Gifts started to arrive; money came in amounts both large and small; the Bank generously advanced a sum of £500 to be repaid by mid-December. At last the happy day dawned when the amount needed to purchase the house had been collected from various sources, and Dorothy entered into possession of Chapel House. There was one gift that Dorothy always treasured which to this day lies on the Altar of the Church, as it has done on the Altars of all her Chapels. It came from a poor woman who said to her, "I am so thankful to God for all He has done for me, I want to give you my most precious possession, and I pray that He will bless and multiply it a thousand fold." This gift was a Jubilee florin that had been given to her by her mother at her confirmation.

By the middle of October, the house was ready for occupation, and on October 25th the Bishop of Woolwich* performed the ceremony of dedication. At the close of the Service, he called Dorothy to him and laid his hands upon her head, asking for God's special blessing upon her for the work He had called her to do. Before leaving, the Bishop asked Dorothy to go quietly with him to the Chapel, as he had something to tell her. They knelt side by side; the Bishop prayed that God would guide, guard and strengthen her, not only for the immediate work of Chapel House, but for all that was to grow out of this work for the future. When he had finished his fervent prayer, he told Dorothy that he saw the house next to Chapel House joined on, and that he was sure that in God's time this would come to pass. Dorothy then told him she *knew* that God had set His seal upon *all* the other five houses in Mattock Lane, with a sixth house, as yet not built, filling the gap between the first house on the left, and that they would all in the fullness of His timing become part of the Chapel House estate.

Towards the end of November, Bishop Loyd wrote from India asking how the money was coming in for the repayment of the loan to

* Bishop Hough.

the bank. Dorothy replied that at the time of writing she had £80, this being the thank-offering of one who had been healed. She had no knowledge of further help coming to her, but as she was sure that Chapel House was in God's pattern for His work, she did not doubt that He would provide, and upon this belief she was content to wait in faith. The following extract is taken from *Fulfilling:*

"On December 3rd, Bruno became desperately ill. In the vet's opinion, he was dying from some poison he had picked up. All through that day and night I nursed and tended him, with very little apparent result. He became weaker and weaker. The following day he was just alive and by night I had to carry him upstairs. I must confess to a very sad and sorrowing heart, for Bruno had been my constant companion and friend, and we loved each other well and truly. He was almost human with an amazing understanding. He had come to be known as 'The Brown Verger' and attended ALL the Services in Chapel. Everybody loved him, and the thought of his not being with us any more was one that had to be faced with courage.

"I was sitting on the floor, with his head pillowed on my lap, thinking and praying about the problem of finding the money for the bank. Suddenly, I was aware of our Lord's Divine Presence, and heard the Voice I knew so well, saying, 'Fear not, I will provide all thy need.' I was then aware of Bruno, who was in an ecstasy of delight, standing up wagging his tail, quite restored. I told him we must go down to the Chapel to thank God for his healing, which we did.

"As I prayed in thanksgiving from a full heart, I became aware that God had promised to provide all the need. I knew this was a test of my faith. I went to my study and wrote the cheque for £500 for the bank, dating it December 13th, and placed this upon the altar. A song of joy and thanksgiving was in my heart. Not that I had doubted God's power to send the money but because it was to me the seal of His approval. I returned to bed and slept. In the morning the joy was still singing in my heart, and I expect was visible in my face, for my mother asked: 'What has happened to make you so happy?' I told her about Bruno, and then added, 'And the cheque is on the altar – ready for our Lord to honour.' Shall we blame her if in her anxiety, she felt that perhaps this was only Dorothy's wish? However, nothing could have shaken my belief, for I knew the Beloved had promised.

"I received a letter from a friend who had been touched and healed by our Lord, in which she sent a cheque for £100, knowing that God had inspired her to do this. This offering implied a great act of faith and meant much to this woman, who was certainly not blessed with an abundance of this world's goods.

"The next day I received two more letters, one containing a cheque for £200, one £100, and both givers saying: 'God has guided me to send you this – you will know why.' This made £480. On the evening of the 13th – the day due for the cheque to be paid, I received from an unknown source a cheque for £20, thus enabling me to post the cheque which God had honoured for His work."*

As the wonderful story unfolds, it will be seen that God's blessing rested wholly upon the work done by His faithful servant in His Name and for His glory. Authentic records exist in number attesting that through the channel of her ministry, dim eyes have had their sight renewed, blind eyes their vision restored. Ears closed to sound have heard once more; bedridden invalids have gone away on their own feet. Diseases pronounced medically incurable have given place to bodily vigour and well-being, while those who have found light flow into their darkened minds, and peace, faith and hope take possession of their troubled souls are beyond computation. These miracles of whole-making wrought in our midst, and which we have personally witnessed, are a powerful refutation of teachings announced today from within Christ's Church by certain of His accredited shepherds, that belief in the supernatural has no part in the religious thinking of 20th-century man, who, they claim, has emancipated himself from the dead hand of so mediaeval a superstition!

For the past fifty years, Dorothy Kerin's life has been a resounding challenge to such views. Her ministry of divine healing has been a constant demonstration of God's concern for the physical as well as spiritual well-being of His children, and of His intervention at the physical as well as spiritual level. It has triumphantly manifested the truth that "*His Hand is not shortened that it cannot save; nor His ear heavy that it cannot hear.*"†

* Dorothy Kerin: *Fulfilling.*
† Isaiah 59.1.

CHAPTER 9

Expansion of the Work

SOON after her move to Chapel House, Dorothy found herself faced with having to make an important decision affecting the future of her work. The Home quickly absorbed its quota of sick, with many more seeking admission as soon as rooms were available. Hitherto, the question of fees had been left to the discretion of those who were accepted as patients. This arrangement soon put too heavy a strain upon Dorothy's slender resources, since the frailty of human nature is such that the greater number were ready to receive help, without regard to their financial obligation to give in return what most were well able to afford. It looked as though Chapel House would have to close its doors almost as soon as they had opened!

Discussing her dilemma with a Harley Street specialist who had sent patients to her, Dorothy received from him the sound advice to register Chapel House as a Nursing Home, and to charge normal fees.

"Chapel House," he told her, "is far too valuable to us to allow anything to interfere with the work being done there."

Dorothy, the least 'money-minded' person in the world, gave the matter much thought, and, as always, sought in prayer her guidance. It was borne in upon her that to comply with this advice would make it possible for her to accept a larger proportion of sufferers whose financial resources were insufficient to pay the modest fees charged. She accordingly applied for a licence, which was granted, and Chapel House became a registered Nursing Home.

Names eminent in the Church, as well as in the medical profession, appeared in the first Chapel House prospectus, as spiritual and medical sponsors to the work being done in the Home. Thus began the partnership between religion and medicine which has always been the policy adopted by Dorothy Kerin in all her Homes of Healing.

This is a side of her work that must never be forgotten. In her public utterances, she has stressed, again and again, that these two instruments of God's healing power must work hand in hand in a harmonious and fruitful relationship. It is no exaggerated claim that her pioneer work has done much to revolutionize the attitude of medicine towards religion as a healing partner, and to bring about their successful co-operation in the field of psychosomatic diseases.

The registration of Chapel House as a Nursing Home necessitated engaging a staff of trained nurses. It was at this juncture that the path of Sister Rose Friend crossed that of Dorothy Kerin, and became thereafter intimately interwoven with the divinely appointed pattern of her life. Their two paths, to the day of Dorothy's death, were to run side by side in a close relationship that successfully withstood the strains and stresses of innumerable difficulties of all kinds, as well as the insistent claims of an ever widening circle of patients and friends, and the adoption of nine war-orphaned babies.

Sister Friend has kept a vivid recollection of their meeting:

"I first heard of Dorothy in 1930 at a tea-party. I was told she had taken an old derelict house in Ealing and turned it into a beautiful Home of Healing, and the story had fired my imagination. Later, when attending a 'Quiet Day', several people had said to me, 'You must meet Dorothy Kerin.'

"On the next morning, I telephoned and heard her soft Irish voice ask what she could do for me. We made an appointment for that evening. That meeting closed a door on my life, and opened another into perpetual joy, service and thanksgiving.

"A few months previously, I had prayed that if it were our Lord's will, I might know what real happiness was. He had now given me His answer. Never shall I forget that wonderful meeting. Dorothy's face was alight with the love that is inspired by spiritual insight and compassion. My problems were all of the soul, and I had a list for fear I should forget, and also that I might not waste her time. There was no need for my list, because Dorothy seemed to know before I could formulate them, the things which were troubling me.

"Dorothy asked me if I would join her staff as Nursing Sister. I could not then do so, but came to her nine months later. Before this happened, I was taken seriously ill with a high temperature. I asked for and received the laying-on-of-hands, and was healed by our Lord. I came to Chapel House to convalesce. It was a lovely chapter in my life. My bond with Dorothy was strengthened, and I eagerly looked forward to the day when I could help her in her work, and perhaps be privileged to lift from her shoulders a little of the great load she was so valiantly carrying for her Beloved Master.

"Although unable, as yet, to become a permanent member of the Chapel House Nursing Staff, I constantly returned to the Home at weekends, and on one of these visits I was again taken ill. Dr. Helena King, known to her patients as the 'beloved physician', diagnosed pneumonia. On the third day I had the laying-on-of-hands by the Chaplain and was instantly healed. There was a reason for this healing that was to reveal itself later."

More and more people from all parts of the country, and also from overseas, were seeking healing, guidance and wholeness through Dorothy's ministry, and many felt the Living Touch of the Living Lord upon their lives.

The original Chapel where Dorothy had knelt with Mrs. Horace Porter and Bishop Loyd the first time they visited the house had become inadequate to hold all those who came to worship in it. It was decided to have in its stead a large room at the right-hand side of the front door, which could accommodate as many as fifty people at a time.

The new Chapel was blessed and dedicated by the Bishop of London, Dr. Winnington-Ingram. He permitted the Blessed Sacrament to be reserved permanently for the sick, a privilege prized above all else, making it possible for those who could not assist at the celebration of the Holy Mysteries to have the Blessed Sacrament brought to them in their rooms. The memory of this Chapel, filled with God's healing power and with His Peace, is enshrined in the hearts of all who knelt there in prayer to find that "they who wait upon the Lord shall renew their strength".* Dorothy wrote with reference to this Chapel: "The prayer that goes up from our Chapel here for all who come for help and healing is that God's will may be done in each one, and that His Peace and Blessing may rest on them." All who entered this sanctuary – and they were many – felt the compelling force of the scriptural phrase in Exodus: "Put off thy shoes from thy feet for the place whereon thou standest is holy ground."†

It was at this time that the then Archbishop of Canterbury, Dr. Lang, gave Dorothy his blessing and commissioned her, in the name of the Church, to go out into the world to proclaim the message of hope entrusted to her by our Lord Jesus Christ, and sanctioned the ministry of her charismatic gift through the laying-on-of-hands.

The Home was always full. As soon as a patient left, another took his

* Isaiah 40.31.
† Exod. 3.5; Acts 7.33.

or her place, and the waiting list became progressively longer. The addition of a new wing was planned and later carried out. There was incessant coming and going of those seeking wholeness of spirit, mind and body, and Dorothy's life was very full. Her correspondence – always an exacting part of her ministry – so increased that it became a heavy tax upon her strength, never robust. Dealing with it necessitated encroaching upon her hours of sleep, already curtailed by the time spent in intercessory prayer. She became very weak. There was no adequate supervision of her meals. Her entourage were inclined to take the line that one so holy and so loved of Jesus could draw upon the spiritual resources of her prayer life for her physical sustenance. The Martha side showed alarming signs of collapse. She caught a chill and developed pleurisy. Dr. King tended her with all the loving care that professional skill could give, but, as every doctor knows, it is the nurse that so often tips the scales on the side of recovery. The reason for Sister Friend's miraculous healing revealed itself in her call to come to Dorothy and give her the nursing essential to her restoration. Sister Friend takes up again her story:

"For many weeks Dorothy was confined to her bed, becoming each day visibly weaker. It was during this illness that I acquired my nickname of 'Jumbo', as I lumbered around the room attending to my patient. In all my years of nursing, I have never, not even in the tropics, had to deal with such terrible fever sweats as befell Dorothy night after night, reducing her to a state of utter exhaustion. She was in every respect a wonderful patient, and it was a tremendous privilege to nurse her; always grateful for the least service, always thinking of others; and enduring without a murmur the utter weariness, sense of frustration, and physical exhaustion that continuously beset her. What greatly increased the strain of nursing was the acceptance on the part of those around her, including the Chaplain, that she would not recover, and her death was considered to be inevitable.

"At last a specialist was called in for consultation. He carefully examined Dorothy, and then asked to be left alone with her.

" 'You will have to make up your mind,' he told her, 'whether you wish to live and continue your work. As things are, you cannot live for longer than two or three months. If, however, you promise to do exactly as I tell you, it is possible for you to pull through, but only on this condition. Now I shall leave you to make your decision.'

"When he returned half-an-hour later, it was to find her ready to obey his instructions. She had received her guidance from her Beloved Master, and, as always, obeyed Him implicitly.

"All physical exertion was forbidden her. She was to remain completely immobilized. She made me pin her sleeve to her sheet to remind herself never to lift a hand. A finger raised was for me the signal that she required attention. All through her illness, Dorothy never forgot to pray for the sick. Too weak to mention them by name, she held them up one by one in thought before God's Mercy Seat, and placed them in the Sacred Heart of our Lord whose statue stood above her bed.

"Once the fever left her, Dorothy swiftly recovered. After her convalescence, the way was open for me to accept her offer, and come as Nursing Sister. I need not say how gladly I responded to the call."

Why did her beloved Master, the Divine Physician, to whose service every moment of her life was wholly dedicated, allow Dorothy to fall ill, just as her work was expanding and her guiding hand essential to its development? This is a question she asked herself without being able to find an answer. She felt sure there was a reason. Perhaps it was in order to deepen still further her understanding of the mystery of pain and suffering, a mystery that eludes our human comprehension. She accepted her illness as being permitted by God, and used it, as in the past she had used all her illnesses, with their accompaniment of pain, as something to be shared and thrown into the common pool of suffering and offered as a drop in the filling of the Cup.*

Dorothy's illness emptied the Home. Patients did not want to come unless they could be personally ministered to by her. Finances were at a dangerously low ebb, and debts were accumulating at a disquieting rate. Boilers burst, and structural repairs were found to be necessary. The expenditure of every penny had to be watched. Dorothy's clothes were threadbare, and at times hunger hovered perilously near the door of Chapel House. While those about her felt anxious and worried, to Dorothy it was a wonderful opportunity to trust in her Lord, and to rest in quiet faith upon His assurance that He would never leave her. And so it proved. When once again the captain's hand was on the wheel of the ship, the passengers clamoured to be taken on board, and Chapel House soon filled to capacity. A period of rapid expansion followed. A wing was added. One of the five houses 'shown' Dorothy in the early days as destined to become a part of the Nursing Home was for sale. It was bought, furnished and put to use in record time. St. Michael also

* Dorothy Kerin: *Fulfilling.*

passed into her possession. On the day of its blessing, Dorothy was conscious of the sound of children's feet and heard their laughter. She decided to move into St. Michael with her mother, and to have there those who sought a place of withdrawal in which they could keep a quiet retreat. In the fullness of God's time, all the other houses in Mattock Lane became a part of Chapel House Nursing Home.

How was the money for all this expansion found? There never was at any time a surplus in the Home of Healing exchequer. God's guiding Hand that brought about the fulfilment of His 'showing' also provided the means. The familiar pattern repeated itself, and money came from all kinds of unexpected sources. The little band of dedicated workers Dorothy had begun to gather around her, which was to form the nucleus of her loved, tried and trusted 'Staff' of later years, were learning that where God guides, the barrel of meal never wastes, neither does the cruse of oil ever fail.

The work at Chapel House had become widely known. Not only were the sick knocking at its doors for admission, but an increasing number of spiritually perplexed souls sought interviews in order to put to Dorothy their problems, and receive from her the wise, inspired and loving guidance they stood in need of. Men famous in the Church, in the world of science, of art, and of letters, took, one after the other, the road to West Ealing. As they journeyed to their destination, they must have wondered what they would find. What they did find was a frail, ethereal-looking young woman who graciously asked them to be seated. She extended to all, famous and unknown, high in the social scale or low in the ranks of the humble toilers of this world, the same courtesy and loving attention to their need, seeing in each a child of God.

Some of the questions put to her were of a nature to tax the intellectual resources of trained theologians, or of technicians in their own field. Each question had a spiritual content bearing upon the subject her interlocuter was interested in. Many of the subjects discussed were outside her experience, and, yet, because the Holy Spirit had given her the great gifts of counsel, knowledge and wisdom, her visitors took their departure helped and illuminated in their spiritual understanding by their visit to her.

The need for a Chaplain had already made itself felt at St. Raphael, and had become still more a matter of urgency with the move to Chapel House. The priest she had in view failed her, and Dr. Langford-James pressed her to allow him to fill this post. Dorothy had strong reservations about accepting his offer. The fact that she had been under his spiritual direction for so many years may have made her fear that he might try to curtail her freedom of action in the directing of her work and its general policy. She decided against his coming, perhaps helped to do so by a letter Bishop Loyd wrote to her from India.

It was the Rev. H. S. Barrett, Vicar of St. Barnabas, Ealing, who assumed the post of Hon. Chaplain to Chapel House. Dorothy has paid him a warm tribute in *Fulfilling* where she says that Father Barrett was unfailing in his love and giving, and that she could never be grateful enough for God's good gift of him, a tribute wholeheartedly echoed by the countless numbers to whom he ministered during the years he was associated with Chapel House.

With the passing of the years there was abundance of evidence that God's blessing rested fully upon the work being done in His Name and for His glory at Chapel House. A group of friends, whose numbers yearly increased, had gathered around Dorothy during the years that had elapsed since the foundation of Chapel House. Their aim was to support the Foundress in her arduous work by their prayers and their faith in the divinely ordained nature of her call to heal the sick, comfort the sorrowing and give faith to the faithless. Some had received wholeness of spirit, mind and body through her ministry; some were still patients, learning to "tarry the Lord's leisure" in the matter of their healing; others had found new purpose in life, and had been given strength to grapple with the very exigencies of living which formerly defeated them; all had known peace and joy take possession of their hearts through their contact with Chapel House. Their one commitment, other than praying for Dorothy and her work, was to say each day the Collect for the Sixth Sunday after Trinity.

Bishop Loyd urged Dorothy to draw this nucleus into closer bonds of fellowship through an association to be called The Chapel House Fellowship. At Dorothy's request, in 1936 he drew up a Circular Letter, signed by Lord Daryngton and himself, in which were embodied their views with regard to the form the proposed Fellowship should take. The following extract is taken from this Letter:

"The only positive obligation involved in membership of the Fellowship is that of saying daily the Chapel House Collect (VIth Sunday after Trinity). Here again, we consider that it is most desirable that no other obligation should be added; because the Fellowship is, and must always remain, primarily an association of prayer. But at the same time when we consider the way in which Miss Kerin has been called and set apart for very special work, and also the heavy burdens (including financial ones) which she has to bear, we cannot feel satisfied that we are doing all that we are meant to do if we content ourselves with just remembering the work of Chapel House in our prayers.

"Can we honestly pray God to bless and provide for her work, if we are not ourselves doing what we can to supply some of the money which is needed for its support? And should we not feel that our connection with Chapel House was a much more real and living one, if we were ourselves helping to provide the means by which it is able to welcome and care for those whom God may send there, however poor they may be?"

No words can adequately express what the Fellowship, under its various guises – Chapel House Fellowship, Burrswood Fellowship, Burrswood International Fellowship – came to mean to Dorothy as the years brought with them an ever-increasing expansion of her work. She loved it deeply as a whole. She loved each individual member. She knew most of them by name, and she was cognizant of their personal problems. Had she not, for many of them, sacrificed in intercessory prayer the few hours allotted to sleep? From their prayers, their unfailing love, their generosity, and their faith in her divinely appointed ministry, she drew strength, encouragement and comfort. How often, when away on missions in other lands, she would exclaim before a Service, "I *know* the Fellowship are praying for us," or "I *feel* the prayers of the Fellowship." On occasions, when important decisions had to be made, after first seeking her guidance from her Lord, and secure in the knowledge of His will for her, she would say, "Now, we must put this to the Fellowship." Their support never failed her. The Fellowship was to her a rock upon which rested the physical structure of her work. It is questionable whether she could have carried on as long as she did, but for their all-enveloping love and trust.

CHAPTER 10

Bishop Philip Loyd

RELIGIOUS history records many instances of friendship between God's saints. In this connection, there comes to mind the names of St. Jerome and St. Paula; St. Francis of Assisi and St. Clare; St. John of the Cross and St. Teresa; St. Francis de Sales and St. Jeanne Chantal; St. Vincent de Paul and St. Louise de Maurillac. Such friendships are inspired by the intercourse of souls who love each other in God and for God. God is the whole foundation of their friendship, the beginning and the end.

Philip Loyd first came into Dorothy's life in 1930 when on furlough from a spell of exacting work in the mission field of India, where he did so much to build up the Church, and where his memory is enshrined in the hearts of countless simple village Indian folk. One of his workers had been healed of a serious illness at Chapel House, and on her return to India had urged him to meet Dorothy at the first opportunity. It so happened that on his first visit it was Dorothy who opened the door to him, and there was an instantaneous recognition on the part of each of the greatness of soul and spiritual integrity of the other. His friendship meant much to her. When their paths first crossed, she had not long left the spiritual director with whom her life had been associated for fourteen years, and she stood in need of someone of great spiritual maturity to whom she could turn for counsel and wise advice. God sent her Bishop Loyd.

Essentially a man of prayer, Philip Loyd resembled in many respects St. Francis de Sales. Like his renowned prototype, he lived 'joyously' in the presence of God. "God is the God of joy," wrote St. Francis, "the spirit of joy is the true spirit of devotion. Joy opens the heart, and sadness shuts it."* It was this spirit of joy, equally possessed by Dorothy, that endeared both these servants of God to men and women in every walk of life.

Bishop Loyd's aristocracy of soul matched his aristocracy of birth. He was consumed by an ardent love of Christ and longed to bring the

* M. V. Woodgate: *St. Francis de Sales.*

souls, that looked to him for spiritual guidance, to experiential knowledge of their Redeemer. It has been said of him by those who knew him best that his life was marked by the holiness, the humility and the gaiety of the true saint, a description equally applicable to Dorothy Kerin. As was the case with her, his life was rooted in obedience to the will of God, and he followed the illustrious Bishop of Geneva in his insistence that we should do everything by love and not by effort. The serene beauty of his spirit communicated itself to others through his letters, his devotional books, his Addresses and in his personal relationships; no one came in contact with Philip Loyd without being the richer for the experience. The letters he wrote to Dorothy could have been penned by St. Francis to Madame de Chantal. The Bishop of Geneva was united to St. Jeanne Chantal by a union of hearts that was the outcome of their complete understanding from the moment they met, and so it was with Bishop Loyd and Dorothy Kerin. "It seems to me," St. Francis wrote to Madame de Chantal, "that God intended me for you, and every hour I become more convinced of this."* There is equally no doubt that God intended Bishop Loyd to be to Dorothy the spiritual guide, inspirer and comforter she stood in need of during the crowded years of her fruitful ministry. Their friendship remained constant in its warmth and mutual trust for twenty-two years, until the day, on January 11th, 1952, when Philip Loyd passed through the gates of everlasting life to his eternal peace and joy. A few of his early letters to Dorothy are here included. They reveal the spiritual bond that existed between these two dedicated servants of God. The first letter, dated July 17th, 1930, was written from Church House soon after their first meeting.

"It is quite time I wrote to you, though it will be only a scrawl while I wait for the committee to begin. But Tuesday was such a wonderful joy, and has made me immeasurably happy. I don't know when I have had such a happy Mass as in the wee Chapel that morning, and it was largely because at the first sight of you, when you opened the door to me, I knew that the Lord Jesus had given me, as I said, a new sister. And then wasn't His Presence wonderful at the Mass? I suppose there is nothing we priests lament more than our coldness in celebrating the Holy Mysteries. Little Sister, pray for me."

There was an undertaking between them that on the 15th of each month the Bishop would say his Mass with special intention for

* M. V. Woodgate: *St. Francis de Sales.*

Dorothy. It was to be her Mass. So we find him writing to her in 1931, from India, the following letters in which he refers to his ability or otherwise to observe this practice.

Bodhegam,
January 15th, 1931.

"I must write to you before I go to bed. You had your Mass this morning: this time you had to share it with fourteen simple villagers (none of whom can read or write), whom I confirmed at 9.0 a.m. I said the Mass in the Travellers Bungalow at this place, alone with a C.M.S. layman whom I have on tour with me; and then we motored over to Golegam, the place of the Confirmation, six miles away, where the Indian priest and two of our Women Missionaries are encamped. I go over there again tomorrow to give them their first Communion. They are such dears; so simple and keen, and I expect it will be a lovely First Communion tomorrow, because they will take our dear Lord straight into their hearts.

"How are you, Dorothy dear? And how is the money coming in? I do so often think of you and pray for you."

Pachwad,
March 16th, 1931.

"This is the week of the month in which I write to you. This month your Mass was said in a schoolroom in a small village in the Aurangabad District, at Kazadgan three miles away from Pachwad, where I am staying for six nights with a fellow Missionary, while we tour the country round about and hold Confirmations. The congregation at your Mass consisted of about thirty simple village people. Later on in the morning there was a Confirmation; and I am glad to say that all the Candidates (there were only six of them) were confirmed. That is not always the case; because in these parts everyone, including the Clergy, is very backward; and so I personally examine the Candidates, and I generally have to put back one or two.

"I am reading the Second Book of the *Imitation of Christ*. I read it every Lent, and really it is just too wonderful. It seems to have everything in it. On every page one feels that if only one could take that and *that* and *that* just literally and live it, one would have got to the secret of all true living."

Aurangabad,
August 20th, 1931.

"Thank you ever so much for your lovely letter. Agnes is so much excited at a typewritten letter coming from you! (Agnes is my typewriter and she will be about six years old next January.) And I am so sorry about the rib. I hope that it is quite all right by now, and that the rest in bed has done you lots of good. I said my Mass with great joy in my little Chapel on Saturday last. The day before I had come out of my annual Retreat at the Cowley Fathers' place at Panch Howd in Poona, and I was so glad the first Mass I said after it was yours. The Retreat was a great blessing to me; but I wish it could have been longer; only three full days; and this year I could not manage to get two days' quiet there preparing for it, but had to plunge into it straight away. But God was very good to me.

"And, of course, the Mass was that of our Lady; and it is a festival which I love. It is such a joy to think of her entering into her rest. I suppose it might then be said of her as of her Son, that she saw of the travail of her soul. And how wonderful has been her life of intercession ever since! While she was on earth her Heart was broken, in order that it might be able to contain all the sorrows of the world. *Mater misericordiae*, what a refuge she is. I do constantly commend you to Her prayers and love, dear Dorothy."

Aurangabad,
August 22nd, 1931.

"Yesterday I wrote to you, and today brought me a letter telling me how dreadfully ill you were, and so I must write again. One of the penalties of being right away in India is that one has to wait so long to hear of things, and therefore cannot always be sharing them just when they are happening.

"I cannot help feeling and believing that you will get well and strong again; because it does seem to me that you have more work yet to do on earth. But, of course, we do not know; so I leave all that in the dear Lord's hands, just as you do. And, as far as I am concerned, I know that I shall always have my little Sister's love and prayers, whereever she may be. Dorothy dear, I feel there is so much I might tell you and share with you; but, whatever happens, I do not expect we shall see much of one another in this world. But that does not matter;

for it can wait; and then there will be all eternity. And when I try to count up my treasure in Heaven, in order to get my heart more firmly there, I number among it a little Sister who will have lots and lots to say to me.

"How great a joy is *Daily Light*. It always has something for us. This morning, it was that wonderful passage in Philippians, 'Christ shall be magnified in my body, whether it be by life, or by death. For to me to live is Christ, and to die is gain . . .' For myself, I hope I shall be allowed to magnify Him by leaving my bones in India, when the time comes. But what *gain* it will be to die! Doesn't it shame one to think of how much He gives and how little we seem to have to give in return? And yet one would not have it otherwise, for then He would not be all that He is in His infinite perfection. When I was young, I used to wonder why we should thank God for our creation in the General Thanksgiving. In my silly indolent youth I did not see what was the great gain of existence over non-existence; but now I thank God that work and sorrow and His comfort and love and mercy have taught me better. Only, *if* one has learnt what a joy it is to know God, or rather to be known of Him, why does not one long more ardently and strive more earnestly to share that knowledge with others? And why does not one sorrow more heartily for the sin of the world?

"God bless you little Sister, and give you back your health and strength, and may the Lord Jesus flood your heart with His peace and fill it with the desire of beholding His Face."

Ahmadnagar,
February 18th, 1932.

"I have never thanked you for a lovely long letter which I got from you at Christmas time. The last month or two has been exceptionally heavy, and then last month I got a go of the influenza. I am all right again now, except that I have got to go a bit slow, which is not what one wants to do in Lent.

"I am reading the Second Book of the *Imitation*, as I do every Lent. In fact I have the whole of the *Imitation* mapped out so that it provides a portion for each day of the year. Book I: Advent to Quinquagesima. Book II: Lent. Book IV: Easter to Trinity. Book III: Trinity to Advent. It is amazing how every year one finds so much more to learn about the Interior Life and the peace.

"It is only when one is suffering that one can be sure that God's will is being done in us. What one does is so little and valueless as compared with what one allows God to do in one. How meaningless and dreary life is, if we regard it in terms of work to be done! And how full of beauty and joy in the Holy Ghost, if it really is a working out of the great mystery of dying to live, of dying that others may live, 'always bearing about in our body the dying of Jesus'. That is why I rejoice over you, even when I hear that you are ill; because I am quite sure that God's will is being done in you, and that you are safe in the Beloved's Arms.

"We have just been having our last spell of cold weather; and now it is beginning to get warmer every day. Already everything is beginning to look brown and parched, and we shall see no more green till June. God bless you, dearest Dorothy. Give my love to Bruno and my thanks for his messages."

Nasik,
Eve of the Feast of the Epiphany 1933.

"It was such a joy to get your and Bruno's letters; and I wanted to answer at once; but Christmas was such a busy time; especially as I had to start off on the day after to Hazaribagh (two nights in the train), in order to conduct a Retreat for the Dublin University Mission. Retreats are hard work, at least for the conductor! But I am very glad that I went; because though it is hard work, it is a real refreshment to spend some days in the atmosphere of prayer which always pervades a Retreat.

"I am so glad about the Tabernacle; how lovely! When shall I kneel before it with you? I just simply don't know. Haven't planned as yet for coming home, and unless something definite turns up to call me home, I don't expect it will be for three or four years at the earliest. And now I must stop and say goodbye to you and Bruno; and ever so much love to you both. May God bless you always & always & always."

In 1936 Bishop Loyd, a tired man, was back in England on a much-needed holiday. We can picture the joy with which Dorothy welcomed him to Chapel House, and we may be sure they did kneel side by side before the Tabernacle to give thanks to God for the blessings of the past years, not the least of these being their friendship, whose bond of union was our Blessed Lord Himself. They must have had much to tell each other of the happenings of the crowded years, since the day in

1930 when the Bishop had celebrated the Holy Mysteries in the wee Chapel at St. Raphael.

After a short holiday spent in Scotland and France with his family, he was back in India to resume the charge of his diocese. No letters have survived of this period, but we shall meet Bishop Loyd again when in 1945, after his retirement from India, he was enthroned in the choir of the great Abbey built by the Normans on the Roman site of Verulamium, as fifth Bishop of St. Albans.

CHAPTER II

Healings

IN her book *Fulfilling*, referring to the period 1930–1940, Dorothy wrote: "God's wondrous power was made manifest in countless blessings and acts of healing." The time has come to make mention of a few of the most outstanding of these wondrous acts of God. God's gift of whole-making sometimes reveals itself as a mysterious travail of the Holy Spirit in the secret recesses of the soul. Its fruits become manifest when the heart and mind have become filled with the love of God to the exclusion of all else, so that this love pours like a mighty torrent over the soul, cleansing and healing it of all spiritual ills. Sin is obliterated, for in its last analysis sin IS spiritual sickness. The value to a soul of such a healing far transcends that of physical restoration of the body, which may or may not follow.

The following account of a soul's experience of the Reality of being, whereby it has become illuminated by the Eternal or Divine Light and filled with Divine Love, is written by Dorothy herself. God wonderfully used her as His channel to bring about the fruition of this spiritual drama, although her humility has made her veil the vital part played by her in its consummation.

THE STORY OF ALAN

"There have been many wonderful and blessed experiences vouchsafed to us in Chapel House during the past years: blessings of healing of mind, body and spirit. I am thinking, as I write, of one, Alan, a young Ordinand, who came on the advice of his Priest to seek healing from his sickness, if it were God's will. The coming of this lovely soul to Chapel House is one of the blessed privileges for which I shall ever thank God. He quickly won all our hearts, where his dear memory is enshrined for ever.

"On August the fourth, Alan came, accompanied by his family, who were also going to stay at Chapel House with him. How well I remember my first sight of Alan: tall, slight with a very sensitive, almost ascetic face, his deep-set grey-blue eyes spoke of his interior life and revealed his true self. He was, obviously, grievously sick. Everything that could be done for him medically had been done; it remained now to await in faith for the Will of God to be made known to us. To this end, we had all united in prayer.

"Alan and I had many talks together; there was never any sort of a barrier between us, and he discussed quite freely and simply his past life, and all his hopes for the future. There was only one desire in his heart now, and this was that he might be given the gift of Ordination as God's Priest. He said one day, 'Will you ask God to tell you what He wants for me? I know He can heal me if He wants to, but if He does not, then pray that I may be given the grace to accept whatever He wills.' I shall never forget the beauty that shone in his face at this time, and the utter peace which surrounded him.

"He was suffering greatly these days, and there was little that any of us could do to relieve him. He delighted in having his family here with him, and was quite content. His priest, his doctor, and indeed all who saw him, marvelled at his courage and spirit. To them, both as penitent and patient, he was unique: it was so obvious to us all that he was being Divinely sustained.

"I had gone to Chapel at Alan's request to pray that God's will might be made known to us for him. As I knelt before the Altar, I saw in a vision Alan clothed as a priest, holding a chalice. He was shining; radiant with an unearthly beauty on his face – utter and complete joy, divine content. It was given to me to know that our Lord had Ordained him, and had given him his heart's desire that he was to go and minister on the Other Side.

"Alan was waiting for me next morning, and almost as soon as I entered his room he asked me eagerly: 'Well, has He told you?' 'Yes, Alan dear,' I replied, 'I think He wants you.' I told him of the vision which he accepted with complete resignation, indeed, satisfaction would be a better word. Then he said, 'I am thankful. It is almost too wonderful: I am Ordained by God! I must get ready, for it will not be long, will it?' He then told me of the Light that had streamed from the wall on to his bed (the wall was that which backed the Altar where the Blessed Sacrament was reserved). He said, 'I felt our Lord looking at me, and I was so happy!'

"From this moment, there was no looking back, or any uncertainty. With the utmost calm he made all his plans, settled all his affairs, arranged about his Requiem, even choosing the Hymns. He constantly told his family, 'I am divinely and supremely happy.' There was never any shadow of fear or any doubt. His patience and fortitude during this time were supernatural.

"Alan made plans for his family and friends, and no detail was forgotten. Father Seymour came and invested him with his Stole, after which Alan gave his family and myself his Blessing. I have never been more conscious of our Lord's Presence, and there is no doubt in my mind that at this time I received His Blessing through the hands of His divinely appointed Priest.

"Alan wanted to give something to the Chapel in memory of him, and with his own pocket money (his dole, he called it) bought a silver Altar Bread Box, which we used for the first time at his last Communion. The Celebrant on this occasion was Father Thompson, Alan's friend. There were present: Alan's father, mother, sister, and myself – a never to be forgotten Service. It was here, I think, during this celebration of the Holy Mysteries that they all gave him back to our Lord.

"The days that followed were full of sacred memories; full of heartache and great thanksgiving for his dear ones, of whom our Lord had asked so great and precious a gift. We owe so much to the coming of this lovely soul to Chapel House, and I thank God for all He taught and gave us through Alan.

"In my heart, I treasure the words he spoke to me shortly before his call came: 'Dorothy, God has given me another sister. I am so happy.'

"His passing on September the second was literally a falling asleep in Jesus. That glorious spirit had, by the grace of God, found complete and utter union with the Beloved, and hastened with joy to be with his Lord.

"He was robed in his priestly vestment, Ordained by God, a Priest for ever, after the order of Melchizedek. May he rest in peace."

The story of Little Louie stands out among the miracles of healing at Chapel House, on account of the circumstances that surrounded it, and because of the '*in extremis*' nature of her case. Louie's story has a delightful prelude.

One day, Dorothy received a letter bearing the postmark Boston, U.S.A., in which the writer expressed her longing to be ministered to by her. She suffered from deafness, and being a physician was finding this physical defect an increasing handicap in the exercise of her profession. She believed that, if only she could get to Chapel House, God would heal her through His servant. Dorothy urged her to come, but promised her no miracle of healing. She always cautioned those who sought her ministry, that they must come prepared to accept God's will for them, leaving their physical healing to the Divine Physician who alone knows what is best for each one of us. What she did promise them was that if they approached the matter of their healing in the spirit of "Thy will be done in and for me", God would not fail to bestow upon them a blessing, although this blessing might not always be the one they were seeking. God knows our real needs far better than we do.

The American arrived, and stayed for some time at Chapel House. Dorothy ministered to her, and together they prayed in Chapel that God's will might be made known. One day, the doctor went to Dorothy and told her that she felt it had been laid upon her, while she was praying in Chapel, that God wanted her to give up the room she was occupying to some sufferer who was in greater need than herself, but who could not come to Chapel House because he or she lacked the means to pay the fees. She wished to allocate what remained to her of her stay and its cost to some such person. Dorothy assured her that money was always forthcoming for such cases, and that she need not go on that account. The doctor insisted that she must follow what she sincerely believed to be her guidance, for she was sure that this was what God wanted her to do. Dorothy gave her the laying-on-of-hands before she left, and as she did so, she *knew* our Lord had touched the woman. The doctor boarded her ship to return to Boston. When the vessel was in mid-ocean, she found her deafness had disappeared, and she sent Dorothy a joyful cable to say she had been healed and that no trace of her impediment remained. The person for whom the doctor had given up her room happened to be Louie, and it is at this point that Little Louie enters the scene. Marina, a member of Dorothy's original staff, has recorded for us her recollection of Dorothy's first meeting with Louie, with whose mother she had for some weeks corresponded.

"It was on Monday, July 13th, 1936, that I went to join Dorothy for lunch at Chapel House, and take her for a drive in the country. This was her favourite form of relaxation, and we discussed with enthusiasm the different places she wished to see. The presence of a visiting missionary, who wanted to return to Cambridge, decided the issue. We would drop her there, and then look for a small town called Wisbech which somebody said was not far away. Dorothy had received repeated requests from a woman living there to come and see her daughter who was desperately ill and who longed to see her, after reading *The Living Touch.*

"Distance presented no problem to us for time was our own; we both loved motoring, and were both free of all topographical anxieties. Not surprisingly therefore we reached Cambridge rather late, and started out for Wisbech slightly confused by the many contradictory directions we received from passers-by. When we discovered it was another forty miles on, Dorothy began to hesitate about continuing further north. She was considering the driver, but I had learnt by then that her hesitations often covered her most cherished desires, so it was not difficult to persuade her that we must pursue our quest at all costs.

"We reached Wisbech at about 7 o'clock, and wormed our way through the narrow streets of a forlorn quarter of the town. The house stood back in a row of small brick buildings, the road was rough, and a narrow pavement barely separated the door from the car. I watched Dorothy go up the few steps and knock. A long pause followed, and then the door opened slowly as an elderly woman peered out at her in silence. Her shoulders drooped and she clutched a shawl round her.

" 'Does Miss Louie Baldwin live here? May I see her?' Dorothy asked.

"The woman stared blankly before she answered.

" 'I'm afraid you can't. She's very ill.' As Dorothy did not turn away, she added sharply: 'She's very ill, she's dying.'

" 'I have come all the way from London to see her. I am Dorothy Kerin.'

"Had the woman been told it was St. Paul standing on her doorstep or an angel out of heaven, she could not have looked more astounded.

" 'Dorothy Kerin!' she gasped, and held her hands out to her. I thought she was going to collapse. Unable to speak, she drew Dorothy into the darkness of the house, and I watched them vanish, wondering what lay within.

"It must have been half an hour or more before Mrs. Baldwin re-appeared, and beckoned to me. She was radiant and tears were running down her face.

" 'Come in! Come in! This is so wonderful . . . so wonderful.'

"I followed her and found myself in a small dark parlour with a low ceiling where a tiny bed was standing behind a partition or screen. Dorothy was beside Louie, and I looked over her shoulders down at the emaciated little figure in the bed. In the dim light I could distinguish a cadaverous face with the unmistakable stamp of death on the pinched features. Then I saw the eyes glowing out of deep sockets, burning with the fire of indescribable joy, the last flicker of life shining out of the dying clay. There was no movement in the face, she was too weak to smile, but her spindly little hand was clutching Dorothy's fingers in her last desperate hold on hope.

"Dorothy was speaking to her in a low and gentle voice, and although Louie made no sign, I felt that not a word escaped her.

" 'You have been refusing all food, Louie, now I want you to do everything your mother tells you, and take a little nourishment every day. When you are stronger, I promise you, you will come to stay with me at Chapel House. I will send a car to fetch you, and I will take care of you until you are well.'

"The burning eyes did not move from Dorothy's face, and they did not move when Dorothy pressed a few drops of warm milk through her lips. There was a release of tension in the air, as Dorothy tenderly wiped her mouth, and tucked the little hand under the cover.

" 'Remember, you have promised, and I am coming to fetch you.'

"As we drove home, we were silent most of the way, and only when we reached Chapel House, and Dorothy saw Sister Friend coming anxiously towards us, she joyfully exclaimed: 'We were just in time, Jummie! Little Louie will live.' "

At last the day dawned when Dr. King, in agreement with Louie's own doctor, pronounced her to be sufficiently strong to stand the journey from Wisbech to Ealing. True to her promise, Dorothy, accompanied by Sister Friend, fetched Louie by car, and deposited her at Chapel House, radiantly happy at the realization of her cherished dream of being cared for under Miss Kerin's own roof.

Louie was not a child; she was a young woman in her late twenties; a small, crippled figure, a hunchback; her right shoulder, forced up above her ear, was immovable, and her back was twisted and misshapen.* She was carried to her room and put to bed. Dorothy visited her that evening, and gave her the laying-on-of-hands; to say that Louie felt herself to be in a paradise of bliss would be an understatement of her feelings. Sister Friend installed Louie in her sick room, and nursed her for a time, but later had to go away to recuperate her strength after a recent illness. News of Louie is contained in letters Dorothy wrote her during her absence. In the first letter she writes, "Little Louie was carried into Chapel yesterday. She is getting on very well, but it is very slow." This was soon followed by another letter:

* A. J. Russell: *Healing in His Wings.*

"Little Louie is getting on wonderfully, and is a joy to us. She sends her love to you and misses you very much. I need not say how much I miss you – but I am trying to be good and do want you to benefit by this rest in the best possible way. You know you are in my heart and in my prayers all the time. I miss your companionship and all that it is – quite, quite impossible for anyone else to give and be. But He will take care of it."

For some little time, there was no striking change in Louie's condition other than a slow but steady increase in strength, a marked improvement in appetite, and daily evidence of her abiding happiness and contentment in her surroundings.

There came the unforgettable day when the great miracle of her wholeness took place, with emphasis more on the spiritual than the physical, although this showed startling improvement. Dorothy wrote the good news to Sister Friend:

"It was a joy to get your letter and to know that Edith had you safely in bed. I know that you will have all that love and care can do, and for that part I am happy about you. You will know, my darling, that I have been very busy, and that is why you have not had a letter. You have been in my thoughts and prayers *all* the time, and I am asking Him to do what only He can, and feel so sure He will bless you. I miss you very, very much, and it felt desolate coming home on Monday night . . . and no Jum! They are doing all they can to look after me for you, and you must not worry. The new Nurses are a joy, and I think will be a great comfort and help. If only we could get the domestic staff right; there seem to be no kitchen maids left in this world!

"Now, for a lovely bit. I went in to Louie last night, she sent an urgent message for me. I found a radiant little soul, saying, 'JESUS HAS TOUCHED ME!' Her shoulder blade has dropped four inches and she is singing away in her bed, and as happy as a Queen. Praise the Lord!!!

"Dogs all well, and send you lickings. I should be able to write more often now, but it has been so hectic. I am going to bed early for you. All my love. Bless you and bless you!"

It was not long before Louie was up and about, enjoying a far more normal life than had been her lot for very many years; assisting at the Healing Services to which she had hitherto been carried; given delightful motor drives in the country; taking an interest in all about her;

enjoying the lovely clothes given her by Dorothy, she literally basked in the sunshine of love, and in the freedom from the frustration and pain of her long years of illness. Her soul blossomed like a beautiful flower; her faith, that of a simple, childlike mind, deepened. Life was indeed full of happiness for Louie. There was however some misgiving in the minds of those caring for her, as to how Little Louie was going to adapt herself to the humble home conditions awaiting her at Wisbech. Fine clothes, motor drives, sympathetic nurses and staff waiting on her every wish – the transition would be very difficult for her! Would it endanger the progress of her spiritual growth, so marked since she came under Dorothy's care, and especially so since the day she had felt upon her shoulder the warmth of our Lord's Living Touch?

God answered these queries in His own unfathomable way. The temptations that could have soiled in Louie the transparent purity of her soul never confronted her. One evening, near the time for her departure, Louie sent Dorothy a message, begging her to come to her, as she had an urgent request to make.

Dorothy came to her when going on her nightly round of visits, and stood by her bed. "What is troubling you, darling?" she asked the bright-eyed, eager little figure, sitting upright in her bed, with her eyes fixed on Dorothy's face.

"Please, please, Miss Kerin, will you take me with you *now* to the Chapel? I have something I want to say to Jesus that cannot wait."

Wrapping Louie in her dressing-gown, Dorothy took her to the Chapel, where together they knelt before the Altar. There, with her gaze lifted to the Crucifix, the little, erstwhile cripple poured her heart out to Jesus, confessing to Him all the sins she could remember ever to have committed, and ended by imploring His forgiveness. We may be sure that Dorothy convinced Louie that Divine Absolution had been granted her by her Heavenly Father, and that the Hand of her Lord and Saviour was fully upon her life – the life He had restored to her, and which she longed to dedicate to Him for the rest of her days. They returned to Louie's room, where Dorothy tucked her up for the night with a prayer and a tender blessing, and left her looking radiantly happy and filled with the Peace of God.

The next morning, Sister Friend, making her early rounds, found Louie curled up in an attitude of peaceful sleep with a look of utter bliss on her face. Jesus had called this little soul to Himself and taken her in her sleep to be with Him in those heavenly places where neither sin nor temptation, pain nor sorrow, could ever more assail her.

Why did God take Little Louie just as she stood on the threshold of a new life, filled with renewed vigour aud hope? The answer, the only answer, to this perplexing question is to be found in the Book of the Prophet Isaiah:

> "*My thoughts are not your thoughts, neither are your ways my ways,' saith the Lord.*"*

Patience, infinite in its range of understanding and its depth of loving insight, was a marked feature of Dorothy's personality. It enabled her, again and again, to overcome resistance, and even hostility, on the part of those unfortunate souls whose mental stability had been deranged through shock or illness, and whose doctors had sent them to Chapel House, after they had proved obdurate to ordinary methods of treatment. Many such cases were cared for in those days, and Dorothy devoted to them hours and hours of her precious time and strength. One case stands out among others on account of its unusual and happy ending.

Sister Friend was asked one day to fetch a girl from a London mental hospital. She brought her to Chapel House and took her to her room, where she immediately proceeded to crawl, round and round, on her hands and feet like an animal. Her hair was unkempt, and straggled in untidy wisps all over her face; her skin was blotchy and swollen; her fingers, with their long uncut nails, were like claws. She kept no food down and refused all treatment. The household had many a scare in regard to her. Early one morning, she crept over her special night nurse, whose bed lay across the window, and slid down a water-pipe to the ground. In a flash she was gone! She was found eventually and brought back by her mother, but had to be kept under constant surveillance.

Dorothy spent long hours with the unfortunate girl, pouring upon her all the the love and pity of her compassionate heart. Gradually she won her confidence, and learnt from her that, while on holiday in Italy, she had fallen in love with a handsome young peasant, whom she had married. Her mother had reacted violently against what she considered to be a disastrously unsuitable marriage for her daughter. She rushed out to Italy and forced the girl to return with her to England. Dorothy gained such an influence over the poor demented creature that she was able to persuade her to take an interest once more in her personal appearance, and even to accept a normal meal and to retain it. She bought her pretty clothes, and took her to a hairdresser to have her hair

* Isaiah 55.8.

shampooed and set. The result was startling, for there emerged a charming and attractive girl, as unlike the wild, unkempt creature that some weeks earlier had entered Chapel House as could be imagined! Dorothy then tackled the unhappy, stubborn mother and persuaded her to get in touch with her Italian son-in-law, to whom she finally consented her daughter should return.

Two years later, Dorothy received from Italy the photograph of a happy, smiling mother, proudly holding in her arms a bonny baby boy.

Among the patients sent by their doctors to Chapel House there were some who revealed themselves to be characters of special interest, whose memory has vividly remained with those who cared for them. Such a one was old Miss Evans, whose story is here told by Dr. King.

"Miss Evans was sent to us as suffering from a nervous breakdown. She was very intelligent, highly cultured and withdrawn. She stayed a short time and then left, returning later for a second visit which proved to be permanent. She became extremely fond of Dorothy. She had periods when she was antagonistic, vindictive and almost satanic in her behaviour, so that the nursing staff were scared of her. Dorothy could always manage her when she was in such moods.

"One day, Dorothy said to me, 'If ever I saw anyone possessed, I have seen Miss Evans!' This occurred after she had been at Chapel House for some time.

"I was visiting a patient in the Nursing Home one morning when I met Dorothy, who said to me, 'I have just had the worst experience I have ever had with Miss Evans. She could have killed me!'

"Somewhat startled, I asked what had happened; to which Dorothy replied, 'I was standing by her bed, when quite suddenly she put her two hands round my neck and shouted, 'You are not fit to live, and I am going to kill you!' As far as I can recollect, making no attempt to loosen the old woman's grip on her throat, Dorothy very calmly and gently said, 'Whatever the Good God tells you to do, you must do.' Miss Evans immediately let her hands drop to her bedclothes, and appeared once more to be sane and normal."

Dorothy possessed a compelling power over disordered minds. She was completely fearless, *for she knew in Whom she trusted*, and those afflicted with insanity were very amenable to her influence.

The senior members of her staff, who worked with her at Chapel House, Ealing, are little likely to forget the evening when a maid working in the kitchen suddenly went berserk and violently attacked the cook. The moment Dorothy appeared on the scene, she ceased banging her victim's head against the wall, and at Dorothy's command meekly followed her to her room. The scared staff waited outside with bated breath. A little later, a chastened and meek young woman emerged and quietly took her departure.

To end these stories, chosen among scores of others, is that of the old lady whose sight was restored to her. Dorothy loved to tell this story, and often included it in her addresses given in churches in this country and abroad, as illustrating what happens when suppliants to the Divine Physician for His Living Touch wholeheartedly accept whatever may be His will in and for them.

A dear old lady in her late seventies came to stay in order to be ministered to by Dorothy whose book, *The Living Touch*, she had read. She was suffering from advanced glaucoma, and had all but lost the sight of both her eyes. She considered herself to be a Christian although her faith was not of the kind that moves mountains; rather was she to be classed among the many lukewarm persons to whom religion is a respectable, and therefore acceptable fact, but far removed from a burning, consuming reality.

The weeks went by without improvement in her condition, but spiritually her life was transformed through her contact with Dorothy. She came to *know* Jesus, and her whole desire was to walk henceforth with Him to the end of her days. God's gifts to her were an abiding peace and an inner joy that shone in her face like a beacon of light.

Towards the end of her stay, Dorothy took her into Chapel and laid her hands upon her head – at that moment she knew our Lord had touched her. On the morning of her departure, the old lady said to Dorothy, "My eyes are no better, you know, than when I came, but I do not mind. God has given me, through your ministry, such blessings that I am prepared to accept in all things His will for me."

A few weeks later, Dorothy received a letter, postmarked Mentone, France, in which she read:

"You will be surprised to read this letter written by myself. Jesus has restored my sight, and I can now see perfectly with both my eyes. Moreover, to His abundant blessings, He has added another. I am going to be married! I have known him all my life, but circumstances have not made it possible for us to marry until now. We are coming to give thanks to God in your Chapel."

She arrived, in due course, with her newly married husband of 83, having herself driven the thousand miles from Mentone. They stayed for a week, and then this old warrior of 79 waved a gay farewell to the staff, assembled to wish her Godspeed, as she sat herself at the wheel to drive a further thousand miles back to the south of France. As the car moved forward, she poked her head out of the window and said to Dorothy standing nearby, "And who knows if God may not bless our union!"

Her faith had indeed become of the kind that moves mountains!

There are many stories of the healing of animals of which records exist. "God made both man and beast," Dorothy would say when using her charismatic gift for the healings of animals, with the special tenderness she displayed towards all stricken creatures. Dogs and horses were specially dear to her and she could do anything with them, for they trusted her as one who understood their needs and could speak their language. She was never without the companionship of some dog whose devotion to her was complete. Of all the dogs associated with her, whose names have come down to us, Bruno stands pre-eminent. He is the *Bruno* so frequently alluded to in Bishop Loyd's letters, and mention by Dorothy of his miraculous healing has been earlier recorded. He was given to her when she was at Thruxton with the Langford-James, and was therefore well on in years by the time she went to live in Ealing.

Many delightful stories of Bruno's uncanny sagacity have been told by Sister Friend, to whom he attached himself if ever Dorothy went away. On these occasions she would whisper in his ear, "You must take care of her, Bruno." This he would do, never leaving Sister, sleeping beneath her bed, although he took scant notice of her when his adored mistress was about; indeed, the moment Dorothy crossed the threshold of Chapel House he would once more ignore her! When the time came for Dorothy's return, Sister Friend would say to him, "Bruno, she is coming back today," without specifying whether morning, afternoon or evening. Half an hour before Dorothy's arrival, Bruno could be seen sitting by the front door, with two of his favourite toys hanging, one each side of his mouth, waiting to devour her with vociferous joy!

A treasured memory is that of the day when Bruno, who passionately loved his toys, of which he possessed a great variety, was seen carrying the broken ones into Chapel, where he laid them side by side on the chancel step. His trust was rewarded and his toys restored to him, beautifully mended by Dorothy. Bruno was given his name of Brown Verger, because of the fidelity with which he attended all the services and the punctilious way he went the round of the pews, politely welcoming all who came.

Each of Dorothy's dogs, as they succeeded one another, accompanied her to Chapel and sat at her feet during the Services, or curled up under her chair. When the Brown Verger was nearing his end, those assisting at Mass were surprised one morning to see him solemnly usher in Dinah, his immediate successor, and initiate her as to how she should behave, showing her the place she was to occupy until the time came for her promotion to his station at the side of Dorothy's prie-dieu.

Dorothy's love of animals was not confined to dogs and horses. There is an aviary at Burrswood. Somebody gave her – she was always being given things – a white budgerigar. It was put in with the others who completely rejected it, and pecked it almost to death. Peggy found it one evening lying on the ground, entirely denuded of feathers, and she rushed it to Dorothy who slept with it that night, snuggled in her hand against her cheek. It recovered, and was soon again in possession of its beautiful feathers.

Over the years, since Dorothy acquired the property in 1948, Burrswood has become a small animal sanctuary. Birds of many varieties abound in its thickets and orchard; wee, furry creatures busily rustle about in its undergrowth; water rats and badgers inhabit the banks of its streams; wild duck have the run of its ponds, which they share with an occasional heron. Pheasants, secure from gunshot, haunt its wooded grounds; rabbits scurry around the fields; squirrels fearlessly cross the path under one's feet; owls, large and small, screech into the night air; foxes bark in the distance, coming close to the houses in winter; nightingales, rapidly disappearing from our countryside, abound in its copses, making the nights in May and June resound to their golden song; pigeons whirr in and out of their dovecot; the rare oriel is a shy visitor.

In the fields by the upper drive, fat old Bunty, once Dorothy's mare, contentedly browses away what remains to her of life. Her handsome son, Barny, has now passed to the ownership of a member of the Fellowship who drives over from a considerable distance to exercise him, because he cannot be separated from his doting mother!

This is God's Burrswood, and God, Dorothy never tired of reminding us, made both man *and* beast to be loved and cared for.

CHAPTER 12

War Years

DOROTHY has recounted how, when seeking guidance one night in Chapel in regard to a particularly baffling problem, she became aware of the Presence of our Lord. He placed an infant in her arms saying, "Nurse this child for Me!" Clasping the baby to her, she felt its weight become so heavy that she could hardly hold it, and had difficulty in rising from her knees. The vision passed, and she realized this was something God held for the future.

This vision heralded the coming of the first of the nine children adopted by her in 1941–1942. Dorothy loved babies. She loved and yearned over all small, helpless and growing young lives: babies, puppies, foals, birds . . . had immediate and direct access to her loving maternal heart.

Sister Friend remembers how one evening, when she was quietly sitting with Dorothy in her room, she appeared to be listening to some message given her from the unseen world. After a time, turning to Sister, she said, "Get pencil and paper, Jummie, and write these names down for me." The names followed in quick succession: Mary, John; Elizabeth, Francis; Faith, Philip; Joan, Peter. She entered these names on the fly-leaf of her Bible, where they can still be seen, faintly outlined in pencil. The name of her first adopted child, Anne, the baby of the vision, is not included in the list, for the reason that she had already come to Dorothy when she was given the names of the eight others. With the paper in her hand, she then went across to her mother's room to give her the glad tidings that our Lord had revealed to her the names of her eight other babies, soon to come to her.

In due course they arrived. two pairs of twins among them: Faith and Mary, Francis and John. With their advent, there entered into Dorothy's life nine potential causes that were to give rise to joy and sorrow, happiness and tragedy, as is the case with every mother who rears a family. Did these children, whom she sincerely believed had been entrusted to her care by God, give her greater happiness than sorrow, or did the heartbreak of their later years outweigh the joy of their babyhood and early childhood? One thing is undeniable: Dorothy paid a great price for them, both spiritually and physically. Her agonized concern over the stresses, the problems, the uncertainties of their difficult adolescent years helped to shorten her life. Where, in the usual course of events, parents together would have sought to control their (ofttimes) turbulent, unmanageable 20th-century offspring, and shared in common their worries and perplexities in regard to them, Dorothy had to carry her burden alone. Being ultra-sensitive by nature, endowed also with a great sense of responsibility towards her Lord for the direction of their young lives, she suffered acutely when they deviated from her standards of Christian ethics. It must in fairness be stated that, during the critical period of their adolescence, they did not enjoy the advantages of ordinary family life. The very circumstances of Dorothy's work, that had grown by then to world-wide proportions; the incessant coming and going of crowds of people: staff, patients, visitors; the administration of a large estate, to say nothing of coping with a vast correspondence: all these claims upon her time and strength did not make it possible for her to give to her children and their individual problems as much attention as a parent normally would be in a position to do. The story is not yet ended, and one must hope that their future will justify her love and her faith in them, as also the great sacrifices she made on their behalf. We may be sure that her intercessory prayers are constantly operating on behalf of these nine adopted children she so deeply loved.

The babies survived the war years unscathed, physically and emotionally, thanks to their devoted mother's constant care and vigilance. We have, however, anticipated events, and must return to the period immediately preceding the great conflict that was to darken the world for six tragic years.

Some Saints are endowed with an additional awareness that science has named extra-sensory-perception. Their consciousness is not confined to our three-dimensional plane. Their prophetic gift enables them to interpret symbols presented to them by their heightened powers of perception. They are the Seers whose attempts to share with us their mystical experiences are all too often treated as fairy tales from a distant, legendary country. Because they possess spiritual faculties far exceeding those of their fellow mortals, there is much about their lives and activities that is susceptible of misinterpretation by those to whom their experiences are a closed domain.

Dorothy knew in 1938 that tragedy on a world-wide scale brooded

Dorothy as she was in 1936.

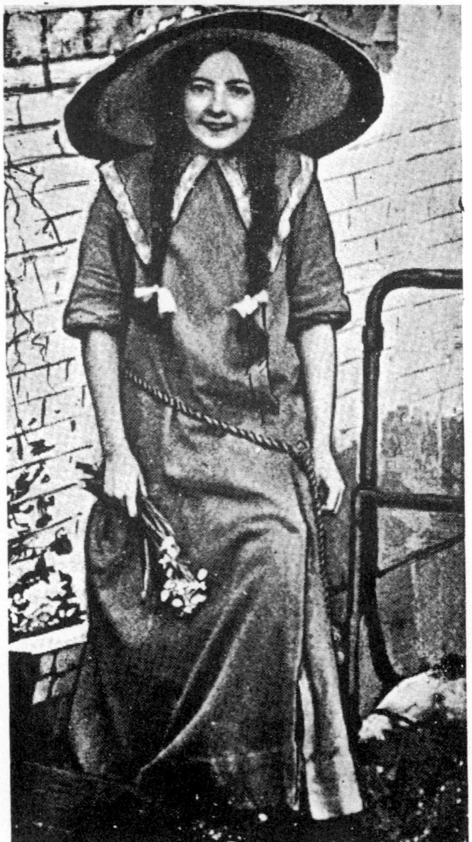

DOROTHY: Taken the morning after her miraculous Healing.

At the beginning of her public ministry.

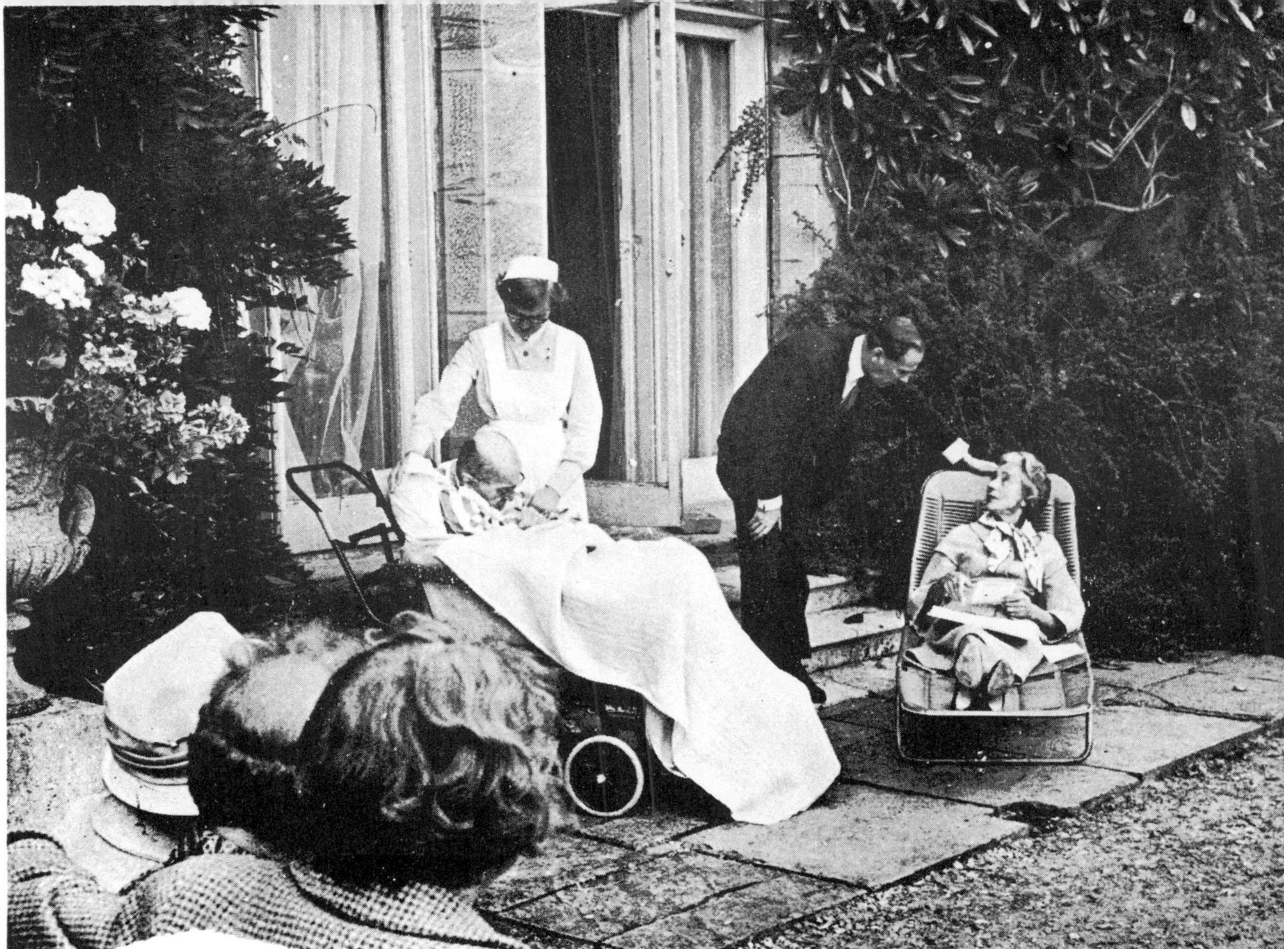

The terrace at Burrswood.

Dorothy and the "Nine"

Burrswood

Chapel House, Ealing.

Church of Christ the Healer.

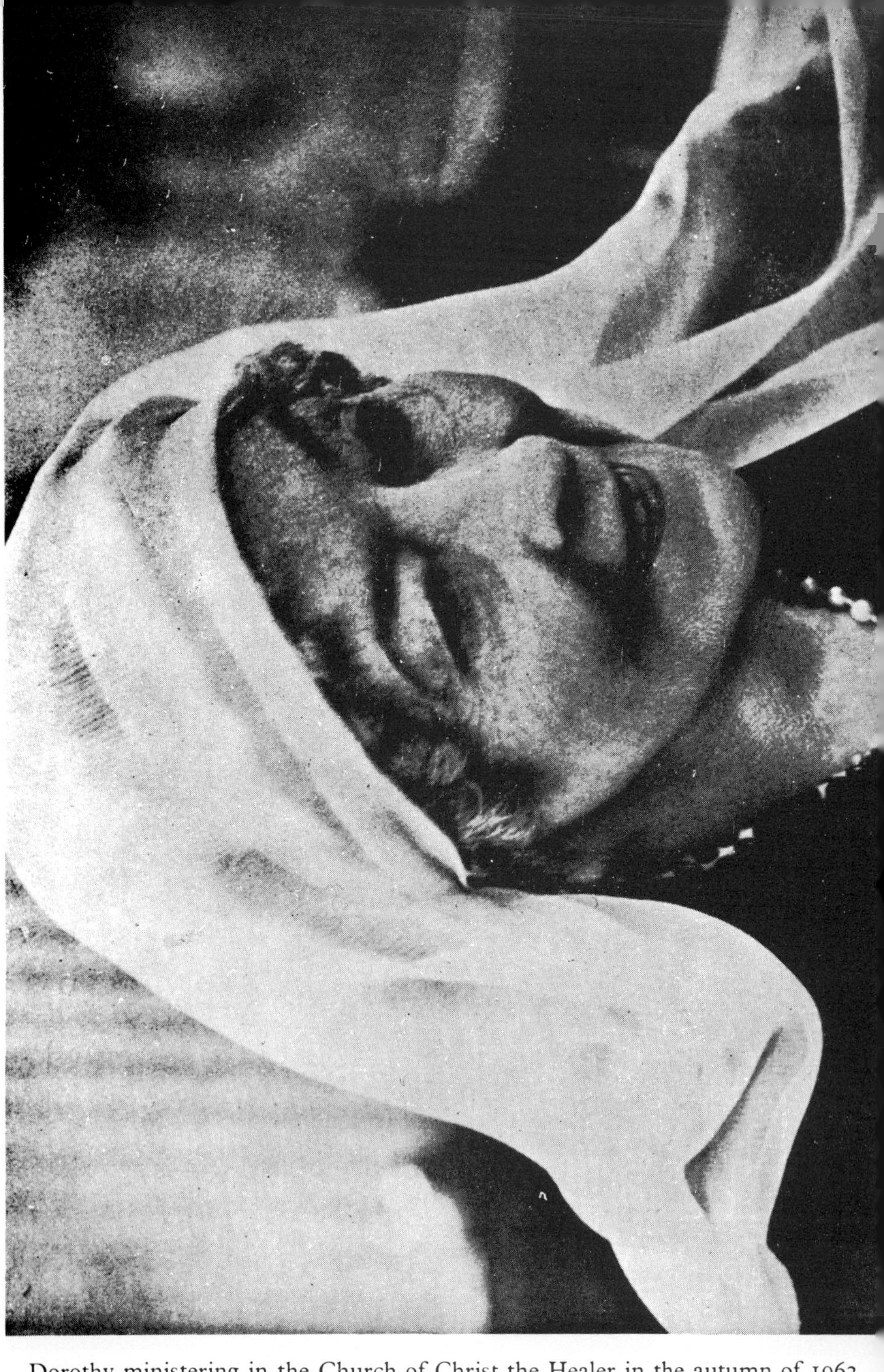

Dorothy ministering in the Church of Christ the Healer in the autumn of 1962.

over mankind. As the months passed, her intimates became aware of an immense longing on her part to be alone, a luxury she had not enjoyed since she left Edgbaston and the household of the Langford-Jameses. This inner urge to aloneness drove her to spend as much time as she could spare at a little country cottage owned by her in Berkshire, called the Ark. To this quiet, rural retreat she would make her way as often as she could. There she found the solitude and peace so essential to that soaring experience that Plotinus has spoken of as the flight of the alone to the Alone, and which to the mystics of the Christian Faith is experienced as union with God.

At the Ark, Dorothy enjoyed uninterrupted hours of blissful communion with the Beloved. She was able to drink deeply of the Living Waters of which our Lord spoke to the woman of Samaria at the well. Refreshed and penetrated by divine joy, her spiritual batteries became charged anew with the Power of the Holy Spirit, and it was undoubtedly this renewal of spirit that enabled her to traverse with serenity and faith the searing experiences of the war years, and to impart to those around her an awareness of God's Protecting Presence that remained with them throughout the war, and which revealed Itself again and again in moments of crisis.

The week before war was declared, Dorothy was shown three symbolic visions. The first took place when she was in the car between Chapel House and the Ark. On that occasion she saw a large, fiery red Cross. The second vision came to her while she was resting. The large Cross was again shown her: in front of it, with wings outstretched, was a dove with a deep wound in the heart, from which fell a stream of blood, that separated into drops of gold. The third vision presented her with the same Cross, but this time the dove was hovering over it with outstretched wings.

War was declared while Dorothy was at the Ark. When the first siren was sounded, the household at Chapel House assembled in the Chapel, considered as safe a place as any they had at their disposal. From there, Sister was summoned to the telephone. Dorothy's clear voice, serene and confident, came to her over the wires: "Tell them all 'in confidence and calm shall be your strength', and give them my love." A pause followed, and then: "He has spoken and told me, 'BE NOT DISMAYED'."

In 1940, Dorothy was told by the local A.R.P. authorities that a shelter must be built for patients. She gives a graphic picture in *Fulfilling* of the nights spent there. It was a shelter-de-luxe, very comfortable, and complete with telephonic communication to the house. The shelter was fitted with bunks for fourteen persons. Dorothy had not intended to go, but her presence was insisted upon. It meant to her the sacrifice of her quiet time at dawn. The shelter was given the elegant name of the "Dorchester", and each evening, a procession of old ladies would wend their way to the safety of the palatial Dorchester, clad in the latest style of siren suits, and carrying bags containing precious bits and pieces.

In spite of deafening gunfire and falling bombs, blazing fires and every kind of other horror by day and night, Chapel House and all under its roof were kept in safety, and seldom did fear rear its head among them. There were many broken windows and considerable damage from blast, but no one received so much as a scratch.

As the war went on it made increasing demands upon the man power of the nation, so the staff at Chapel House dwindled to skeleton proportion. Even the skeleton threatened to vanish, and so leave Dorothy stranded without domestic help, with all the houses filled with sick and old folk. Then it was that four members of the Fellowship, who had been her patients, volunteered to undertake the housework, and the situation was saved by this team of truly dedicated, joyous and willing workers.

No one of our generation is likely to forget the shock of hearing of the catastrophe in Belgium!

Early one morning in June, 1940, Marina turned on her wireless to hear the shattering news: King Leopold of the Belgians had surrendered unconditionally. She says that when the full import of this fact broke over her, it sent shivers down her spine: our little army, all we had was trapped in Belgium, and what would happen now? Was this the end? She flung her clothes on and ran across the garden to the main building to find Dorothy. She could feel her legs shaking as she ran. People were coming out of the Chapel; there had been a Communion Service, and she waited in the Hall, watching for Dorothy. Father Barrett was the last to come out, and still there was no Dorothy. Minutes passed and Marina could bear the suspense no longer. She opened the Chapel door and saw Dorothy coming towards her, her face alight with extraordinary joy!

Marina burst out: "Have you heard the terrible news?"

Dorothy's expression did not change, although Marina's words and her fear must have reached her.

She shook her head. "No, but I too have news. You tell me yours, and I will tell you mine."

Marina told her, "They have just said on the wireless that the King of the Belgians has surrendered. That is the end, Dorothy!"

"Oh no, it isn't. Our Lord has just said, 'I will protect the Isles of the Blessed.' "

Marina goes on to say that at this astonishing message, it was impossible to doubt any more. After that day those at Chapel House were privileged, for they knew that all would be well in the end.

For Dorothy, the most wonderful event of these hazardous war years was the coming to her in 1941 of Anne, whom she declares was God's most precious gift to her. In a letter to an old friend she writes:

"I expect you know I have a daughter, Anne, now seven months old, and she is quite the loveliest thing that ever happened. I held her when she was two weeks old, and now the Beloved tells me I am to have eight more!!! I hope He does not send them all at once!"

By August, 1942, all the eight other babies had arrived. Dorothy's heart was filled with joy, and the nursery filled with cots! They were legally adopted and so became her own children in every sense. She had very little to contend with in the way of baby ailments. There had been a cessation of bombing, and for a time undisturbed nights prevailed. There were several remarkable incidents of supernatural protection such as on the day when Dorothy told Mary, her devoted Nannie, to bring in all the prams from the garden quickly. "But there has not been a siren," objected the maid. "At once!" Dorothy insisted. The last pram had only just gained the shelter of the house when a shell came whizzing down, the cap of which landed where the last pram had stood.

Morrison shelters were installed for the protection of the children in St. Michael's dining-room, and when the bombing was resumed, nine little cots were placed round the room. At the first alarm, Dorothy and Sister Friend would dress and sit with the children, who were lifted, some asleep, out of their cots and placed in the Morrison shelter. They were soon all awake, and many nights were spent in story telling and singing, an exhausting occupation for weary adults who had spent a strenuous day, with the prospect of a similar one before them!

The incessant bombing and the disturbed nights began to affect the children adversely. They showed signs of nervous strain, and Dorothy decided to move them to the quiet of the countryside. As was her invariable custom, she prayed about it before making her decision. A few days after the idea came to her, she received a letter to say that a small cottage was available in Buckinghamshire. The Lady Abbess of the Community of St. Mary at the Cross, a much-loved friend, wrote to tell her that a furnished cottage near them at Burnham would be shortly vacant. She asked Dorothy to come and see it, and this she did. She was delighted with the cottage and the surroundings, and thought it an ideal place for the children. The old lady who inhabited it was ill and lonely. She was taken in and cared for by the nuns, thus liberating the cottage for Dorothy to use. She and the children moved in, and for some time remained there. One night they were all awakened by a queer and unknown sound. It was a flying bomb, and thereafter the locality was daily visited by them. Dorothy decided it was useless for the children to remain at Burnham, and arrangements were made for their return to Ealing, where they stayed until the war ended.

Dorothy's mother lived long enough to take all the babies to her heart. She was able to rejoice in the sound of children's laughter, and the pattering of their little feet in St. Michael (as had been foretold by her daughter), before her death. Marina, who tended "Mum" with great devotion, has this to say of her last days on earth:

"Dorothy's mother was gentle and lovable. In spite of her age, Mum, as we called her, had that youthful spirit which remains unaffected by the weight of years. She also had a child-like simplicity and the gift of a pure heart, forgiving easily, and easily pleased. Dorothy shared many of her characteristics, especially her sense of fun and an intense love of music. Even when Mum was confined to bed, we would hear them singing in unison or reciting from her songs, for she once had a lovely voice, and had even sung in the Albert Hall. It was a charming sight to see them together. Theirs was a true relationship, although Dorothy was, of course, the adult, and Mum forever the child.

"During the last years of her life, she became increasingly confined to her room, because of her failing sight and hearing. This caused her endless frustration, for she found difficulty in accepting the limitations imposed by the War, and she grew to depend more and more on her elderly friends for the luxury of a homely chat. The crowning joy of her day was Dorothy's visit, which usually took place at mealtime; a tray was then brought to Mum's bedroom, and Dorothy rested after the endless interviews and letters of the day. At such times, Dorothy would come to her exhausted, and would stretch herself on the bed beside her and fall into a brief but deep sleep.

"This quiet rhythm of Mum's life, uninterrupted in spite of the air-raids, was suddenly broken by her illness. On November 9th, 1942, she collapsed with a heart attack, and two others followed, leaving her totally blind and deaf. For four days her condition remained critical, and Dorothy hardly left her side. We were all waiting to hear of her passing when, unexpectedly, she regained consciousness and, to our amazement, her sight and hearing were restored. She came back into life radiantly happy, in a sort of ecstasy, her features transformed by a new and youthful beauty. Her friends came to see her and wondered at this change. It was to Dorothy she confided her spiritual experiences, and they were of a nature rarely recorded by those who have crossed the river of life and returned again. Dorothy, having herself crossed that bridge, understood what she was saying.

"Mum told her that she had been to a most beautiful place, where there were trees, water, the scent of flowers, and where the whole of nature was filled with light and inexpressible beauty. The atmosphere was alive with a joy such as she had never experienced before. 'And then,' she said, 'I saw Him coming towards me, and there were others with Him. He told me you were very dear to Him, and that He would always take care of you. Our Blessed Lord also said you were not coming yet. He made that very clear, and He added that He was very pleased . . .'

"Dorothy did not repeat the concluding words, but the context was obvious. She had wept as she had listened to this message from the Kingdom for which she yearned: her heart was divided between the joy of it, and the sorrow of all it implied about her mother. Thus it followed that a month later, Mum became critically ill once more, and this time Dorothy went down with a temperature of 103°.

"Jummie (Sister Friend) nursed them both, with only me to help her, dividing her time between the two invalids as best she could. Then, on December 13th, in the early hours of the morning, as Jummie and I were watching over Mum, Dorothy suddenly came into the room, hardly able to walk, and collapsed into a chair beside her. Hastily we wrapped a blanket around her and bolstered her up with pillows, and then we sat and waited, praying for the approaching end.

"Mum lay very still, her hand in Dorothy's, and I could see the outline of both their faces in the shaded light, both so withdrawn and yet at one, in that moment of separation. I became conscious of the stillness that lay about us as a cloak of peace, and the room was filled with an invisible Reality, impossible to describe. This peace and its activity deepened with our silence; only occasionally, Dorothy's gentle voice could be heard murmuring a prayer, and then the silence would flow through us on its progress towards eternity.

"I wondered how Dorothy would know whether Mum was still with us or not, but shortly I heard her say:

" 'Into Thy Hands, O Lord, I commend her spirit.'

"As she spoke, Mum gave a little sigh, and bowed her head in a movement of assent. She had fallen asleep."

By the goodness of God, everyone at Chapel House was kept in safety throughout the war, and brought through perilous times unscathed. There had been hard days when every ounce of faith and strength were called upon, but though the flame of hope grew dim at times, it never went out.* Had not our Lord told His servant at the onset of the war, "Be not dismayed," and had He not later said, "I will protect the Isles of the Blessed?"

When once again travel was possible, a friend came from Switzerland to visit Dorothy, who asked her if she knew of anyone who would help her to bring up her nine adopted children, by then sturdy youngsters of from four to five years old. The friend happened to know the very person with the ability to dedicate her life to this exacting task, provided she felt this was God's Will for her. She came to England to see Dorothy, and instantly *knew* that God was calling her to this work. Kathleen, known to so many of the Fellowship in later years as Dorothy's personal attendant, vigilant watch-dog and close personal friend, has written for us a vivid account of those early years.

* Dorothy Kerin: *Fulfilling*.

CHAPTER 13

Kathleen's Story

A WHITE-PAINTED door, with a large black knocker. St. Michael, Mattock Lane, Ealing, the home of Dorothy Kerin and her nine adopted children. My heart sank within me. My hand raised to knock, fell to my side and I hastily beat a retreat. But the *inner voice*, merciless and unrelenting said:

"Go back. This is where you have come to serve your Lord!"

So back I went and knocked. The door opened on to a large, square hall. I was shown into a room at the far end of it. This was Dorothy's study, and this was Dorothy Kerin. As my 'inner' eye looked and saw the soft haze of light that surrounded her, I felt the impact of something that no words can define. In a flash, I knew for a certainty why I had left the mountains, the rushing streams, the pine trees, the luxury of solitude. It was to find just this that I saw before me in the face of Dorothy Kerin: selfless service and sacrifice; suffering, joy, happiness all mingled together, but above all Love, Compassion and the Cross.

The children whom I had come to help look after were then at the ages of four to five; beautiful to look at, beautifully dressed. Nothing was too good for them. Dorothy herself wore the same coat and skirt, bluey-green in colour, week in, week out, until it was quite threadbare. But the children were given only the best. Debenhams or Marshalls smocked the girls' dresses, and Rowe's of Bond Street tailored for the boys, and later there were riding clothes for all. Dorothy felt she must give them of the best to compensate for their lack of a father.

I well remember my bewilderment in the early days in trying to pair off, and search for leather gaiters, socks and gloves for all, the gaiters having at least twenty buttons per leg, and eighteen legs to cope with! As you can imagine, the cloakroom was the scene of many a conflict and scramble: buttons missing, gloves hidden, odd socks, Wellingtons full of water, caps thrown out of reach! Mummy would come along, and it seemed a hundred little voices screamed –

"Mummy! he's got my cap! Mummy! Tell Peter to give me my ball. Mummy! can I sit by you?"

A walk in the adjoining Park would follow, complete with dogs, sundry dolls' prams, dolls and teddy bears. There was always the temptation to climb trees to be coped with, or leaning too far over the pond with the ducks, not to mention the talking parrot's strange fascination.

Mummy was very occupied all day. There were about sixty patients in the seven houses which comprised the Nursing Home, and many outside callers. She would come up to the Night Nursery in the evening, and go round to the cots to hear their prayers, 'Gentle Jesus' being one of the favourites; then, she would often sing them a song or two, or we would all sing 'Gentle Jesus' together, if she had less time than usual. They all adored her, and of course there was one continuous fight for her attention. She never failed to come into the Day Nursery for a few minutes to talk over the day with me, before she went down to her solitary meal on a tray. She always preferred to eat alone, except on Sundays when we all had lunch at a huge round table in St. Michael's dining-room.

In the evenings, Dorothy's closer friends were expected to gather in the study to talk or listen to good music. It was summer when I came to Chapel House, and Mr. Temple never failed to bring his bunch of sweet peas he had grown specially for her. Mr. Temple lived in one of the seven houses. There were seven rambling gardens, and Dorothy loved to go out with her basket and dogs, and either pick flowers and fruit or pull out weeds. She was particularly fond of weeding, and could never understand how people could pass a weed without extracting it!

Bishop Loyd was a constant visitor when I first arrived. Dorothy had her own little Chapel on the top floor of St. Michael's. Here, the Bishop gave me the laying-on-of-hands to bless me into the work; here Dorothy brought her problems and cares in the silent night hours, for in those days she had very many. The move to Kent was imminent, and there were both financial and other problems in plenty.

That first summer of 1946, there was a very big gathering of the Fellowship at a Garden Party which Her Royal Highness Princess Marie Louise had promised to come and open. She was very gracious and charming. Seated in the drawing-room of one of the houses, she received "Purses" from two of the little girls who made their wobbly little curtseys at her knee.

In September of the same year, we moved to Speldhurst in Kent. The story of how Speldhurst passed to Dorothy's possession is beautifully told by Miss Modin (whose home it was) in *Fulfilling*. Before the move, Dorothy went down frequently with one or two of the children for odd weekends to get everything ready. On the great day itself, Dorothy, the children and the dogs, and I all packed into the large brake, driven by James, the young chauffeur.

There followed the blessing by Bishop Loyd, and I refer readers to *Fulfilling* for details of that unforgettable day.

Dorothy had a bedroom overlooking the garden and the pool, from where, later, water was to flow. I was given a little room adjoining hers. There was the most holy and wonderful atmosphere in her bedroom . . . I can still feel the urge to take off my shoes before entering.

One evening, I was sitting on the hearthrug in Dorothy's bedroom. She had fallen asleep, which she did habitually quite suddenly, and I dared not move for fear of waking her from her few precious moments of sleep. Twilight was giving place to night, when, by the firelight, I saw her get out of bed in her sleep, as though intent on some purpose. She moved behind the dressing-table to the window, and standing there, she obviously communed with SOMEBODY or some PRESENCES outside. Was it with our Lord or His Angels, I remember wondering. It made a very strong impression on me, as the whole atmosphere seemed to be fraught with POWER that was not of this world. Afterwards, she told me, she was told to go and look out of the window, and from there she saw a long stream of people, the sick, the lame, the deaf and the blind, passing by the pool and coming up the lawn to her to be healed.

In the early Speldhurst days, Brenda, the daughter of an old friend, came to stay. She had cancer of the breast. There was only one spare room, and Brenda went to bed for a fortnight. The first evening, when the children were in bed, Dorothy asked me to go with her, and we knelt one each side of the bed, each holding one of Brenda's hands. This seemed to connect a current of Power, and my whole being felt as if on fire. Dorothy prayed, and then, in silence, we would leave the room. This continued for about a week. Then, one morning, Dorothy told me Brenda was well, that the lump had gone, and that she was going to stay and help to look after the children as a thank-offering. This she did, and in fact she was the only person who ever successfully exercised any discipline over the turbulent nine. During these two years, we had an interlude when the daughter of an old Indian friend of Dorothy, Judge Nanavhati, wanted – or thought she had been led – to come and teach the children. She was Froebel trained, and for some days there was great excitement when the children swarmed around her. Little saucers were prepared to demonstrate islands, isthmuses, lakes, mountains, rivers, etc., but soon the schoolroom floor was a mass of spilled ink, damp sand, and the chaos and noise were beyond description, so after a few days Pareen shook the dust off her feet and returned to India, and we settled down to our military discipline again!

Dorothy was away in Ealing, where the Nursing Home was still in full swing, for half of the week, so her home-coming was always a great event, and presents were made in the schoolroom, flowers were gathered, garlands plaited and preserved for her. Our days were full, as between the two of us (Brenda and myself) we not only taught the nine children, but looked after their well-being, which included their clothes, washing, ironing and mending. In addition, there was riding in pairs, music lessons, supervised practising, French and outdoor games.

I well remember the day Dorothy said to me that she was going to have riding lessons in order to be able to ride with the children, but, she said, "I don't want them to know until I can ride!" So she and I stole out across the fields to meet the Riding Master waiting with the horses in order to fulfil one of the dreams of her life. From the moment she got into the saddle, she rode as though to the manner born, and it was not long before she was able to join the children.

Another activity she enjoyed at this time was haymaking. There was one field which 'belonged'. Here we raked, and carried the hay, all mixed up with children, dogs, favourite dolls and discarded bicycles, while Mummy stood on top of the haystack, making it into the most perfect and beautiful shape, just as though she had been making haystacks all her life . . . and how she loved it. This ability to do well whatever she put her hand to amounted to genius with Dorothy, and we never ceased to marvel at it.

Peggy, who looked after the horses, one day asked me to help her give Boy (Dorothy's horse) a dredge. This resulted in his rearing up and dragging my hands against the bars of his stall and almost severing a finger. Normally, I suppose, I would have had several stitches, but with Dorothy's care it soon healed.

One day, the three little ones, as Priscilla, Peter and Philip were called, were out riding when Priscilla's pony shied and threw her. An ambulance was called and brought her home. Mummy returning from London at that self-same hour, met the ambulance at the door, and had Priscilla taken up to her own bedroom. X-ray experts were sent for, and she herself never left the child. The X-ray showed fractured skull, which meant a dark room, six weeks at least . . . if . . . etc., Dr. Perkins and the specialist said, both looking very grave.

That night Dorothy said to me, "Leave me with her, I believe our Lord has something to give her," so I left her to a long night vigil. In the night, Dorothy was told to lay her hands on Priscilla who said, "Mummy, Jesus came, and all fwee headaches have gone!" Within a few days, Priscilla was out in the garden, playing with her brothers and sisters!

About this time, too, Dorothy was given the money to buy a horse. This particular beast was sold to her as a quiet hack. We afterwards learnt that it was the bane of the neighbouring hunt! One day it bolted before our eyes, Dorothy sitting tight until she was a tiny speck in the distance. The Riding Mistress and I did not dare to gallop after, for fear of making things worse, so we followed as quickly as was advisable, and were astonished to meet Dorothy coming towards us still seated. She told me that she seemed to be held by unseen hands, and that when approaching a big ditch at breakneck speed, she breathed the name "JESUS", and the horse stopped almost immediately, and she was able to turn round and come back quite quietly.

This horse used to buck regularly in the yard, but on one particular day, when I was exercising it, we got on to the road making for the beech wood, when round the bend came a fast sports car. We bucked and bucked, and bucked again, until I was thrown with a very hard whack on to the tarmac road flat on my back! A passing car stopped, and carried me in, and I was laid on the drawing-room floor. I thought every bone in my body was broken. Dorothy was away in London, but was expected back that night. When she arrived she at once said in that amazingly commanding and reassuring voice, "Take her upstairs, she's all right." The next day a visitor arrived from Switzerland, and Dorothy sent me a message to the effect that she expected me down to tea! Stupefied, and feeling rather resentful, but knowing that Dorothy must be obeyed, I moved very cautiously to see if the bones would hold together. They held, and so I crawled downstairs, and by the end of the afternoon was practically healed.

Dorothy spent happy days at Speldhurst, perhaps the happiest she had known. The war years, and the move from Ealing, had brought a curtailment of her work. The children had become her first care. She was living a normal life, and doing all the things she had always longed to do. She was well in health, she loved the riding and the horses, and all the country pursuits: walks, gardening, riding, haymaking, etc. After the children had been put to bed, having been bathed and brushed, she would do the round of the cots hearing their prayers, perhaps singing 'Gentle Jesus' to them or some other lullaby. Nanny left about this time. Nanny had been sleeping with the more nervous ones, and I offered to take her place. This was not a success, and Mummy said she was going to sleep with them herself . . . to the great delight of the children. There were three night nurseries, all leading out of each other, and she slept in the middle one with two of the children. As soon as they awoke in the mornings, about 6 a.m., they all rushed to her bed, and she used to pretend that her bed was a ship sailing to America. The children had no mercy. They literally bounced on her, tumbled all over her, shrieking with delight. These were indeed happy days for Dorothy. The little Chapel amongst the clump of trees on the mound, within a stone's throw of the house, saw many a healing. Daily prayers were held there too, after breakfast, when each child had the opportunity of opening its heart to God. The word "JESUS" was constantly on their lips. The two youngest boys were taught to serve at the Altar at a very early age, and Dorothy herself made their little cottas.

On Mummy's birthdays there was always great excitement, and at the earliest possible moment of the day Mummy would seat herself in the drawing-room, and the excited children would come in one at a time to make their bow or curtsey and hand their present to Mummy: little raffia mats, blotters, hand-painted shoe trees, coat hangers, etc., to each she gave such extraordinary attention, expressed such pleasure and delight, praised the maker and teacher so warmly . . . that teacher and child alike swelled with pride and satisfaction. When this ceremony was finished, they all joined hands round Mummy and sang "Happy Birthday to you . . .", ending up with hurrahs which rent the air for some considerable time. Later in the day, the horses would be brought to the front door to express also their birthday good wishes. There was an occasion when one horse insisted upon walking right into the Hall – to the great delight of Mummy and the children! Once on her birthday she was given two lambs, Buttercup and Daisy, and also two geese, by the same patient. They used to live in the orchard, and when I took the washing to hang on the line one of these geese used to fly straight at me. I was terrified! *Par contre*, it used to sit on Peggy's lap to be fed, and afterwards twist its neck around Peggy's neck!

One winter's night, we were woken by an S.O.S. from St. Raphael. They had a burst tank and the water was two or three inches deep all over the ground floor, and pouring down the stairs. Brenda, Peggy, Bocky and I all rushed over with buckets, cloths, and any other receptacle we could lay hands on, and started baling out frantically. Suddenly, there was Dorothy in our midst, standing on a table in the middle of the sitting-room playing a musical box, and singing the accompaniment! Always full of fun and joy and humour . . . with a hidden strength and serenity when faced with any emergency that gave confidence in the gravest of situations – a leader to the finger-tips, with dynamic driving force, and expecting, therefore getting, only the uttermost from all, yet with such gentle humility and love that she won the hearts of all those with whom she came in contact, and not *only* the heart; but in winning it, turned that soul to God.

Dorothy never remained static for long! Soon a new Chapel was planned on the site of the old cowshed. A cedar tree, keeping light and sun from the house, was felled and seasoned and made into the panelling. An artist, Wallace Wood, was commissioned to design and make the stained glass window for the east end. (This window is now in the east end of Christ the Healer, in the organ loft.) Pews seemed to appear from nowhere, and all the Church furnishings supplied. The Altar was the one from Ealing, but a Reredos was carved by a craftsman from Southborough. This man was mortally ill, but would not give in, such was his love of the job that he was doing for his Lord. It was his last piece of work, however, and one which is surely precious in the eyes of Him for Whom such sacrifice was made. It is the Altar which stands in the Lady Chapel of Christ the Healer. The Chapel was blessed by Bishop Loyd, and its memory is very precious to those who worshipped in it. Next, the Bull Chamber was turned into a delightful little residence, furnished and blessed and named St. Francis. It was in this little cottage that Miss Modin lived when she directed the Nursing Home after it moved from Ealing to Speldhurst, and Dorothy herself and her children had taken up their residence in Burrswood.

PART THREE

The Gathering of the Sheaves

CHAPTER 14

Burrswood

IN 1944, Bishop Loyd said farewell for ever to the country to which he had given the best years of his life. Those years had taken a heavy toll of his physical strength and health, and he returned to England a sick man, whose tired heart cried out for a prolonged period of rest. He was, however, far too valuable to be left in retirement for long. He had hoped to be given a country living, helping when needed with Confirmations, and with time to spare to write more of his devotional books which had proved so popular with the religiously minded section of the British public. Archbishop Temple had other plans for him, and when the official offer of St. Albans came he felt he could not disregard the call. He had a cardiograph taken of his heart, and was told that by the New Year he would be fit for a strenuous life again, and could look forward to five years of active work. In 1945, he was enthroned in the great Abbey Church of St. Albans, with all the solemnity and ceremonial that the Church has ordained for such an occasion. He entered upon his episcopal duties with the same zeal and selflessness that had distinguished the tenure of his episcopal office in India. He was the first Bishop of the Indian Church ever to be translated to an English see.*

It was a great comfort and joy to Dorothy when Bishop Loyd came to live in England permanently. Her loved and trusted spiritual guide, whose wise counsel had never been at fault, was now within easy reach, and a constant visitor at Chapel House. Her children were fast growing up, and the need for help in their upbringing was beginning to make itself felt. The aftermath of war showed itself, among other drawbacks, in that very few capable persons were free to assume this charge. We have seen how Kathleen, on hearing of Dorothy's predicament, was led to leave Switzerland to devote her life to God's servant and her work, in whatever capacity she could be most useful. For some years her activities were confined to the care of the children. Life in the metropolis was not easy in those 'ration-minded' days. The conflicting demands of a Nursing Home filled with sick and old people in need of quiet, and

* R. P. Stacy Waddy: *Bishop Loyd: Missionary and Bishop* (Mowbray).

a house filled with growing and noisy children, created an uneasy situation that must have been a strain for all concerned.

The Bishop observed, prayed much as was his custom, and drew his conclusions as to the course he should advise Dorothy to follow. One day, he came to her and said he believed it to be in God's plan that she should take her young family away from the vitiated atmosphere of London to the health-giving air of the countryside. Dorothy looked at him aghast. "But," she objected, "where my children are, there I must be; and, yet, my work is clearly in Chapel House!" To which the Bishop replied, "God will find a way. Let us leave it to Him." There for a time the matter was allowed to rest. It was not long, however, before it was made clear to Dorothy in her prayer, that the Bishop's advice was inspired by God, and that the removal of her children from Ealing was, in fact, a part of His plan for them. Readers must turn to *Fulfilling* to learn how, through the instrumentality of Miss Modin, Etherton Hill in Kent passed into Dorothy's possession. It was an ideal place for the children, perfect in every detail, despite its rough handling by the Army which had occupied it during the war. They were all moved from Ealing to this delightful country home in September, 1946. Henceforth, Dorothy divided her time between Speldhurst and Ealing. It was not a satisfactory arrangement, as it exacted time being spent by her in travelling to and fro between the two homes, each of which clamoured for her presence. It was obvious that such a way of life could not be indefinitely maintained.

In 1948 the Bishop again intervened. He told Dorothy it might well be that God was asking her to give up the Chapel House Home of Healing, and transfer her work to some large country house that could accommodate herself, her nine children, and a few patients not dependent upon skilled nursing, leaving Speldhurst to take the place of Ealing as the official Nursing Home. It would necessitate finding a place within easy reach of Speldhurst. Dorothy felt the bottom was falling out of her world! Leave Chapel House! Abandon the flourishing work that had reached its zenith at the cost of so much love and labour! Turn her back upon the place in which God had gloriously manifested His Healing Power! Close the doors of this shrine of healing in which so many of His suffering children had received the gift of their Lord's Living Touch! Surely He was not asking this of her? She could only stare at the Bishop in utter consternation.

"Little Sister," he gently reminded her, "the Holy Spirit of God can never be confined within brick walls. We know that It bloweth where It listeth. If it be His Will that your work be carried on in some other environment, then He will guide you, and provide for you, as He has never failed to do in the past." Taking her hand in his, he drew her into the Chapel where, kneeling side by side, they laid this tremendous problem upon the Altar, and left it there for God to make known His Will. It was in this heroic spirit of selflessness that Dorothy surrendered to God the seven flourishing houses of her greatly loved Home of Healing at Ealing. Who of us would thus have given up a life-work of such magnitude with the unquestioning readiness to do God's Will, as she did on that April day long ago? Only God's Saints, in whose hearts flames the "measureless, endless, ineffable Love Divine", are able to assume the crown of renunciation whose thorn-twisted strands are woven of their constant and unhesitating obedience to God's Most Holy Will.

The decision having been made, the sacrifice accepted, Dorothy, as always, lost no time in releasing the springs of action. She at once put the Ealing houses on the market to be sold at the best obtainable price, and the news was circulated among her wide circle of friends and acquaintances. She also began her search for a country home.

Each Sunday, since she had acquired Etherton Hill, accompanied by Peggy, Kathleen and the children, Dorothy had been in the habit of attending Mass at the parish Church of St. Thomas in Groombridge. They would often stay to breakfast in the village hall after the Service. Fr. Gilbert, the priest-in-charge of the parish, brought to Dorothy's notice that there were two large houses for sale in the neighbourhood. One, called Leyswood, was in his parish, and the other, known as the Manor House, or Burrswood – its original name – was situated close to the Old Village of Groombridge which was attached to the parish of Speldhurst.

One afternoon, Dorothy and Kathleen set out to look at both these properties. Leyswood, rambling and unsuitable, proved to be in too bad a condition for consideration. There remained the hope of Burrswood.

Many years ago, wealthy people owned the valley with the wood called "Burrswood" stretching for miles at the upper end of it. A tributary of the Medway wound its way across the meadows; a carriage drive ran from the Big House right through the woods to Speldhurst parish Church; four lodges and the Home Farm completed this property. The parkland was sown with truckloads of bulbs, imported from Holland: in the spring, the fields were a golden glory of daffodils.

Fifteen gardeners cared for the property, which was one of the show places in Kent; people travelled from near and far to view the splendour of its gardens, whenever these were open to the public. Then came the war years. The land was sold off in bits; the house was occupied by troops; the gardens became a jungle. Ammunition was stored in the woods and down the drives – the property became more and more derelict. When hostilities ceased the troops moved out, but they left behind them a desert where once beauty and order had reigned.

On arrival at Burrswood's front door, Dorothy knew at once that this was the house she was looking for; this was the one her Mother had seen in a dream years before. It had what she had then depicted: a long stone terrace, along which she had seen children running. Dorothy turned to Kathleen, as she put her hand on the knocker, and said, "This is the one" – then she gave three loud knocks that reverberated through the house.

On account of its dilapidated condition, Burrswood was offered at a comparatively low price, well below its real value. With the financial security represented by the prospective sale of the Ealing property behind her. Dorothy had no difficulty in arranging to put down the required deposit. While negotiations were in progress, she and Kathleen and Peggy would go over from Speldhurst to work in the garden. The grounds, that had become an impenetrable jungle, were tackled by the head gardener from Ealing, assisted by German prisoners. They literally had to hack their way through from one part of the property to another. Dorothy would sickle and pull at the ten-foot brambles that were choking everything, and then have a gorgeous bonfire. She adored bonfires, and these bonfires became quite famous. Kathleen affirms that she worked like a black, and those who know her propensity for work can well believe it! Her vitality was astonishing, and she seemed possessed of Herculean strength. Once, in her enthusiasm, she got so close to a bonfire that her eyebrows were singed off! She believed that Chapel House, Ealing, would soon be sold; there was, therefore, an urgent need to get Burrswood ready for habitation.

Dorothy was, however, to encounter one of the grievous 'rebuffs' that had been foretold in the vision of her Beautiful Day recorded by her in *The Living Touch*. The Archdeacon of London had intimated his wish to buy the Ealing Home for use as a Diocesan House. After Dorothy had signed the agreement to purchase Burrswood, she learnt that the Archdeacon had withdrawn his offer. It was decided to sell the houses separately, and St. Michael was bought by a doctor. She was on the verge of favourably disposing of Chapel House, when the Middlesex County Council suddenly intervened, and made her an offer for the property. Their offer proved to be so much less than it was worth that Dorothy was advised to turn it down. Whereupon, she received a notice from the Council stating that they were applying for an order for compulsory requisition of the property! She sought legal advice, and was told the Council had powers entitling them to do this. She had no option but to accept this offer, or else go to Court and fight the case. Dorothy felt that to do this would be wrong, so she accepted the offer on condition that there should be a speedy settlement. Two years were allowed to pass before the Middlesex County Council took steps to complete the purchase of the five houses they had requisitoned. Much publicity was eventually given to the scandalous delay. A reporter from one of the national newspapers investigated the scene and found dozens of windows smashed, doors broken, cupboard drawers torn out and burnt in the fireplaces, door handles and electric fittings stolen, and wanton damage caused to the houses and gardens. The County Council insisted that Dorothy remained responsible for the condition of the houses, and that she would be held liable for any damage or deterioration during the interval between the original valuation and the Council taking over! As one official concerned in the matter said, "So many Authorities are interested that Miss Kerin is caught in a murderous machine. Nothing can be done unless pressure is brought to bear on the Ministers to give immediate decisions." Eventually pressure was brought at a high ministerial level, after Questions had been asked in Parliament, and the sale was finally completed.

The move from Speldhurst to Burrswood took place in September, 1948. Dorothy applied for permission to register Etherton Hill as a Nursing Home: this was granted, and Etherton Hill became Chapel House, Speldhurst. The aged and sick of Ealing, who had nowhere to go, were installed in the newly registered Nursing Home, with the remaining nursing and domestic staff, as soon as Dorothy's occupation of Burrswood was an accomplished fact. Miss Modin was put in charge of Chapel House, Speldhurst. Dorothy has paid her this tribute: "I will not try to describe her selfless giving, not only of herself, but all she has and is. Her efficiency and tireless devotion to the work to which both she and I believe God has called her is one of the greatest blessings He has bestowed upon us, and for which I am eternally grateful."

The early days at Burrswood were in many ways a repetition of those at Chapel House, Ealing. As the days passed, the sense of peace grew, and the Presence of the Beloved Master dwelt with the household. Bishop Loyd blessed the house, which was dedicated to St. Michael and All Angels. He ended his Address with these words:

"Chapel House at Ealing has been a place where for years God has done many wonderful things. His work will go on here, and for that purpose is the blessing of this house. There are few places on earth where there is FAITH for God to do His mighty works, but here are people who believe He can do them."

This living faith, of which the Bishop spoke, was the motive-power behind all that was done through Dorothy's ministry for the glory of God, and the healing of the sick. It is the source of every grace God has bestowed upon this shrine of healing; faith is a lamp in the darkness whose light illumines our way in our progress towards Reality. Faith has opened the door to the flow of supernatural life whose effects at Burrswood are visible for all who have eyes to see; faith continues to inspire the dedicated community Dorothy left behind her to carry on her work.

Those first years at Burrswood were for Dorothy a period of good health and great vitality. The Speldhurst Nursing Home was always full, with a waiting list of sick, eager for accommodation. There was room in Burrswood for half-a-dozen guests, who were in need of help but not dependent upon skilled nursing. A Healing Service was held every Thursday morning in the small Chapel, that has now become the Staff sitting-room. It was the scene of many wonderful healings, and there was every indication that God was abundantly blessing, as well as guiding, the ministry of divine healing that Dorothy quietly built up again from this centre. She visited Speldhurst each day, and people came from many parts of the country to ask for her help and guidance.

There was time also, in those days, for gardening, and into the work of beautifying the gardens Dorothy threw her energies and her love. One by one, those parts of the estate that had been sold during the war came on the market and were bought back, to become once more a part of Burrswood. Somehow, Dorothy achieved the necessary deposits and gathered them all in: St. Mary's Cottage, the kitchen garden, the orchard, the Stone Court Farm. The latter acquisition was a source of great entertainment, for Dorothy was determined to run it as a farm. Kathleen tells an amusing story in connection with this enterprise:

"Dorothy was given by the donor of the geese and lambs of Speldhurst days, a small herd of Jersey cows. They were very fierce, but gave wonderful milk. The first day they arrived, no arrangements had been made to dispose of the milk, so Dorothy said she would make butter. A member of the household dashed off to buy a churn, and lots of milk bowls – large, round, flat things. The cream was put into the churn and we took it in turns to turn the handle. Then someone said, 'Let's put it under the tap, it will set quicker.' This was done, but unfortunately it was the hot tap . . . and the result can be imagined!"

In the afternoons, Dorothy, the children and Kathleen would often make their way to the part of the garden that was still a wilderness. While the children amused themselves making houses in the trees, she and Kathleen would fell small trees and uproot bushes, raking and sickling, and always ending with the famous bonfire. The ordered beauty of the carefully tended terraces, as we know them today, came into existence only at the cost of tremendous labour on the part of Dorothy and her helpers. The Burrswood of those days bore little resemblance to the stately, well-kept place that is our delight today. The gardens were created out of chaos, and the smooth lawns rose from a wilderness of brambles and small bushes.

They would return to St. Michael exhausted: Kathleen to put the children to bed, Dorothy to visit her patients. When, at last, quiet prevailed and all duties were fulfilled, the pair would often go for long country walks. One evening, as they were going along the ridge at Withyham, a tractor pulling a truck passed them, and the driver laughingly asked them if they wanted a lift. Nothing daunted, Dorothy climbed on to the coupling between the tractor and the truck, and rode thus for a mile or so. She was in those days game for anything! Another evening, when returning from one of their excursions and coming down the back drive, they saw the whole sky above Burrswood lit with such intensity and vividness that they both ran, thinking the place was on fire, but when they arrived breathless, both the house and the sky overhead were normal in appearance.

When Dorothy first came to live in Burrswood, no doctor was in regular attendance. This was remedied, however, when late in 1948 Dr. John Elliott first came to see Dorothy through a chance summons for an emergency. Within minutes he was in the house attending to the sick patient in a way that impressed Dorothy and appealed to her. She invited him to become Burrswood's visiting physician, and he accepted although he knew nothing of her work and regarded her "healing" with the suspicion common to the medical profession at that time.

Dr. Elliott can be described as a typical doctor of the modern school, up-to-date with all the latest techniques, dispassionate and scientific in his approaches, equipped with psychological as well as medical training. He soon became a familiar figure in Burrswood, enjoying increasing and ever enlightening discussions with Dorothy, not only about medicine as a whole, but also in regard to particular cases, and especially, in the early years, concerning her family. In fact, he soon felt a "part of Burrswood." His first big stand for what he came to believe in whole-heartedly was taken when Miss Friend sustained a serious head injury as the result of an accident, and was healed.

Dr. Elliott is much loved by his Burrswood patients. His long association with Dorothy and his loyal support of her healing ministry has secured for him a permanent place in the affection and esteem of the Burrswood community.

In the winter of 1949, Bishop Loyd had a bad attack of bronchitis, and he came to stay with Dorothy until his recovery. He was back at St. Albans for Easter, but was feeling very tired. After a busy summer, he had a holiday in Wales, and found how quickly he tired compared with the previous year. In December he went to his doctor for a heart test, and was ordered to bed. For a time he seemed to make progress, until suddenly a clot developed, and he was brought back from the very threshold of death. He gave in at last, and in April, 1950, his resignation took effect. His biographer tersely states that his time at St. Albans was "one of prodigal self-spending upon a task beyond his strength, which left him emptied and dying".* But Philip Loyd would probably not have had it otherwise. His was a nature, akin to that of Dorothy, impelled to the uttermost degree of self-giving without counting the cost.

Dorothy rejoiced to have living under her roof the beloved counsellor and friend whose wisdom had helped her to solve the many difficulties that had beset her path over the past twenty years. She was able to discuss with him problems concerning her children, as also those affecting her ministry, while giving him all the care he stood so sorely in need of. He was cherished back to health, and by Easter was strong enough to celebrate the Holy Mysteries in the chapel and to assist the priest-in-charge of the parish Church. He began to dream of a further ministry, such as conducting retreats and resuming direction of some among the many who looked to him for spiritual guidance. He had a great gift for spiritual direction: a sure insight into the souls of his penitents, and an instinctive knowledge of their needs. He adhered closely to the wise precept of Charles de Condren, founder of the

* R. P. Stacey Waddy: *Philip Loyd: Missionary and Bishop.*

Oratory in Paris, that directors should be nurses and not masters. God desires gentleness from them above everything else, and Philip Loyd possessed great gentleness allied to patience.

Despite an appearance of renewed strength, his heart remained in a parlous condition, and he was dependent upon drugs to keep going. As the months passed, he became increasingly restive, and in June, 1951, he left Burrswood, bent upon leading a more active life. It is possible that his decision was influenced by the fact that the nine children were fast becoming unmanageable, and their noisy demonstrations of high spirits had reached disquieting proportions for the peace and quiet of patients living at Burrswood. This was clearly harmful to her work, and presented Dorothy with a real problem. We shall see how wonderfully God took care of the legitimate needs of His servant's ministry, and provided her with the means to overcome this difficulty.

Dorothy voiced her misgivings as to the wisdom of the Bishop's leaving Burrswood, but he was not to be persuaded to remain, and he settled outside Dorking for the summer. From Pixham End, he wrote to her:

"You are constantly in my thoughts and prayers, and I wish I could do more to help you. But it is *you* whom God has called to Burrswood, and to whom He has given it all, in order that you may give it all back to Him. And if He is to use your offering as He wants to use it (and the welfare and salvation of so many souls, old and young, depend upon it), then it must be a very costly offering, which the Beloved has stamped with His own Cross. So we who love you so dearly must needs leave you to make your own offering in the way that God has appointed for you. But we are there in love and trying to help with our prayers: and I believe that God does use our prayers to support you and strengthen your faith, even at the times when you feel most alone – and yet not alone, because He is with you.

"And you may indeed be sure that God's grace is sufficient for you, even as His strength is made perfect in weakness. You are not going to fail Him; and He will never fail you; and His purpose will be accomplished to the glory of His Name. In all our sufferings and trials let us endeavour by the grace of the Holy Spirit to thank Him sincerely for the means which He takes to effect in us the sanctification which we so greatly need."

Bishop Loyd felt the cold terribly after his long years of residence in the East, and he moved to Ellerslie Mansions, Bournemouth, for the winter. Before leaving Pixham End he again wrote to Dorothy:

"This is Sunday evening, and there does not seem to have been any time till now to write to you. Now, I have a clear week before me, in which to get ready for my migration to Bournemouth. My heart is very full when I think of all that God has given me through Burrswood in the last year and a half. He has been so good to me, and has had such great mercy upon me, and helped me so much in my great need. And I see so clearly that it was His loving plan and gracious will to give it to me through you and through the life at Burrswood. If I was allowed to contribute to that life while I was there, that makes it all the lovelier, and is one more sign of His Goodness and most loving Condescension. I just keep thanking God for such a priceless treasure, which is all the more precious because so many others – according to their many needs – are allowed to share in it day by day.

"In the Epistle for this last week (Trinity XXII) came the words 'I thank my God upon every remembrance of you, for your fellowship in the Gospel . . . being confident of this very thing, that He that hath begun a good work in you will perform it until the day of Jesus Christ; even as it is meet for me to think this of you all, because I have you in my heart.' So lovely and so true! And remember that the *good work* of which St. Paul speaks there to the Philippians is not the work of personal sanctification (tho' that of course is necessarily involved), but the 'fellowship in the Gospel'; that is to say, the work of making God to be known to others, and glorified, and that chiefly by the common life – the fellowship – which we live together. That is the good work that is going to grow and grow at Burrswood. And oh, how confident I am of this very thing. And you may humbly and thankfully be very sure that the growth and growing effectiveness of this 'fellowship' and 'good work' at Burrswood is a very sure and certain seal upon your own personal life and work there; a seal by which He reassures you that you yourself are indeed responding to His call, and allowing Him to fulfil His gracious will and purpose in you. How wonderful and lovely this is, but how *costly*! – as you know well enough, for there always has to be the 'dying of the Lord Jesus' which we bear about in our body; for only so can His life abound in us, and through us in others. Read what St. Paul says about it in Corinthians 4. 7, 15."

At Bournemouth, the Bishop was within easy reach of St. Peter's Church. There, to his joy, he found the Blessed Sacrament was reserved, and a daily Communion Service held, which he attended until the renewal of his heart pains drove him to bed. He wrote regularly from Ellerslie Mansions to Dorothy. For a time there was an improvement in his condition, and then it worsened. In the week before Christmas, he received the Sacrament of Holy Unction.

The Bishop's last letter, dated December 31st, was written eleven days before his death.

"I still get very little writing done: because the doctor keeps me fairly well doped, and I do a tremendous lot of sleeping. It is answering very well so far as my heart is concerned, and he is greatly pleased with that. Yesterday, he said that in a fortnight's time he hoped to be able to say where we were, and whether he wanted to keep me on here for the present, or whether he would send me over to you.

"You know how gladly I shall come: and I am sure that God will show me what His will is, and with your help and prayers I will try to obey. You say that you felt I ought never to have left Burrswood: and indeed at that time you did show that that was your opinion. But I just don't think that I could then have made up my mind to another year there, without trying to go out and be a bit more active. For me it would have meant sinking into a kind of semi-invalidism; and I did not believe that that was God's will for me."

The following paragraph is taken from R. P. Stacey Waddy's biography of Philip Loyd:

"Philip Loyd died in a Bournemouth hotel about eight o'clock in the morning of January 11th, 1952. He had not been able to go out for the past few weeks, and that morning a priest was bringing the Blessed Sacrament from St. Peter's Church to give him Holy Communion. The room was ready to welcome our Lord; he had been up to light the candles, to set out the table with its Cross and a bowl of snowdrops. Soon he would stretch forth his hands to receive the Host and say, as he always did, *Amen* to the words of administration. But today there was to be no need of bread and wine to pledge the Saviour's presence and veil the sacred Mysteries. When the priest came, his body lay on the bed. In a single moment he had passed through the gate of everlasting life into that joy of which the Real Presence is a foretaste, and beheld His glory Whom he had loved and served his whole life long."*

* R. P. Stacy Waddy: *Bishop Loyd: Missionary and Bishop*. Quoted by kind permission of A. R. Mowbray & Co. Limited.

CHAPTER 15

Successor to Bishop Loyd

THE day came when Dorothy reluctantly decided the children would have to go to school. Brenda had gone to Australia, and governesses and tutors followed in rapid succession. Bishop Loyd had left; Dorothy was absorbed by the pressing needs of her ministry. There was nobody sufficiently authoritative to curb the boisterous spirits of the 'nine', who, as they increased in stature, demonstrated forcefully their assertive and self-willed personalities! The house in consequence was suffering. Kathleen has kept a vivid memory of the day when Dorothy revealed the news of their adoption to the children.

"On the eve of their starting their first term at Forest Row, Mummy said she wanted to speak to them. So, when they had all had their baths, they collected in the room at the top of the backstairs. Never shall I forget that evening! Mummy started off by telling them that she herself had never been to school, but that she thought they would love it. They would hear lots of things that they had never heard about before. There would be beautiful things, and things that were not beautiful, but they must try hard to remember only the beautiful. They probably would hear they were adopted children.

" 'Now,' she said, 'I want to tell you that it is a very special thing to be adopted, because it means that you were wanted very much, and that Jesus Himself is your Father. He chose you and sent you to me to look after. Therefore, if anyone says anything to you about being adopted, always remember that you are very specially Jesus' children . . .'

" 'But . . . but, Mummy, aren't you our *real* Mummy?'

"And then the howls began. John started off, but very soon they were all, without exception, howling. Useless to try and comfort them! Useless to try any more explaining! In the end, they were given some disprin, tucked up ten times over, sung to far longer than usual . . . and, at last there was peace!"

School discipline was not to the liking of the 'nine', and a number of schools were given a trial before they settled down to acquire the rudiments of learning. Although in term time they were absent from Burrswood, there remained the long holidays to be coped with at Christmas, Easter and in the summer. The endeavour to reconcile the needs of patients requiring rest and quiet with those of growing youngsters demanding an outlet for their exuberant activities imposed a considerable strain on the household. Once again, as had happened so many times in the past, the prevention of Providence showed how vigilant was the exercise of divine protection over Dorothy's ministry and its needs.

Among the patients residing in Burrswood was a cultured lady of advanced years with no experience of divine healing before she was led to Dorothy, to whom she became devotedly attached. She knew the spiritual deeps of a genuine prayer life, and quickly became aware of the constant flow of supernatural life which enfolded the Home of Healing. Winifred, as she was called, fully realized the difficulties created for Dorothy's work by the children's presence in Burrswood. God ordained that, through the unfolding of circumstances which read like a fairy tale, she would be used by Him to remedy the situation.

One day, long before his illness, when Bishop Loyd was staying at Burrswood, he said to Dorothy, "Let us go for a walk, and perhaps we shall find bamboo dry enough to make a needle case." He had picked up a needle, and at once his ordered mind sought a practical way of keeping needles elsewhere than on the floor!

Their walk took them past Court Lodge, where, as usual, they paused to admire the beauty of this old building. The Bishop said to Dorothy, "How lovely it is; I should like to know its history." To which she replied, "I know nothing of its history, but I do know that one day it will belong to Burrswood!" "If you see this," said the Bishop, "I am sure in God's own time, it will be so. When this happens, I pray it may be a place of escape for you and the children."

Years later, a local doctor remarked to Dorothy, "Do you remember saying you were interested in Court Lodge, and that one day it would belong to Burrswood?" "Yes," she replied, "of course I do. Why?" "Well," he asnwered, "its owner has died, and it is on the market!"

Dorothy has narrated how, during the silent watches of that night, she knew of a certainty that God had a plan to reveal, and as the days passed she prayed to know His Will.

Her Silver Jubilee* was approaching: there was to be a Quiet Day

* Not the Silver Jubilee of her miraculous healing, but that of her ministry started at Ealing on October 20th, 1930.

of Prayer. She asked the priest conducting this to pray that God's Will would be revealed. During that morning, it came quite clearly to her that she was to "ask Winifred". She was completely mystified by this command, for command it was. She knew that Voice – and she knew she would obey. But what was she to ask Winifred? This question repeated itself over and over again. She waited for further enlightenment, and had the utter conviction that God would show her His plan.

Some days later, early one morning, the same doctor rang her up, asking if she had done anything about Court Lodge, adding, "If you want it, you had better take steps at once, because several people are interested." Dorothy said she would go and see the place, and she made an appointment to do so that morning.

The daughter of the late owner welcomed her, and showed her over the house. Dorothy then knew of a certainty that the seal of the Lord was upon this venture of faith. She asked for the first refusal to purchase, and obtained it. It then occurred to her to enquire the price, and was told that as it was a unique property, the purchase price would probably be in the region of £15,000!

On her way home, halfway down the hill, the enormity of what she had commited herself to dawned upon her: she had asked for the first refusal to buy this property! At that time, it was humanly impossible for her to do so, for there was no available money anywhere, so far as she was concerned. She stood still, asking, "Dear Lord, what have you led me into now?" To her inner knowing came the reassurance – "Leave it to Me."

There was no further need for questioning. Dorothy knew that already the Master's plan was fulfilled, so with heart overflowing with thanksgiving she made her way to the Chapel to offer thanks to God. On returning to her study, she was met with a request to go to Winifred.

Winifred, unknown to Dorothy, for the past three months had been waiting to hear whether or not she was going to inherit her cousin's money. He had died in Australia without making a will. Although Australian law only recognizes relationships down to uncles and aunts, Winifred being a first cousin and the only remaining relative, her lawyer had appealed on her behalf. She had been waiting to hear the result of this appeal. On the very day that Dorothy had arranged to be given the first refusal to buy Court Lodge, she heard that she had won her appeal, and was able, therefore, to request Dorothy to come and see her!

As Dorothy went up the stairway to Winifred's room, wondering what she had to say to her, there surged up within her the answer, "To see the wondrous works of God!" She found Winifred in a state of joyous excitement, and was welcomed with these words: "Darling, the post has brought me the most wonderful news – that a cousin of mine has died and left me a large sum of money. I know God has sent it for you in order that you can have all you need."

In the course of the next few days, it was all signed, settled and sealed. The vision of many years ago was fulfilled, and once more Dorothy was blessed and strengthened in the knowledge that where God guides, God provides.

Court Lodge was dedicated to God's service by the Bishop of Coventry on November 30th, 1955, when a large concourse of Fellowship members gathered together in joyous thanksgiving. Winifred was called to the fuller life on May 21st, 1956, and the little garden Chapel at Court Lodge was dedicated to St. Winifred in the same year by the Bishop of Chichester.

This story of how this beautiful old house was given to Dorothy for as long as was necessary for the good of her work, shines with special lustre among the many remarkable instances of God's unfailing providence in safeguarding His servant's ministry. Readers may wonder why Dorothy was given so costly a property to house herself and children. At the time, the answer was hidden in the folds of God's pattern for her life-work. A few years later, when her adopted sons and daughters had left, or were about to leave, their respective schools to make their way in the world, she was shown in a Vision that the time had come to unite *all* the work under one roof. It was the money realized from the sale of Court Lodge which enabled this Vision to be fulfilled. It was sold for exactly the same amount as it had cost to buy.

A successor to Bishop Loyd had to be found. Who was he to be? God guided Dorothy to ask Bishop Bardsley, at that time Bishop of Croydon, if he would assume the charge of Bishop Warden to the Fellowship. To her joy he consented, and in her Whitsun News Letter, 1954, she was able to announce the good news: "You will be thankful to know that the Fellowship is no longer a flock without a shepherd, as, alas, it has been since our beloved Bishop Loyd passed on to the fuller life. The Bishop of Croydon has most kindly consented to be our Warden. This is immensely kind of him. We all know how full his life is, and are therefore doubly grateful."

Dorothy has frequently acknowledged the great debt of gratitude Burrswood owes to Bishop Bardsley. His unfailing concern for the welfare of her ministry; the inspiration of his challenging addresses delivered from the pulpit of our Chapel; the gift he has of revivifying in his listeners their sense of commitment to Christ and to His Church; the healing quality of love that emanates from him to all who cross his path; his sympathetic understanding of the needs of those who seek his advice; his zeal to win souls to God – all these qualities make of him a true Shepherd in Christ's service, and have endeared him to every member of Burrswood's Fellowship and community. It was feared that when the great call came to him to be translated to the see of Coventry he might not feel able to continue his connection with Burrswood. Happily, these fears were groundless, and he is today our loved and trusted Bishop Visitor. No words can express the source of strength he was to the stricken community when they were suddenly bereft of their beloved Foundress.

The Bishop's first message to the Fellowship was written after a visit he paid to Burrswood on October 28th, 1954, Feast of St. Simon and St. Jude. In it he bears witness to the supernatural life so abundantly at work in the Home of Healing.

"The atmosphere of the House struck me most forcibly – an atmosphere of peace and harmony. It was a privilege to meet people who have experienced wonderful spiritual and physical healing through the work of the Fellowship. The light of God was in their eyes, and their hearts were filled with gratitude. The one supremely glorious thing about Burrswood is that Miss Kerin and her fellow workers believe in the Power of Prayer. They pray expectantly, confidently, and so must we. The Bible does not put forward arguments for the existence of God, the Bible takes for granted the existence of God, and lays claim to His Power, believing that His Power is available for all of those who really trust Him. This was true of St. Simon and St. Jude, and it is true today of Miss Kerin and the Burrswood Fellowship."

The year 1954 was one in which there were many healings. In her Christmas Letter to the Fellowship, Dorothy wrote:

"There have been many outstanding healings since my last Letter came to you. Some have received complete healing, many more the release from fear, the renewal of hope and the courage to 'tarry the Lord's leisure' – the latter, I believe, is the most precious gift of all, for when we receive peace enabling us to wait patiently and be still before God, we begin to realize something of His infinite Love for us as His individual children."

Ever since Dorothy started her work at Ealing she had been in the habit of holding a Christmas Market with the object of raising funds for the needs of her work.

In the autumn of 1954, a Market was held whose target was to raise the considerable sum of £1000! There were those who thought this target to be unobtainable, but not so Dorothy! It proved to be an occasion for the glorious demonstration of the bountiful goodness of God towards her to whom He had entrusted the great work of bringing back to His Church His ministry of divine healing.

"Those who were unable to come to the Christmas Market will want to hear the result of their efforts, and as I look back upon these last weeks, my heart is very full of thankfulness to God, for His goodness to us; for again we have been permitted to know that where God guides, God provides, and how abundantly! As you know, the target we had set was for one thousand pounds, because this sum was needed to enable us to carry on God's work. There were some faint and doubting hearts, but there were also those who *knew* that if it were in God's pattern the need would be supplied, and they were not disappointed – thanks be to God.

"On the day preceding the closing day, we totalled exactly four hundred pounds. When I retired to bed that night, I had to remind myself that God still had another day in which He could supply the need; whereupon, I composed myself to sleep. Suddenly, remembering a pile of letters I had not had time to open, I sat up in bed, put on the light, and the first letter I opened contained a cheque for six hundred pounds with a letter from the donor saying: 'This is not from me, it is from God.'

"Surely, the most exciting and wonderful adventure in life is when we put our hand in God's Hand and trust Him utterly, for indeed His ways are not our ways, and His ways are best."

No fitting comment can be made upon such an amazing evidence of the way in which God honours the faith of His Saints. One can only bow one's head in wonder and thanksgiving!

On October 25th, 1955, the Fellowship celebrated the Silver Jubilee. Before calling on the Bishop Warden to address the Members of the Fellowship, Dorothy gave them this message from the chancel step of the Chapel.

"My heart is very, very full of things that my lips cannot utter. What I can say is that I am immensely happy and grateful that so many of you are here today to share this wonderful occasion with us. Some of you have come long distances, some of you from over the seas.

I do ask for your continual help in prayer, the encouragement you have always given, as well as your love and generosity in every way.

"At the end of these twenty-five years in which it is true to say we have seen, by the grace of God, all those promises in the Bible fulfilled, we have seen those apostolic acts performed by our Lord; and we are left in no doubt that it is the same Jesus that we serve and follow today who walked and wrought miracles along the shores of Galilee. We know His arm is no shorter, His power is no less. I believe now He is opening up fresh opportunities of service for all who are engaged in this ministry of healing. Let us pray that wherever He may call us or lead us, it may be for His glory, and not for ours."

Bishop Bardsley then gave one of his unforgettable Addresses. He took as his text a verse from the Old Testament: "This is a day of good tidings; let us not hold our peace." Some extracts from this Address follow:

"It is a fact that the Church is once again becoming aware of God's great longing to make men healthy, but God is concerned with the whole man, not just the body. Burrswood has given *that* as a great challenge to this day and age. Miss Kerin and others with her have shown that we do not come to God to be healed only of our bodily infirmities, to be made 'cushy, cosy and comfortable'. If that was all I would have nothing to do with this place whatsoever! People flock to places where they can be made cosy. But that is not the heart of the Christian Gospel. God desires that we may be effective in our service. That effectiveness may comprise a wonderful radiant suffering as God's way in us of giving our witness.

"We have seen a pageant of triumph in Christ. That is the story of the last twenty-five years. We have seen God guiding and providing in a quite wonderful way. The moment we come within the doors of a place like this, we feel the impact, the power of the supernatural.

"Men need to see the power of God in healing and in the raising of money. In them they see the supernatural materially at work. There is nothing so intensely evangelistic as Healing, because in the healing of the physical body men are brought so in touch with our Lord that their hearts are changed. That is what we have seen in these past twenty-five years – the power of God to heal men, and to make them whole for His service. In story after story, case after case, home after home, has been seen the impact of the supernatural. One of the most triumphant evidences of the work of God here is the way in which He has provided for the raising of money. There where we have to badger, badger, badger for money is a clear indication that the Gospel is not being preached; because if men's hearts are touched their pockets will be at the disposal of the Almighty. In these last twenty-five years we have seen that demonstrated in a glorious way.

"The loss of the sense of community was caused by the industrial revolution, the uprooting of men from the soil and putting them into slums, housing estates and suburban life. The answer is that the Church should once again present community within its walls and outside them. One of the glories of this work here has been that it has not just been one person, but a team of people drawn together by the Holy Spirit, living and loving and laughing together, and *together* demonstrating the Holy Spirit at work.

"The greatest Master, Leader, and lover of adventure that this world has ever seen made total demands upon people. He never said that life would be easy. He said: 'He that will take up His cross and follow Me, he is my follower.' So we follow and throw ourselves away in the service of this glorious, eternal, reigning CHRIST."

Two outstanding events took place in 1956: they were the coming of Robin to Burrswood in January, followed by Dorothy's visit to Guernsey in August.

Robin was the eldest son of the Rev. Frank Drake, Headmaster of the Monnaie School in Guernsey. In 1954, Fr. Drake had been summoned to the Princess Elizabeth Hospital to hear from the lips of one of England's most famous surgeons, then on a visit to the island, that his eldest son had been stricken by what was considered to be practically an incurable disease, although some cures had been known to occur. Nevertheless it was a rare disease, and there was very little chance of Robin's recovery. Robin, a young man in his twenty-sixth year, had been called to the Bar, and during the winter of 1953–4 had studied French law at the University of Caen in Normandy, with the intention of becoming a barrister in Guernsey. He had been greatly exhausted by his studies. A young man wishing to become a barrister in Guernsey must work particularly hard, for, after being called to the English Bar, he must read French law and, finally, take an examination in local law in Guernsey. After a course of treatment at Guy's Hospital, he returned to his home in Guernsey. For some months his health had shown signs of remarkable improvement; those parts of his body which had been affected were X-rayed and found to be free of the disease, although he remained in indifferent health and became very easily tired. Almost exactly a year after his disease had been diagnosed, his health began again to deteriorate, and despite a temporary improvement of some months after his father had given him the Church's Sacrament of Holy Unction, a condition of increasing deterioration manifested its effects.* The doctor attending him had no doubt that the disease was once more active.

Early in the new year of 1956, Robin's parents brought him to Burrswood. In his moving book, *Thy Son Liveth*, Fr. Drake has written:

"During the weeks which followed Robin learnt to experience, through the warm love of Dorothy, the wonderful Love of our Lord Himself. Then one morning Dorothy came, at our Lord's command, to lay her hands upon him, and shortly afterwards he wrote to us saying that at last he believed himself to be really healed."

Robin returned to Guernsey in August, accompanied by Dorothy and Marina. This was Dorothy's first visit to the island and it was to have important repercussions for her ministry. A branch of the Fellowship was started, and Robin undertook to be the secretary. He believed he had received a call to serve Christ as a priest in His Church, and his whole heart was set upon the realization of this project.

The days Dorothy spent in Guernsey were taken up with visits to the sick and dying. She gave her great message of hope to a congregation of five hundred assembled to hear her in St. Peter's Church, the town church. She also ministered to the sick in St. Martin's Church under the auspices of the Guild of St. Raphael. By the time Dorothy and her companion bade farewell to the friendly little island, the corner-stone of a new venture had been well and truly laid.

Robin died at the age of twenty-eight. His apparent healing proved abortive. Why was this so? Why did God allow this promising young life to be cut short by death? In her Foreword to *Thy Son Liveth* by Frank Drake, Dorothy wrote:

"The story of Robin Drake is one of the most moving I have ever read. Here, we have glowing and irrefutable proof (if we need it) of Life after death. We see also the glorious fruits of obedience in the acceptance of God's Will. Robin desired most passionately that our Lord would heal him physically, that he might become a witness of God's power and serve Him in the Church as a priest; so far as we can

* Frank Drake: *Thy Son Liveth* (Hodder and Stoughton).

judge, he had complete faith supported by the faith of many others who were praying for his healing. Why, then, did he die? The answer to this question – one that is in the heart and mind of many committed Christians – can only be answered if we humbly remind ourselves that Almighty God in His infinite love and wisdom refused the request of His only begotten Son Jesus Christ: 'Father, if it be Thy will let this cup pass from me.' In His refusal was bought for all mankind eternal salvation. We who had the privilege of knowing and ministering to Robin, thank God with all our hearts for His perfect answer to our prayers, and rejoice in the knowledge of His call to further service in God's will."

There were remarkable healings in 1956, and in her Christmas News Letter we find Dorothy referring to them:

"Many wonderful healings have taken place for which we thank God, and humbly pray that those who have felt His Living Touch upon them may be kept humble and obedient so that God can use them as He wills.

"Let us not be discouraged or dismayed if all those for whom we pray do not receive physical healing, for we know that God has other precious gifts to bestow upon us. If His answer seems long in coming, let us humbly ask Him to give us grace to tarry His leisure, and in obedience seek only His will, for in His will is our peace and nothing else really matters.

"I want to ask you all for a special remembrance in your prayers; ask that I be lost in Him, for in this loss of self is the true finding of Him. How often one sees the hideous vision of what one has wrought by self, but there is always that tender, encouraging promise: 'My grace is sufficient for thee,' and how often we have proved the truth of this! Forgive me if I digress. I was trying humbly to suggest that we do not primarily regard our Fellowship as one seeking, and asking, for physical healing, but a complete wholeness in Christ Jesus, of body, mind and spirit."

CHAPTER 16

Speldhurst and Burrswood Amalgamate

"As Christmas lasts for ever, may I include in my good wishes for the New Year those that should have reached you on, and for, the Birthday of our Lord? I hope you all had as happy and joyous a Christmas as we had here, and that the Festival was full of peace and blessing. We were signally fortunate in having with us the Reverend Gordon Kenworthy, who made it possible for us to have a Midnight Mass in our Chapel at Burrswood. This will be a precious memory, for it is the last time we shall gather together in this Chapel to meet and receive our Lord on His Birthday," wrote Dorothy in her News Letter of January, 1957.

Christmas has always been a time of joy at Burrswood. The prelude to the Midnight Mass is the gathering of the household shortly before midnight to assist at the blessing of the Crib by the Celebrant. This little ceremony is a reminder of that transcendent event in the history of mankind when, moving out of Eternity into Time, the "Word became flesh" and took upon Himself the robe of a human frame to live among men a human life.

The Chapel has always been the glowing heart of Dorothy's work. There are many who know the beauty of Burrswood's Chapel; many who have felt the warmth of the love, the healing of the Peace that pervades its atmosphere, and have experienced the Reality of the Divine Presence that fills its sanctuary. This awareness of supernatural life is intensified at the Church's great Festivals: especially is this so on the Birthday of our Lord. As the Mass moves to its sacred culmination, a sense of dedication in fellowship unites all who are worshipping there.

Dorothy's Christmas presents were placed on the large round table in the centre of the hall. Each one was a personal gift to patients, visitors, friends and staff, chosen by herself, and wrapped in bright paper with that loving attention to detail that characterized all she did. She had sacrificed quite a number of nights to this considerable task, for there were literally piles upon piles of parcels, but she felt amply rewarded, each year, by the evident pleasure of the recipients of her gifts.

A feature of Christmas is the midday dinner to which all who live, or are staying, on the Estate are invited. This practice continues, but there was a radiancy about this meal in Dorothy's day that made of it a veritable *agape*. The loveliness of the table decoration was a labour of love on the part of herself and her staff, and over this festive table Dorothy, diffusing the radiant joy that emanated from her on these occasions, presided with the charm and graciousness that were her special gifts. All who have assisted at these Christmas dinners will never forget them, and they thank God for their share in the blessing of its fellowship.

The year 1957 marked a great expansion in the work, both as regards Dorothy's ministry and the erection of buildings at Burrswood. This amazing expansion was to continue to the day of her death, which left a number of projects as yet unrealized.

The small Chapel next the kitchen could no longer hold all who came to attend the Healing Service held in it every Thursday morning. Dorothy decided to convert the old schoolroom, no longer needed, into a Chapel, and to build on to it an extension that could serve as its sanctuary.

On February 18th, the Bishop Warden, now Lord Bishop of Coventry, came to bless the new Chapel to the commemoration of the 'Beloved Physician' St. Luke, in whose name and to whose honour the Chapel was dedicated. He invited the congregation to stand with him in front of the Gate known as the Gate Beautiful, one of the gates leading into the old city of Jerusalem. There they would see a man who had been lame from his birth. Day by day he sat there with his begging bowl, and as people passed by he looked up and said, "Spare a copper!" Simon Peter passing by looked at him and said, "Silver and gold I do not possess, but in the Name of Jesus of Nazareth, get up!"

"Now," said the Bishop, "something of that order happened thirty-five years ago today, when our Lord Jesus Christ came and stood by one who was dying and gave to her life for a purpose, which was to communicate His touch of Healing to a world that desperately needs it . . ."

The Bishop closed his Address with these words:

"And so I end by saying with all my heart, I believe this lovely Chapel will be for many a Gate Beautiful. It will be a gateway into Life, into that divine Life, where our Lord Jesus Christ, the living and eternal Saviour, will bring to diseased souls, health through holiness and wholeness. It is my prayer that that glorious ministry which began thirty-five years ago today, will be with us for many years, and that through her many others may come to be modern Simon Peters to this distraught and disunited age, bringing the touch of the divine Lord to those restless, unhappy souls, that they may find through Christ wholeness, holiness and health."

In her News Letter of March, 1957, to the Fellowship, Dorothy told of the sense of joy and expectancy that filled her heart on this occasion of the dedication of the new Chapel of St. Luke. Referring to the Bishop's hope "that this lovely Chapel will be for many a Gate Beautiful", she wrote, "I refer to this particular sentence for the reason that already, as one peeps through the Gate Beautiful, one sees the ever-increasing goodness of God, stretching out and opening up new fields of service in this, His Ministry of Healing. I humbly believe that God has shown me that another prophecy of our beloved Bishop Loyd is now to materialize. We are to go forth in faith and build a new wing on to Burrswood and so consolidate the work under one roof. It is becoming increasingly difficult, as the work expands and grows, to convey and to administer God's gifts to those He sends to us for help. The fact that we now have three bases inevitably means wastage of strength and time. This God-given strength, I am convinced, must be conserved for the purpose for which He gave it. I believe this new venture of faith to be God's plan which has unfolded in the watches of the night with Him. I ask you all to make a matter of earnest prayer that God's will may be done in this, and that through His grace, we may go forth fearlessly commending the issue to Him.

Dorothy later told a Diocesan Conference at Hawyards Heath, "It was revealed to me in a vision that God meant all the work to be united under one roof. The estimate for the new building was £20,000. There was nothing at all for this, but there was the command of God to do it, and I am so sure of that Voice, that, in the face of the whole world, I would have gone forward fearlessly with that plan, because I *knew* in Whom I had believed. And so the work was started and in ten months the building was completed. At no time was any appeal made for funds, because there was no need, and now that house is built and fully occupied."

Whitsun has always been an exceptional Festival, for it has been a time when God in some special manner showered His blessings upon His servant's ministry. Therefore we find her writing in her Whitsun News Letter:

"I hope this Letter will reach you in time for Whitsun, for, as you know, it has been our Lord's good pleasure to pour His Blessings upon us abundantly at this great Festival. Year by year, we look back with thanksgiving upon the road along which He has led this Fellowship – a road which at times has been stony and difficult, but always illuminated with the light of His guidance. We see His milestones all along the way, encouraging us to further efforts and perseverance.

"I ask you, therefore, as a Fellowship, to join with me at our Whitsun Communion in prayer that we may be guided and kept in the way of His will concerning all that is done for the greater effectiveness of His work at Burrswood, and that as we go forward in faith with the building of the new wing, God will make known His plan for providing all that is needed. He *knows* where the necessary money is to be found, and *I* know that if we do our utmost in offering Him our Love crumbs, He will weld them into a loaf—as He so often has done in the past. So let us go forward in the strength of the Lord, nothing wavering."

The new wing, known as St. Faith, was blessed and dedicated on February 15th, 1958, by the Bishop of Edinburgh.

While this expansion was taking place at Burrswood, Chapel House, Speldhurst, continued to function as a registered Nursing Home under the devoted and efficient supervision of Miss Gladys Modin. The Home was regularly visited by Dorothy, who was finding it a great tax upon her time and strength to be constantly moving between the three houses. The time had come at last for the divided family to be reunited, although its Head still had her home at Court Lodge. The time was close at hand when she also would take up her residence in Burrswood.

In March, the amalgamation of Chapel House with Burrswood became an accomplished fact. Dorothy paid tribute to the efficiency with which this move – no small matter – took place:

"The move was achieved with unhurried smoothness and skill. Our thanks are due to Miss Modin, Miss Nest, Sister, Nurses and Staff who put all they had into this gigantic undertaking. Speaking for myself, I am thankful that the work that was under three separate roofs is now under two. Very soon, God willing, it will be entirely under one, for God has shown me that I must go back to Burrswood to take, under His guidance, the Captain's wheel, and steer, with His help, that little ship for so long as He wills."

The amalgamation of the two establishments was not exempt from difficulty. It called for the selfless surrender of what may be considered as the 'particular' atmosphere of each house, in order that this particularity could be absorbed into a climate common to both. Burrswood, very naturally, had become a closely knit unit, most of its staff having worked for years under Dorothy's direct guidance. The process of rubbing shoulders in the performance of their daily tasks had revealed both their weaknesses and their strength – they had in fact acquired a common 'soul'. Speldhurst, to some extent, had lived its own life, and although the divided body possessed a common Head, to whom both gave in equal measure their complete and loving allegiance, nevertheless, Chapel House had for some years made its own individual and valuable contribution to Dorothy's God-given work.

Soon after the family had been gathered under one roof, Dorothy called her Staff around her to share with them her vision of the future:

"Beloved Friends, we have met together to look at a picture, a pattern which I believe with every fibre of my being is a pattern that our Lord Himself has made for us, and of which He will unfold to us the design as the days go by, provided we strive faithfully and selflessly to make of ourselves the instruments of His will. It is a wonderful pattern, and for a moment I want to take you back about a year ago when I put before you a plan* which I believe our Heavenly Father revealed to me. I told you then that I did not know what the fulfilment of this might involve of sacrifice and hardship, but that what I did know was that without question I was going to follow wherever He called me, and, you remember, I asked you all, 'Are you coming?' Without a moment's hesitation, you all answered 'I am coming!'

"Now, it is through obedience that that building (St. Faith) has come into being, obedience to the heavenly command. I believe I have said this before. I cannot over-estimate its importance. I believe with all my heart that when our Lord commanded me, a dying girl, to get up and walk, had it not been through the grace of obedience to that heavenly command, nothing would have happened. I want you all to remember this, because obedience is the foundation upon which this work is built. Obedience was the secret of our Lord's triumph. It was not the Cross that was so important, but His implicit obedience to His Father's will. The human side of us does not always want to do God's will. Our Lord did not want to be crucified. He prayed, 'If it be Thy will let this cup pass from me; not My will but Thine.' That is the most revealing thing for our encouragement.

* Dorothy was referring to the occasion when she first disclosed the plan to build a wing on to St. Michael.

"We are starting on this venture as a fellowship of friends, all dedicated to the service of our Lord. Every one of us in this room has been called to serve Him in this particular work. Without each other, it would be impossible to carry out His work, whether it is sweeping a floor or listening to people's troubles. It is our Lord who has given us each our particular work to do. You will see that as we embark upon this great adventure some wonderful acts of God will take place, and I know that we go forward together in faith. Of course difficulties lie ahead of us, but we can only face these difficulties if we face them as one solid company. If we are going to achieve our Lord's work, we must not ask ourselves how the new régime is going to affect us individually, but how it is going to affect the work, for that alone matters.

"I am aware there has been a good deal of conjecture as to what is going to take place. There will be no difference in the policy of this house. Our Lord appointed a captain of this ship, and however unworthy she may be, that captain *was* appointed by our Lord. That captain has been placed by Him on the ship with her hand on the wheel, and so long as she is left there by our Lord, she has no right whatsoever to delegate her responsibility to anyone else.

"I know that I can count on your love, your loyalty and your obedience, and so what I ask every one of you to do in the Name of God is to give to each other some of the love and forebearance that you give to me. God has given us a wonderful opportunity to renew this venture, and I believe He has asked each of us to love each other. You know the hidden meaning of what I am saying. Harmony, peace and love must rule this family. Of course there will be difficulties, but if we are obedient to God's will, and forbearing to each other, we shall be given the strength to do what God has laid upon us. I do not know whether it will be more difficult for you here, or for those coming from Speldhurst, but I do know they have come to us with heart-whole desire and intention to give God everything they have. Their wonderful love and obedience are such that they send me on the knees of my heart. I know that each and all of you will face every difficulty and trial in the spirit of 'How much can I give?' and not 'How much can I spare myself!' That applies to me also, but with all your prayers, God may enable me to guide this little ship into safe waters."

A situation fraught with possible friction was transmuted through Dorothy's leadership into an occasion for glorious co-operation. Eight months later she was able to write, "The amalgamation between

Burrswood and Chapel House has become a solid and established fact. We are all so pleased with each other, we cannot imagine how we managed to exist apart!"

1957 was also a momentous year as regards the extension of Dorothy's ministry, for it heralded the outset of her apostolic journeyings to feed God's hungry sheep in pastures far afield. Her loved and trusted Master, the Good Shepherd, was soon to lead her to visit lands in the Old and New Worlds to proclaim His message of hope and healing. At the time of her release, appeals for her presence were coming to her from countries far away in the Southern Hemisphere, and, undoubtedly, had she lived, these would have been included in future itineraries.

Among the many Churches visited by Dorothy during the years that remained to her was one that stood foremost in her affection. This was the famous Church of St. Martin-in-the-Fields in London. It was this Church that saw the start of her fruitful public ministry. Although, over the years, she had occasionally spoken in Churches of all denominations, it was after her appearance in St. Martin-in-the-Fields that scarcely a week was to pass without her voice being heard in two or more churches in counties often widely separated. These visits frequently necessitated long night journeys by car, for she always insisted upon returning to Burrswood to fulfil, the next day, her heavy commitments.

In the late spring of that year, a Service of Divine Healing was held in St. Martin-in-the Fields that will never be forgotten by those who were present. This Service was held under the auspices of the Churches' Fellowship for Psychical Study. Its Secretary, Canon Elliott, introduced Dorothy to the congregation. When the time came for her to speak, an expectant hush fell upon the large gathering, a silence that remained unbroken throughout her Address. She began by saying how, on receiving the invitation, her first impulse had been to refuse it, when suddenly she had been carried back many years to an occasion when she had come to St. Martin-in-the-Fields with Dick Sheppard, who had said to her as they stood in the centre aisle, "Dorothy Kerin, God has given you a message for the world!" Pointing to the very spot she was standing on, he had continued, "I want you to give it here." To this she had replied, "God has not yet told me to deliver that message here. When He does, I will do so." At the moment of her rejection of Canon Elliott's invitation, she had been taken back in spirit to hear once more the voice of her old friend urging her to deliver in St. Martin-in-the-Fields her God-given message.

"At that moment," she said, "I knew that I was hearing God's Voice telling me to speak to you here, and so I wrote to Canon Elliott to say I would be willing to give an Address under the auspices of his Society, provided this could be done in St. Martin-in-the-Fields."

Her Address was a clarion call to faith in the supernatural, a poignant reminder that those miraculous happenings, which changed the lives of the men and women crowding the slopes of the Galilean hills two thousand years ago, can and do take place in this our twentieth century, and would always do so to the end of the world, for had Jesus not said, 'Lo! I am with you alway, even to the end of time'? She closed her Address with an appeal:

"I know that many of you are coming to the Laying-on-of-Hands in the hope of being cured of your physical ills. I want to say to you that that is not the most important thing, and that you must not be disappointed if you are not immediately healed. Physical healing is not always of the greatest importance – of far greater import is the quickening of the spiritual life within us, the restoration to spiritual health of our souls, and this, if you sincerely ask it of Him, our Lord will surely grant to you."

The tumultuous life of the great city flowed on as usual outside the old Church, but within its walls there brooded over the scene the peace of a profound stillness: a stillness filled with the Blessing of a Divine Presence. As an illustration of the sincerity of the impact which their spiritual experience was making upon those who that day had knelt at the Altar rail, Dorothy afterwards told her friends:

"My own heart was full to overflowing when, at one moment during the laying-on-of-hands, I noticed that my shoes were wet with tears: tears that had fallen from the eyes of those who had come to receive the blessing of our Lord's gift of renewed life."

CHAPTER 17

Holiday in Italy

THE spell of Italy was to capture Dorothy in 1958. Italy, land of beauty and sunshine, home of the Madonna whose shrines adorn every corner of the countryside, claimed her for its own, and thereafter, each year, she took her brief holiday in that lovely country to which she felt herself akin in spirit. It was the second time she had gone abroad since she left the Langford-Jameses in 1929, and the first time she had taken a holiday since the advent of the children in 1941. Hitherto she had only visited France and Switzerland. Now she was to know Italy, and this was to be for her an enriching experience. Through every pore of her being she absorbed what Italy has to give those who love her. Her inability to speak the language was no impediment to her contacts with the vivacious, loquacious and friendly Italians. Through the play of her hands, the glance of her expressive eyes, her varying facial expressions, she communicated her needs to them, and expressed her appreciation and delight in the beauty surrounding her. By means of some invisible channel of communication, this interchange of thought and feeling was in constant evidence. Italy and her warm-hearted, beauty-loving sons and daughters took Dorothy wholly to their hearts.

The first visit was on a pilgrimage to Assisi; subsequent holidays were spent in Florence and Venice. Dorothy had always had a special love for St. Francis and a sense of nearness to him. She had seen with the eyes of her spirit the little brown monk at different times in her life, usually during periods of crisis, and had been made aware of his protection. Francis, that tremendous lover of Christ, must rejoice in the possession by this sister soul of an equally flaming love for the Supreme Lover of all mankind. Only saints know how to love: we lesser mortals grasp at the shadow, they enjoy the substance.

The friend accompanying Dorothy, who had persuaded her to allow herself to be given this holiday (she never consented to spend "God's money" on a holiday, no matter how well earned or needed), was privileged to enjoy many facets of her multifarious personality. Her sense of fun; her love of beauty; her natural and undisguised enjoyment of the culinary delights of the countries she visited; her sparkling interest in all she saw and came in contact with; her absorption in the pleasure of the moment, and her ability to put aside for the time being problems connected with her work; the joy that welled up to spill over in rapturous delight, as the lovely Italian countryside unveiled its beauties: all these characteristics combined to make of her a perfect holiday companion.

The two pilgrims stayed at Perugia, and from there drove over each day to Assisi. It is a lovely approach from Perugia across the plain to the little town on the hill with which, in the days of the Saint, she was constantly at war. Unfortunately, when they arrived at the great Basilica of St. Francis, where they had expected to feel the presence of the loved Saint in stillness and peace, all was noise and confusion. Crowds poured out of the huge char-a-bancs all through the day. They strode into the Basilica, talking at the top of their voices and effectively shattering whatever quiet and peace may have existed prior to their arrival. Dorothy's visit had coincided with Ascension Day, and an Italian crowd in holiday mood has little use for reverent silence!

In the crypt of the Basilica, kneeling by the tomb of the Saint, Dorothy was lost for hours in contemplative prayer. There happened to be a wedding taking place at the Altar rail, and people were incessantly coming and going. Little did the milling crowds of sightseers realize, as they brushed past the small figure so withdrawn and absorbed in prayer, that for a brief moment their transient lives had impinged upon the Eternal! They were quite oblivious to the spectacle of a human mind inflamed by divine fire, a human heart possessed with ecstatic love, receiving before their eyes the 'touch' of God upon the substance of her soul! When the two friends eventually made their way from the dark crypt to the brilliant sunshine, Dorothy, encountering the enquiring look of her companion, said to her very simply and humbly, "A Ray from the Divine Love pierced my heart!"

The highlight of this visit to Assisi were the hours spent in the Church of San Damiano. No char-a-bancs could make their way down the narrow street that led from the city to the little church. Sitting in the old cloisters surrounding the garden, Dorothy was steeped in stillness and peace, and felt herself close to the radiant spirits of St. Francis and St. Clare. It was on this spot, in what was then an inconspicuous, ruined Church overlooking the Umbrian plain, with the wooded slopes of Mount Subasio rising behind it, that St. Francis knelt one day amidst the broken stones and weeds covering the floor of St. Damiano before a simple stone altar with a Byzantine Crucifix painted upon wood behind it. His eyes were fixed upon the image of the suffering Christ and he was wholly absorbed in his prayer, when suddenly a Voice spoke, "Build up my house for Me!" It was a divine command, and St. Francis, the prayer of whose whole life was that he might in all things do God's Will, immediately set himself to the task of repairing the ruined Church.

Dorothy and her companion felt themselves immersed in peace; swallows swooped in and out, flying low to their very feet, and, close by, a turtle dove, whose mate was sitting on her nest high in the rafters, contributed to the soothing atmosphere by his gentle cooing. In the afternoon they returned to San Damiano, as Dorothy wanted to compose her News Letter to the Fellowship, and found an old lady sitting by the corner where Dorothy had earlier sat. She was dressed as a member of the Tertiary Order of St. Francis. They spoke to her and found to their surprise that she was English. As they were conversing, a tall monk entered the cloister, who, she said, was her son. She asked him to take the English visitors round and show them everything. His name was Brother Francis, and he was a gentle soul with an ascetic face lit with a lovely smile. He was immediately drawn to Dorothy, sensing her rare quality of spirit. As a result of their mutual attraction, he disclosed his great knowledge of the two Saints and shared with her the lovely, intimate stories and legends concerning St. Francis and St. Clare, some of which have never found their way into print. He took them to every corner of the monastery he could; he showed them the refectory where Clare and her daughters took their meals and where a vase of fresh flowers is always kept at the corner of the table at which the Saint habitually sat (it is still the same table of solid oak) ready to attend humbly to the needs of her nuns at all times. He encouraged Dorothy to uproot a small plant from the tiny garden in the upper building where Clare grew lilies for purity, violets for humility, and roses for love. It is the merest strip along a wide window ledge. Finally they returned to the cloisters where they found the old lady still sitting, her rosary dangling from her hands. Dorothy knelt by her and asked Brother Francis for his blessing. Three times she humbly asked the monk to bless her, and each time the humble monk protested, "But I am only a Friar Minor, Madame!" until at last his mother sharply bid him do as he was asked. Then, with great gentleness and love, he placed his hands on Dorothy's bowed head, and gave her St. Clare's blessing:

"I bless you in life and after my death, as much as I can, with all the blessing the Father of Mercy blesses. God be with you, and you yourself be everwhere and always in God."

Was the monk aware that there knelt before him one whose life was rooted in the Eternal Life? There is little doubt that both his mother and himself felt themselves to be in the presence of a rare and lovely spirit, a child of God, journeying in the footsteps of His Saints.

The return journey was broken by a stay of some days at Fiesoli, the little town perched on a hill overlooking Florence. Every day, Dorothy and her companion drove down to the city to visit its art treasures, and ferret among its antique shops. Dorothy loved to do this more than anything else. With uncanny intuition she would unearth from some dust-laden corner artistic treasures with which to adorn her Chapel. All the furnishings in the main body of the Church of Christ the Healer, with the exception of its pews and pulpit, were brought back by her on her various trips to Italy, or, if too heavy, freighted to Burrswood. Dorothy was a child of the Renaissance. She responded in every fibre of her being to the beauty that is to be seen on all sides in Florence, so rich in artistic treasures of every kind. The city's ancient culture took full possession of her beauty-loving nature. For a time she was saturated with beauty, and Beauty, it must never be forgotten, is an essential manifestation of the Godhead. In the Florence of the Renaissance Period, Beauty reigned supreme in the hearts of her children, and because they so loved her, Beauty sprang to life under the hands of the greatest artists and craftsmen the world has known since the 6th century B.C. It was these men who took over from a rediscovered Greece the torch of Beauty with which for a time they set aflame the rest of Europe, and which in our utilitarian, hustling 20th-century civilization still awakens nostalgic echoes in our hearts.

It was during her stay at Fiesoli in an Italian Albergo that Dorothy came closest to the Italians. It was delightful to see how completely they fell for her, and the extent to which her heart went out to them.

On the last evening of their stay at the Albergo, the head waiter prepared for Dorothy and her friend a special farewell supper. Dorothy was in festive mood. She had enjoyed her day in Florence unearthing treasures in the antique shops, and, with her flair for bargaining, had secured some really lovely art objects. They enjoyed their dinner, sitting on the terrace overlooking Dante's city with its lights twinkling, and in the distance the silvery ribbon of the Arno. Over their heads hung clusters of purple wisteria. The head waiter hovered around the beautiful English Signora, bringing her roses that he had himself cut in the gardens and placing them in a silver vase before her. A troup of Italian singers sang "Santa Luce" and "Regina" to her, in which songs she joined wholeheartedly. After dinner, as Dorothy was making her way to her room, a young Italian waiter, standing in the middle of the terrace and gazing towards the distant hills suffused with the pink glow of a late sunset, confided to her, "Signora, I like food, I like wine, I like women, but this", with a wide sweep of his arm heavenwards, "is the best!" So deeply is the love of beauty embedded in Italian hearts!

A thrilling moment of the return journey was the drive over the Simplon Pass, after having stayed for the night at Stresa on beautiful Lake Maggiore. On the way to the summit of the Pass, it was Dorothy who first sighted the gentians waving in the breeze all down one slope of a mountain, and, at the top, it was again she who spotted the solitary cluster of edelweiss.

Dorothy's ability to put aside, when on holiday, problems connected with her work did not extend to her sick. These she never forgot, carrying remembrance of their needs wherever she went. She continued, as she had always done, to awake at dawn and give herself to intercessory prayer for the suffering in soul, mind and body, who, all over the world, had asked her to pray for them. No matter how great the distance that separated her from Burrswood, she remained acutely aware of the needs of her patients.

The name of Eileen was often on her lips as she neared home after her Italian holiday. Sister Frances Bennett has recorded her memory of Eileen's determination to await Dorothy's return before her passage to the next world, on whose threshold she had hovered for many weeks.

An intrinsic part of Dorothy's ministry was the helping of souls to effect in peace, and without fear, the often difficult transition from this world to the next. There was a time when, owing to the difficulty of getting dedicated nurses, she had wondered whether God wanted her to give up having trained women, and refuse those cases that required professional nursing. The two doctors whom she had consulted were horrified that she could entertain such an idea, and told her that from a medical point of view it would be a disaster if she were to do so, because Burrswood, in their experience, was the only place they knew of where their patients were enabled to accept without fear the thought of death. Burrswood is essentially a shrine of whole-making. Healing covers a wide field far beyond its physical manifestations, and the elimination of 'fear' with its calamitous effects is to the forefront of its effective ministry of divine healing.

"During the early months of working for Dorothy," writes Sister Bennett, "I was astounded by her profound knowledge and true understanding of each individual patient. She was undoubtedly guided by the Holy Spirit in her compassionate and unerring handling of each case with its particular need and problems. Eileen had become a dear friend of Dorothy: the bond of love between them was mutual. She was a wonderful patient, making few demands, never openly asking for Dorothy, although eagerly awaiting her visits. For years she had suffered from a severe chest disease, and eventually came to Burrswood. Here she found peace and came to know, through Dorothy, the love of Jesus, and to experience the joy of participation in the sacramental life of the Church, and to receive into her soul the Living Touch of the Divine Physician. Physical healing was not granted to her, but she did receive the 'precious pearl which is hidden from the eyes of many'.*

"The Sunday before Dorothy's return, she surprised me by saying, 'Wouldn't it be dreadful if I were to die before Dorothy returned home!' Reassuring her over this, I reminded her of Dorothy's expected return late Tuesday night, or early Wednesday morning. Needless to say, I was puzzled by this remark, because my patient appeared no worse, if anything more active and alert. She finished knitting a pullover for her son, and wrapped it in a parcel ready for posting; then paid her laundry bill and paper account one week in advance. During Monday morning, she became considerably weaker, and as the day passed we became anxious for her. With the aid of drugs and oxygen, she rested quietly that night: during Tuesday, she appeared only to be waiting. Refusing night sedation, she explained her desire to be awake when Dorothy visited her.

"Late though it was, upon her return, Dorothy went at once to the bedside of her waiting friend. The next day, Eileen decided she wanted to see her 15-year-old son, and he was sent for. To me she confided that Dorothy was the only one who could tell him she was not going to recover.

"Dorothy visited Eileen on Wednesday morning, and said she had to go that day to London on urgent business, a sick call, but would return later that day. The son arrived and spent a happy hour with his mother, who was truly God-inspired, looking radiant and speaking clearly.

* *The Imitation of Christ:* Bk. III, ch. 32.

When Dorothy went to her that evening, Eileen said to her, 'Dorothy, do tell me what Heaven is really like.'

"Quietly leaving the room, I, too, pondered this question. The next morning, Thursday, Dorothy came early to administer the Laying-on-of-Hands to this courageous soul, who had waited so patiently.

"As we entered the room together, we found Eileen fast asleep, looking so happy and peaceful. Kneeling beside Dorothy, I listened to the familiar prayers and heard her commend Eileen to our Lord, 'If it be Thy will.'

" 'Stay with her,' she said to me softly, 'I will be with her son in the study.'

"The peace in the room was transcendent, an air of blessed triumph seemed to pervade the atmosphere, when suddenly Eileen said, quite distinctly, 'Oh, Dorothy, Dorothy! It is just as you said – beautiful, beautiful!' No more. With these last few words, she passed to the glory of the Heaven world.

"I knocked at the study door and, without waiting for permission, entered the room to find Dorothy seated on the couch with Eileen's son to whom she was talking earnestly. She gave me one look, and then turned to the boy. As I closed the door, I heard her say, 'Our Beloved Lord Jesus has just called your dear Mother home to Him. She will suffer no more.' There were tears in Dorothy's eyes, and I realized how much she would miss this particular patient, possibly because Eileen had suffered so much, so patiently, and yet in the midst of all her suffering had remembered Dorothy, her staff and all in Burrswood in her frequent prayers each day."

A sequel to this story of Eileen revealed itself in a letter found after her death, that she had addressed to the Chaplain a few days before her call came to her:

"I have been thinking a lot of what you were saying the other day, and you know I have a lot of time in which to think!

"What I am going to say could only be said (if it was to carry any conviction) by a patient. When I first came here, I used to think (as others do) that more frequent visits from Dorothy would be a help to me. And although I loved her from the first time I met her, I thought the acceptance by her staff of her every word, always and without question, slightly besotted. 'After all,' I used to think, 'she *is* human, she could be wrong!'

"Now, after many months, it is all beginning to dawn upon my feeble intelligence. The thing is that we have come in on something far more terrific than we can imagine.

"Dorothy prays for us always, and outside that knowledge, we can only know that she is under the direct guidance of our Lord, and who among us, once they realize that, will ever again feel aggrieved, or indeed anything but infinitely privileged? I feel only someone like myself, so near to the other world, can say this. She never talks about herself, but I know now she is in touch with a realm which someone like myself can in no way imagine. Dorothy never forgets us. If it is really necessary, she always *knows* and makes time to come. All the increasing work she takes on is only done in answer to prayer. Perhaps it is your business to put this across.

"The main thing is that it is all right, and we *must* know that, and try to help Dorothy in the only way some of us can – by not making demands upon her."

Following this testimony by a soul about to pass to that 'far country' whither we are all journeying is an appreciation by someone, the nature of whose arduous and self-sacrificing work in the world of the living made it very acceptable and precious to Dorothy. It happens to have been written by a tired and busy Bishop, but is typical of the feelings of many who have gone away from this Home of Healing refreshed and renewed in body, mind and spirit.

"In my Quiet Time this morning, I wrote these words which I feel urged to pass on to you:

" 'Praise God for this glorious interlude on my journey; for this haven of peace – for this quiet and holy sanctuary. Thou, O God, hast given it to me and I thank Thee for it. May I learn much from it and be worthy of the privilege of it. May I communicate to others the peace and the joy of Thy Presence that I have rediscovered in this lovely place. O holy and eternal God, I thank Thee and praise Thee and worship Thee – and love Thee.'

"These words attempt to sum up what I feel, but no words can express *all* I feel, for my heart is full to overflowing. I have discovered in this place, peace, devotion, quiet effectiveness. It is a power house of healing—the whole place is healing.

"And now, today I come down from the mountain into my particular busy valley. Another year of service opens up with many and constant and heartbreaking demands, but I shall tackle them all with a new inner spirit of quietness and harmony. Thank God for Burrswood."

CHAPTER 18

Church of Christ the Healer

IN the still hour of dawn, one morning in the spring of 1959, Dorothy had a vision while in her prayer. She saw a Church, complete in every detail, standing on what was the rose garden at Burrswood. From within this Church, a wonderful golden light was streaming forth, lighting up everything it touched. As she gazed, spellbound by the significance and beauty of this Vision, she heard these words: "Build this church for Me!"

The same unquestioning obedience that characterized the Saint of Assisi has always distinguished this equally dedicated servant of God. Like St. Francis, her instant reaction to what she believed to be God's Will has always been, "With joy, Lord, will I do whatsoever Thou wishest," and to this cry from her heart can be added, "At no matter what cost to myself."

A few weeks after this vision, one Thursday morning, at the end of a Service of Divine Healing, Dorothy stood on the chancel step of St. Luke's Chapel and told the congregation what she had seen. She also told them of her intention to fulfil God's command to build for Him the Church of Christ the Healer, no matter what obstacles she might encounter in the way of its realization. She said that before entering the Chapel that morning she had had no thought of disclosing this vision, but that it had been laid upon her by the Holy Spirit to do so during the Service. "And now," she ended, "I am going into the rose garden to turn up the first sod of earth. Who will come with me?" The entire congregation streamed after her into the sunshine of a lovely June morning, and stood watching, with prayerful hearts, as she dug a spade into the ground. The Chaplain asked for God's blessing upon this undertaking, which was to be dedicated to His Glory and Worship, and the healing of His sick children. The brief little ceremony was quickly over, and the crowd dispersed, but it marked the beginning of a venture in faith that was to be the crown of glory upon Dorothy's long years of ministry. It stands as a fitting monument to the memory of a saintly soul who spent herself in service to all who sought her guidance and help, and, through her ministry, the Living Touch of our Lord Jesus Christ. She later wrote of the Church in a Letter to the Fellowship in these terms:

"We have to thank God for the knowing that His Power and Goodness made possible the offering to Him of the Church of Christ the Healer at Burrswood. It is no exaggeration to describe the building of this Church as miraculous. Twelve months ago roses were blooming in the rose garden. Now, the Church of Christ the Healer stands there in beauty and strength, the crowning glory of a little city set on a hill."

At the time of Dorothy's vision, there was no money with which to pay for so costly an enterprise as the building of a Church. But true to her knowing that where God guides, He never fails to provide, she went forward fearlessly with the project, ignoring the pressing counsels of caution that were showered upon her on all sides. A number of extraordinary happenings occurred during the building of this Church in a period when it was almost impossible to obtain delivery of building materials. Among such happenings must be numbered the granting by the local authorities of permission to build a church! It seemed as though every obstacle encountered faded away before the power of some supernatural agency constantly at work – as, indeed, was the case.

The work of erecting the church was entrusted to a small firm of local builders, who had never before built a church. Yet, after the plans had been drawn up by a local architect, carefully supervised by Dorothy, who was insistent they should be true in every detail to the church of her vision, these village builders set to work to build the little gem of a church which is the admiration of all who visit it. These builders had undertaken a number of jobs for Dorothy to her satisfaction over the years, including the building of St. Faith and Chapel House, but a church was a proposition before which they quailed. Mr. Ted Russell, the senior partner in the firm of Russell Brothers, has recorded his memories of many of the occasions when his work brought him in contact with Dorothy, for whom his admiration, his loyal and affectionate regard grew ever greater as he was privileged to come close to the workings of her clear, quick and incisive intelligence. This seems a fitting place in which to embody his impressions, that are here included just as he set them down:

"I will start from the day I first came to see Miss Kerin. In June 1948, I was asked by the Vicar of the Village Church to go and see her. She had asked him to find her a local builder and send him up to Burrswood. I arrived at Burrswood and was shown into the study, where, by her manner, Miss Kerin immediately put me at my ease. This manner she had is not very easy to describe. She asked me questions about myself, and then said she would like me to do some small jobs about the place. We soon found out that Miss Kerin was a most unusual woman who seemed to know all about work and how to get it done. In those days, Burrswood had not even started to grow, and on my second visit she said to me, 'Take care of yourself, as I have a lot of work for you to do.' How very true this turned out to be!

"Miss Kerin had a habit of turning her thoughts to the next piece of work half way through the first one. She would send for me, and ask me to start on another job. One day, I said to her, 'Aren't you going to let me finish the job I am on, Miss?' I could see she was taken aback by what I had said. After a moment she replied:

" 'Mr. Russell, God has only given me so long on this earth. I have got a lot to do, and not much time in which to do it. I want you to do everything, as arranged, as quickly as you can.' She again insisted very seriously, 'I have a lot to do, and not much time to do it in.'

"The first Burrswood Chapel was very small. A sitting-room, that in years gone by had been the servants' hall, was altered into a chapel. Soon things began to happen. People came, and received great benefits, and they wanted to give in return. One day, Miss Kerin said to me, 'I have a lovely oak door that has been given. Will it fit?' Yes, strangely, it did fit perfectly! Other things came along. No effort was required. Then came the day when Miss Kerin said, 'This Chapel must be enlarged.' This began a series of ever larger chapels inside Burrswood, because no sooner were they finished than they had become too small.

"The first enlargement was of the first chapel in what is now known as the oak room. During this enlargement, Miss Kerin sent for me and said, 'I have been given £150 from someone who has received a great blessing at Burrswood. I can think of nothing better than some nice oak panelling for the Chapel. I know where there is some to be had, but this is priced at £1000!' She then said to me, 'Mr. Russell, you go out and look around for some.' 'But,' I protested, 'where?' And I insisted, 'I have no idea where to look!' She replied, 'You will find some, Mr. Russell, I know you will.'

"I came away thinking this was impossible, because panelling is very difficult to find, especially to fit. But three days later I telephoned to say I had been put on to some lovely oak panelling! After measuring the walls of the Chapel, we proceeded to check the sizes of the various bits of panelling available. Lo! and behold! there was a piece for every wall of the Chapel! What is more – all to be had for £75! In a fortnight all the panelling was in place.

"Even at this stage, Miss Kerin was planning an even larger Chapel, because she said to me, 'In a few months, this will be too small!' This proved to be correct. The old schoolroom was converted into a Chapel able to hold a hundred people, and work was started on what seemed to us a colossal task – cutting right through a stone gable at the west end of the house to build on an extension that could serve as a sanctuary to this Chapel. But true to Miss Kerin's words, it was only a matter of months before this chapel had also become too small. This time, we were faced with a real difficulty: the main stairway of the house was at the rear of the Chapel, and Miss Kerin said, quite simply, 'Put it by the Front Door!' My brother and I went into all this, and finally decided it was quite impossible. 'But,' said Miss Kerin, 'I know it can be done.' She would not accept our conclusion. Again we examined the project and again decided it was not possible to carry out this major operation. On my way to her with this news, I met her and very briefly told her we did not believe it was possible to do as she had asked. She put her hands up in the air and said, 'Impossible?' Then she smiled, 'Why, I have seen it there. I just will not accept your verdict.' Well, we felt nonplussed, but by now we *knew* that if Miss Kerin said it could be done, then it could and must. So we started, just to prove she was right! The staircase is now standing just where she said she saw it by the Front Door at Burrswood.

"Burrswood was steadily growing during all these building operations. Moving the stairway was just a small item in Miss Kerin's vision of the future. Very soon she sent for me again. 'We must have some more bedrooms, Mr. Russell, there are so many sick people wanting to come to Burrswood.' Then she went on to say, 'The east wing is not in a very good state. We will pull it down and build twenty more rooms.' Within a few weeks we were at work. She came to me and said, 'I would like you to finish by February 18th.' This was the anniversary date of her miraculous healing. I replied we should love to do it, nothing would give us greater pleasure, but that it was an impossible task, beyond our capacity to achieve. Nevertheless, I told her I would speak to the men involved, and tell them her reasons for wanting this building done by February 18th. They responded magnificiently, and after a tremendous effort we actually finished by that date. Then followed the building of Chapel House. We started building in September, 1958. I remember there was no place in which to hold the Christmas Market, because St. Michael and St. Faith (the new wing) were full. Miss Kerin suggested it should be held in what was to be the dining-room of Chapel House. The roof was not yet on the house, but the Market was one of the most successful ever held.

"The roses were still in bloom when Miss Kerin sent a message, asking me to meet her in the rose garden which was at the west end of the Burrswood terrace. I thought to myself, 'What has Miss Kerin got in mind now?' When I presented myself to her in the rose garden, she was all smiles, and turned to me and said, 'How would you like to build a church here?' I was speechless! I thought to myself 'Here!' I said to her, 'You don't mean *here* Miss?' She replied, 'Yes, on this rose garden. God has said to me I must build a church here. He has told me to start it.'

"I just thought to myself, 'I have got to tell Miss Kerin that this is too big for us!' Before I could say anything, she said to me, 'You have nothing to fear, Mr. Russell. You are a part of the Plan. I have seen you build it.' Then she added, 'When you require some money, come to me. I have not got the money, but God will provide it. When will you get the turf up?' I said, 'We cannot start all that soon, Miss. We have first got to get the plans passed.' To this she replied, 'Do not worry, Mr. Russell.' When I insisted we were not able to tackle such a big job, she answered, 'God will provide you with the knowledge and strength to build this Church.'

"After hearing these words, and seeing the expression on Miss Kerin's face (something which I cannot put into words), I came away convinced that we could and would build that Church.

"The plans came along, but they were not quite as Miss Kerin had seen the Church, the architect having put a pent house roof on top of the tower. She pointed to it and said, 'It is as though it had a weight on top of it!' This was re-designed and before long we were at work. We were given a glorious summer, and in a country starved of bricks, a quarter of a million bricks arrived! We were never held up at any time. All the stone needed for door and window-surrounds, and enrichments came and fitted into the sequence pattern of design, so that there was never at any time an interruption to the smooth flowing of the work. Always in the background there was Miss Kerin, spurring us on to make every effort, always ahead of our thoughts, constantly sending for me and constantly asking, 'What have you done about flooring, and ornamental ceiling, stained glass windows?' She was actually leading us in everything, so as to be sure that nothing was overlooked. Sometimes she would say with a twinkle in her eye, 'If you have not dealt with these matters, why not?' She never failed on her next visit to enquire about the things she had mentioned on her previous visit. There was one thing we marvelled at: Miss Kerin never bothered to take any notes about our building operations, she always remembered everything she had said on the previous occasion. She told me one day that the dedication date had been fixed, and she stressed the importance of getting the work done in time. She was always very keen to help us in any way she could.

"As the date for finishing drew near, all around said, 'You'll never do it!' But Miss Kerin, calm as always, said, 'I have no doubt whatsoever!' She herself brought out refreshments to the men, and seemed to inspire the final effort needed to get the work done in time. We worked overtime three weeks prior to the dedication, and on the great day itself, we were complete in every detail, except for a couple of door handles!

"As regards the Church of Christ the Healer, we always considered Miss Kerin as having built it. We did the actual work, but she was the inspiration, and only Miss Kerin could have got the work done in time. She was a 'lady' Churchill in a physical sense, because she had a way of getting the impossible done – and that was what Churchill did during the war!"

The Church of Christ the Healer was dedicated, free of all debt, on May 14th, 1960, exactly eleven months after the building was begun, by the Bishop of Coventry, assisted by the Bishop of Lewes. It had cost £30,000! Where did all this money come from? At no time was an appeal made for funds, yet the money came in a steady flow from people all over the world, in amounts small and large, given by them in thanksgiving for blessings received through Dorothy's intercessory prayers, as also through her direct ministry at Burrswood.

The building of a church of the size of Christ the Healer necessitated the presence of a full-time Chaplain. The spiritual needs of the community since 1957 had been take care of by the Rev. Gordon Kenworthy, Burrswood's much loved Honorary Chaplain. His gaiety of heart, warmth of sympathy and unfailing concern for patients and staff during his years of devoted service endeared him to all. His place was taken by the Rev. Frank Drake, M.A., who left his home in Guernsey to follow God's call to serve Him at Burrswood.

Visitors are invariably enchanted with the beauty that makes of this

Church of Christ the Healer a gem the perfection of which renders it worthy to be offered to Him whose command brought it into existence. The furnishings belong to the period of the late Renaissance, and have for the most part been acquired in Florence. The prevailing colour scheme is of gold and blue, and its effect is one of harmony and grace. The glass of the Rose Window over the Altar is from Venice. The Altar, whose design is 17th century, came from the private chapel of a princely Italian family whose origins go back to the 9th century; it was redecorated by Dorothy herself. The panels on each side of the Altar depict St. John the Divine and Catherine of Siena. They are believed to have been painted in the workshop of Andrea del Sarto, possibly under the Master's eye. The glazed terra-cotta of the Virgin and Child over the altar in the Lady Chapel is a genuine Andrea della Robbia. The arresting Angel, serving as lectern, is an early Baroque of singular beauty.

The four windows on the north side of the nave depict the Archangels: Michael, captain of the angelic hosts; Gabriel, messenger of God to Mary the Mother of Jesus; Uriel, sent to warn the Prophet Esdras not to meddle with things beyond his reach; and Raphael, who restored his sight to Tobit, and is the patron of the Church's Ministry of Healing.

These beautiful windows were given by relatives to commemorate a much-loved patient, Hilda, whom God called to Him only after her heroic fortitude and living faith had brought her entire family – husband, children, brothers and sisters – into membership of the Church of Christ.

Worshippers entering the Church by the little Italianate cloister that connects it with the main building have an impression of Light prevailing everywhere: they are conscious of being bathed in a Radiance that is vibrant with the love, the peace and the power of the Spirit.

In the days of Dorothy's ministry, the Church was full to overflowing, as was also the Lady Chapel. She several times hinted at the necessity to enlarge the Church on its north side. There was a striking proportion of men and little children, of whom many had travelled considerable distances to receive through the Laying-on-of-Hands the Healing Touch of our Lord. An impressive absence of emotional excitement of any kind was very noticeable. Those who kneel in worship in this beautiful Shrine of Healing know they are taking part, within the framework of the Church, in a rite that is sacramental in character. They believe themselves to be in the Presence of Jesus the Divine Healer, as they expectantly kneel at the Altar-rail to receive from Him the blessing which He knows them to be most in need of, whether this be of a physical or spiritual nature, or, as is often the case, both physical and spiritual, so interdependent are soul and body. Prayerful devotion, quiet and reverent, is the keynote of the Service. This attitude, which the Psalmist has summed up in the phrase "Be still and know that I am God", became intensified when the time came for Dorothy to kneel before the Altar to say the prayers that precede the Laying-on-of-Hands:

> O Blessed Lord, Who has promised that when two or three are gathered together in Thy Name, there Thou art in the midst of them to grant their requests: we come to Thee now just as we are, and we pray Thee, behold Thy servants, who, kneeling now before Thee, seek Thine aid.
>
> We pray Thee pour upon them the fulness of Thy blessing: abide with them, and never leave them: and if it be Thy Will, stretch forth Thine hand and touch them, and make them to be witnesses of Thy Power, and use them for Thy glory. O my God, our hope is in Thee, because of Thy promises and power.
>
> And now, O God, I give myself to Thee, Empty me of all that is not of Thee; Cleanse me from all unrighteousness, And if it be Thy Will, Take my hands and use them for Thy glory. Be it unto us according to Thy Will.

Who among us can ever forget the beauty and the poignancy of those moments when, in her clear soft voice, Dorothy offered up before God's Mercy Seat the incense of her humble petition on behalf of those to whom she was about to administer the Living Touch of the Living Lord? With the Chaplain at her side, she then went to the Altar-rail. As she placed her charismatic hands on the bowed heads before her, the Priest said the accompanying prayer:

> In the Name of God most High, and through His infinite Love and Power, may release from all sickness be given thee. In the Name of the Holy Spirit, may new life quicken thy mortal body, and mayest thou be made whole, and kept entire, to the Glory of our Lord and Saviour Jesus Christ.

Faces bearing signs of severe mental and physical distress often seemed as if transfigured as they turned from the Laying-on-of-Hands to resume their seats, having shed in that transcendental moment of contact with the Divine Physician their burden of fears, despairs, doubts, worries, and, very often, their physical ills as well. Bending over a kneeling child, or pausing before a heartbroken mother carrying in her arms her stricken baby, Dorothy would say in her gentle voice, her face alight with compassionate love: "Jesus said, 'Suffer the little children to come unto Me, for of such is the Kingdom of Heaven.' " Having thus ministered to all who were able to come to the Altar-rail, the small white-veiled figure then moved down the long succession of wheeled chairs, which lined one side of the centre aisle, to bring to each immobilized sufferer her Master's Whole-making Power, that awoke in them a sense of peace and joy to which most had long been strangers. The sacramental act of the Laying-on-of-Hands having been ministered to all who wished to receive it, she returned to kneel before the Altar to say the final prayer:

> And now, O Lord, we pray Thee, give us grace to tarry Thy leisure, and to await with hope the fulfilling of Thy promise. For they that wait upon the Lord shall renew their strength.

Dorothy's attitude towards her God-directed mission to heal the sick, comfort the sorrowing and give faith to the faithless is best stated in her own words which embody the very essence of her Gospel message:

"I believe that some of you are coming to receive the Laying-on-of-Hands. Before you come, I would ask you to remember three things: first, that there is no magic about the healing of our Lord Jesus Christ. It does not come always immediately, sometimes it does not come at all in the way we hope. Therefore we must come with one prayer in our hearts and minds, and that is that God's Will may be done in and for us. Secondly, the one thing our Lord asks of us is that we should come in faith. So, unless through the grace of God, you can come, believing you are coming to touch the hem of His garment and hear Him say, 'Go Thy way, thy faith has made thee whole,' remain quietly in your seats, and pray for those who do come in faith. Thirdly, and perhaps most important of all, that you should lose sight of Dorothy Kerin, who is nothing, has nothing, who can do nothing, except offer herself as an empty channel. There is only one healer, our Lord Jesus Christ, Who in His love uses His human instruments, unworthy though they are. It is His Power and His Power only. Therefore, unless you can come, bringing these three things in your hearts, I would beg you to remain in your places and pray that the Holy Spirit of God may use me, and that He will empty me of all self, and that what will be done shall be done in accordance with His Will and for His Glory."

CHAPTER 19

Witnesses to Healings

WHAT Dorothy's personal ministry: what the Services in the Church of Christ the Healer: what the peace that overshadows Burrswood, and the love which is its mainspring MEANT to people, is best told by quoting some among the countless tributes received by her from those who, over the years, experienced blessings of one kind and another.

Innumerable hearts will echo this tribute from our Bishop Visitor on the occasion of a Fellowship gathering:

"We have come here with hearts full of thanksgiving to thank God for what must be one of the most remarkable and significant works of Divine Healing going on in the Church of England – may I venture to say, in this country, today. Very many have come here with thanks in their hearts for the experience of Divine Healing brought to them, in their souls, minds and bodies, during these past months or years. Every single one of us must thank God that He raised up Dorothy Kerin to give this work and service to the glory of God in this day and age."

The Bishop then recalled the wonderful story in the Bible that tells how Elijah was sent by God to Zarephath to request from the starving widow the gift of a handful of meal in a land where famine was rife. On hearing the Prophet's assurance that her barrel of meal would never waste, nor would her cruse of oil ever fail, she shared with him the meagre portion she had reserved to serve as a last meal for her son and herself. Her faith was amply rewarded for "she and her house did eat many days". We have seen how this Bible story was, in essence, repeated many times throughout Dorothy's ministry. There were days when the bottom of the barrel had to be scraped, when the remaining drops of oil could be counted, but always God's prevenience averted the threatened disaster. The Bishop went on to say that we all have our Zarephaths, our point of encounter with God:

"We all have our places of encounter, but for very many your Zarephath has been this lovely place – this place of Peace, this place of

Holiness, this place of Healing. Here, whether directly or indirectly, the Lord God has reached out His hands to touch your life and you have been made whole and, maybe, healthy. You have caught a vision of Holiness, and at that moment you knew that the Lord was the great Other. It may be for many that Burrswood will have been throughout our life, the Zarephath where we met the Lord."

In his book, *Thy Son Liveth*, a former Chaplain to Burrswood has written: "The place is filled with a profound Peace. I knew at once, because I could feel it, that Christ Himself walks those corridors and enters the rooms."* Nearly every letter expresses its writer's gratitude for God's guidance of him or her to Burrswood, where the Peace and Love that are enshrined in this Home of Healing are felt the moment its threshold is crossed.

"What can I say to you about our wonderful day! I cannot put into words what we all felt. I know I speak for all when I say we were very, very moved and deeply touched by the beautiful love that comes from every corner of your beautiful Home. I think many of us feel that we have found something, and I hope we may have the pleasure and the privilege, because PRIVILEGE it is, of coming again. If any of us doubted before we came (and I for one did not) the Power and the Love, there was not one single doubter when they returned (a bus load of some forty people). The Chapel is the most beautiful I have seen, and its peace cannot surely be equalled."

"My wife and I feel we must write and tell you of the deep spiritual experience we had on Saturday at Burrswood. From the moment we entered the beautiful Chapel, we felt the very near, the almost overwhelming, Presence of God, and we were moved more deeply throughout the Service than we can tell. We were both inspired by the Service which seemed as natural a Sacrament as Holy Communion, and so very much in keeping with our Lord's command."

"Life can never be the same. It was my experience of Burrswood, the most wonderful thing that has ever happened to me. I am so very happy about your wonderful work. It was something I thought I would never live to see, although I have dreamt of it. Will you please give my sincerest thanks to everyone, including the doctor and the nurses, for all the wonderful help they gave me. And what of your dear self? All I can say is that you have brought me nearer to our Lord than I have

* Frank Drake: *Thy Son Liveth* (Hodder and Stoughton).

ever been. The only way I can really thank you is to assure you I shall now hold you and your work up to God in very sympathetic prayer."

"How can I find words to express the gratitude I have for you and for Him? At Burrswood I have discovered something which I only imagined existed: the Fountain Head of all goodness; the Reality; the Heaven on earth; the Truth I have been searching for in suffering and frustration all my life."

"I have seldom, if ever, felt so genuinely sad to leave anywhere, as I felt when leaving Burrswood yesterday. The wonderful kindness which greets one and upholds one is something I have never experienced before. The peace and joy of that beautiful place will, I hope, remain with me always."

"I feel I must write to express my gratitude for the wonderful week I spent at Burrswood. As well as being a tremendous 'build-up' and re-charging at every level, it was a great inspiration and comfort to see the wonderful work that is being done. There is so much beauty at Burrswood, in the sympathetic kindliness of the Staff, as well as in all the lovely things around, and I feel this stays with one long after leaving."

"My husband and I were deeply grateful to you for telling me to come to Burrswood; having been there for over a week, we want to thank you even more (a hundredfold more) for your goodness in arranging it. This is indeed a Home of Healing – an abode of peace and joy. My experience hitherto having been chiefly of mental homes, I had no idea there was anything remotely like Burrswood."

"Words are quite inadequate to describe all I felt at Burrswood, so I can only thank you from the bottom of my heart for the wonderful time there, so rich in a new vision of life. The love and caring of all your Burrswood band was wonderful to experience."

The elimination of FEAR – that arch-enemy of mankind whose tentacles reach into every corner of our modern civilization – was among the most fruitful consequences of Dorothy's effective personal ministry.

"I am the man who, with my wife, attended your wonderful Service for the first time yesterday. I feel that you would like to know that the Power which was vouchsafed through you is already at work. The *fear* which has nagged at me for years has gone, and this morning, for the first time for years, I attended two Services without difficulty of breathing. I know where my thanks must be given, but I am deeply grateful to you for being the channel, and also for your kindness in giving me a twenty-five minute interview before the Service."

"It was such a joy to meet you and talk to you yesterday, and I loved every moment of the Healing Service. The feeling of fear and tension about which I talked to you left me very soon after the Service started. I shall always remember the feeling of heat that came through your hands on my head at the altar-rail."

"I write to tell you what help and comfort you have brought to us. Everything seems to have come right in my mind, and I think all the fear, worry and sadness have quite gone."

"Jane, the woman for whom I asked prayer in March, is better, and I believe the danger of breakdown (due to long mental cruelty, fear, anxieties) has now passed. Thank you for interceding, and God bless you."

A number of the letters contain expressions of gratitude for the restoration of a happy relationship between husband and wife, as the result of an interview with Dorothy, or through her intercessory prayers.

"I want to thank you from the very bottom of my heart for all your wonderful help and kindness to us. Through your loving-kindness we are at unity together. When I came to see you last week, I just didn't know what to do, and everything seemed so dark and bewildering. When I left you, I felt I was no longer alone, and that the armour of the Holy Spirit was about me. Thank you for your wonderful strength and help. It is your loving-kindness that has done this for us."

"Whenever I see them (husband, wife and children) restored to happy family life and the weight of anxiety and misery lifted, I want to give ecstatic thanks and I hope to attend one of the Services soon. I think of Burrswood so gratefully, and feel thankful, again and again, even in buses and waiting for trains, and at all times of day for what has been done by God through you."

In his Foreword, our Bishop Visitor affirms: "that Dorothy Kerin was used of God to heal diseases apparently unresponsive to any other treatment is undoubted and amply proved".

Letters containing ecstatic thanks for healings of all kinds are legion. It is not possible to include more than a few of these records of cures taken at random from the files in which they are being carefully preserved for the edification, inspiration and comfort of future generations who were not privileged to know Dorothy Kerin personally. It is to be devoutly hoped that many more of these wonderful acts of God will find their way into biographies that are yet to be written of this unique woman. God, in His goodness, manifested His whole-making Power through His servant, because she was able to open herself to the Divine Source, the Fountain Head of all LIFE and offer herself, emptied of self, to be used as a channel. Her dedicated life of great spiritual beauty bore much fruit. "God deigned to touch her life with a supernatural touch of redemptive, creative, healing, life-changing LOVE, and from that moment she went out into the world to be one of our Lord's servants in His Ministry of Healing, and thousands of people from all over the world have known, that when they came across her path so they have come across His path, and as they have walked down the road of life, Jesus of Nazareth has passed by them through His servant Dorothy Kerin."*

"Although this won't be in your hands until two weeks hence, I feel I simply must write to you before I go to bed to try to tell you some of the joy in my heart. I shall never forget that moment when I knelt in 'our' lovely Church and felt His Power through your hands on my head – it seemed like an electric current. Just before you came to me, my head seemed to be lifted up to look at the Crucifix and it seemed to be shining, so golden and bright, as if the whole power of the sun was behind it, and as you came towards me, the light seemed to envelop you too. It was too bright for me to keep my eyes open. As I went back to my seat, I knew with complete and absolute certainty, not that the lump had gone (that came after), but that whatever the outcome, it was all right, that our Lord had been there as surely as any human being; but so great was His radiance one couldn't bear the sight. Then just before you asked the Priest to give the Blessing, quite unconsciously I put my hand where the lump had been, and lo! and behold!, it had gone in the 'twinkling of an eye,' and 'I was every whit whole!' I tried to tell E, but the tears were falling so fast I could not get the words out, until after the Blessing."

"These few lines come to tell you how profoundly inspired and grateful I was, and am, by everything at Burrswood – yourself, Divine Healing Service, and the Fellowship meeting. I believe that the Living

* From *A Series of Addresses delivered to members of the Burrswood Fellowship:* The Right Reverend the Lord Bishop of Coventry.

Touch of Jesus has come to me through the channel of your hands, because some ataxic movements and unbalance are no longer with me. Consequently I am full of thankful praise."

"I can hardly put into words my gratitude for the Healing Service on Thursday, and for my talk with you. I know that the hard crust of my resistance has clearly been broken, and that our Lord has truly come to me in a new, and hitherto unknown way. When I walked across to Church this morning early for the Eucharist the tears were streaming down my face, and they were tears of gratitude and not just mere emotionalism. I also knew that the peace of Burrswood has already in some small way descended on our home and family."

"I cannot work this morning, without first writing to you, to express, in all humility, my deepest gratitude to you, and to God, that through your hands yesterday evening, I sensed the Presence of Jesus Christ, more surely and wonderfully than ever before in my life. My spiritual development has only recently begun, and I am afraid that often I find it difficult to believe the fact that God is constantly guiding my life, in spite of the countless signs of His Love and interest that I cannot deny, but which make me feel even more unworthy. But last night confirmed for me, as never before, that God has accepted me with all my failings and unworthiness, and that Jesus' Power will help me to overcome them, and become at last a worthy servant of God."

"It was during the Healing Service on Saturday evening that God spoke to me. I slept that night better than I had done for a very long time. It has given me a feeling of confidence that I shall be able to do away with sleeping pills altogether. I have been taking them for about six years."

"I feel I must write to tell you about Audrey. Following her operation, she got a pulmonary embolus which gave her very great pain. She was whisked back into hospital again, and was told that she would have to have three weeks' complete bed rest. Last Thursday, I came over to Burrswood to receive the Laying-on-of-Hands especially for her. I wrote to tell her about this, giving her the time of the Service – 'Hospital dinner' is usually at 11.45 – but by a series of different happenings, she was left undisturbed between 11.0 and 1.0. She had ten hours' normal sleep without drugs and woke up on Friday morning with no pain. The Doctor when he did his rounds examined her thoroughly and said she was perfectly fit and could go home."

"When I came to you I was suffering from cancer, now it is not so. If you think it will help other people I will gladly testify that this is so. My doctors are pleading with me to have another biopsy but I have refused to submit. They cannot understand. I asked my specialist how many cases of a biopsy proving fallacious he had known. The answer was 'none'."

"I am so glad to be able to tell you that my Mother has made a wonderful – in fact what seems to us a miraculous-recovery. Even the specialist told me that her recovery did not tie up with her symptoms, so convinced was he that she had cancer of the liver. No words of mine can express to you the heartfelt thankfulness for your prayers for her because I am sure they turned the tide for her. She was a dying woman when I arrived in New Zealand and my sister had been told by the doctors that her days were numbered."

"You will remember I came to one of your Healing Services to receive the Laying-on-of-Hands last September when I was suffering from 'incurable cancer' of the stomach. As a result, the severe pain I had been suffering from left me. I have since attended the Westminster Hospital for treatment, and I am very pleased to say I have now been discharged, remarkably well, and able to lead a normal life."

"I thought you would like to know that I am feeling a lot stronger in myself. I have also got the sight back in my left eye since I stayed with you at your Nursing Home."

"I must write at once to tell you the good news! It was so good of you to spare some of your valuable time to go into the Church yesterday and give Annabella your Healing Power through our Lord, and I know how happy and thankful you will be when I tell you what has happened. It was some weeks ago, that she found she had a lump the size of an egg in her abdomen, and after seeing her doctor she went to hospital for X-rays. It showed on the plate as a black patch and the doctor suggested an operation might be necessary. *But she was determined not to have this before coming to you.* So I wrote to you to ask if you would give her 'The Laying-on-of-Hands' on the 18th, and you so kindly said you would. We looked forward so much with faith and prayers to the 18th; then the day came, and now the 19th, and the lump has entirely disappeared. She has seen her doctor who confirms this. Isn't it absolutely wonderful! We are so happy and thankful, and we went straight to Church to say 'Thanks be to God for His wonderful gift through you.'"

"Though very new members of the Fellowship, Burrswood has quickly become a focal point in our lives. We both look forward to our weekly visit, and if for some reason are unable to come, there is a feeling of loss. I wanted to tell you before you go away, that the specialist at Guy's is amazed at the extraordinary progress my husband has made. He can find 'nothing', and they are beginning to wonder if they made the wrong diagnosis."

"I write to send my profound and most grateful thanks for saving my sister last night. She is looking well again today. We are for ever in your debt."

"She sees what Burrswood has done for me. All my friends are quite astounded at my wonderful wellness. I can never thank God and you enough for all He has done for me through you – and all *you* do by your help and kindness."

"I came out of the hospital Wednesday. I went in Sunday, and the doctors all found the lump in the same place. Three of them. So on Monday at 12.0 I was cut open by the surgeon, who took the other breast off, and he *had* found the lump there. But when he opened up the breast this time, he could not find it! Isn't it wonderful! I knew you'd got my letter and that you would all be praying for me. I was so sure of that, and I was happier because you knew about me. I had your Cross with me that belonged to you. Miss Modin sent it to me. Well, I couldn't have faced it without knowing you were praying for me. And to think that God in His great Love and Mercy took the lump away. How can I express what is in my heart? The wonder of it has caught the hearts of hundreds of people, who were praying too, in many churches."

"Last Saturday I had the pleasure of attending the Healing Service in your Church. I was most moved and impressed by the beauty of the Church as well as the wonderful atmosphere of peace and tranquillity. In no other Church have I ever felt that JESUS was so near us, and I received not only a wonderful blessing but healing as well. When you laid your hands upon me I felt a new strength come into me. For a year I have suffered from a heart condition and have been unable to walk very far. The Sunday after my visit to you I walked to the bus and went to church, and did not get any pain. When my Doctor visited me on Wednesday he said there was a vast improvement. I was overjoyed. I know now that I will in time get completely well. I hope to have the pleasure of attending yet another Service of Healing later on, when I am well enough to travel by public transport. In the meantime, I would like to know more about your work and would be glad to receive any literature that is available."

"I want to thank you with all my heart for all the fresh hope and inspiration my visit to Burrswood has given me. It was so very good of you to see me alone. And your assurance that you have such a sure feeling that I shall be healed has made me feel that, every day, I must ask Him to give me the faith I need, so that His Power can take possession of every bit of me. You have implanted such a wonderful spirit of love and kindness into your Staff, that, as I said to you, Burrswood to me means 'Christianity in action'. If everybody followed Christ as your helpers do, there are no limits to what can be done in the world."

"The child of twelve with an inoperable cancer, of whom I wrote to you in October, I think, and whose name you added to your prayer list, is wonderfully better than she was, has gained two stone in weight, and has now no pain."

"Will you please tell Dorothy that the little boy who was born without any gall bladder or bile ducts, and of whom it was said by doctors and surgeons at the Gt. Ormond Street Hospital, and by doctors and surgeons here (Portugal), he could not possibly live, and for whom we asked Dorothy's prayers for God's healing, has just come back from a visit to London with his mother for a check-up, and these brilliant doctors and surgeons are all absolutely mystified over the child's condition! They say he can now be treated as any normal child and that there is no reason why he should not live to any age, and they add they simply do not understand what is happening inside him!"

"I am writing to thank you for helping to renew my faith in God. I am suffering from leukemia. Since my friend wrote to you on my behalf, I have made slow but sure progress. Previously, since June 26th, 1962, for five months I have made no progress whatsoever. The doctor kept giving me blood transfusions, but within 3–4 weeks the blood was all eaten away, and I was back where I started again. The doctor then tried me on some new tablets, but my blood gave no reaction to them either. When my friend wrote to you, she gave me your book to read in hospital. On the night I was finishing it I was having a transfusion at the time. I prayed to God with my free hand on my left shoulder blade (where I had a lot of pain) and asked Him to take away the pain. I slept on and off a few hours. When I awoke, I was aware that something wonderful had happened. I suddenly felt secure and also that there wasn't any need to worry any more. The pain in my shoulder had disappeared completely. I prayed again thanking God. For you see, Miss Kerin, I hadn't been to church for about three years nor had I prayed properly, so I was most surprised to receive help from God so quickly. The same morning the nurse came and asked me to take my old tablets again, as the doctor had turned to them as a last resort. Again God must have given him a sign telling him to do so, for within ten days the abormal blood cells had reduced from 25,000 to 16,000 – the highest result ever. Well, since all this happened I have found out that your reply to my friend was received the day before, saying that you would pray for me and that my name was now on the altar in your Chapel. So that was no coincidence was it? My friend, her husband and child came to see you a few weeks ago, travelling 400 miles to do so. She is nearly cured now, but would you please pray for her to ensure that her illness does not recur, and would you also continue to pray for me and also send me your fellowship card so that I may feel closer to you and all that you do."

"In my last letter I tried to explain to you the things that happened after my visit to you on Saturday last. I would now like to tell you about my wife's condition today. About 95 per cent of her body was racked with pain, now it is only 5 per cent. The doctors now say that the original diagnosis wasn't confirmed, and that she has improved so much that she looks like getting better. This is very surprising as she is supposed to have cancer throughout her whole body! There was no treatment that could be given. Her appetite is good, complexion good, morale good. I hope that you have her name still on the Altar and that you will continue to pray for her as she isn't completely cured yet, but I am positive she will be, given time."

"I am very sorry to bother you again about my daughter, but she is very ill in hospital with her mind in a torment, living in a world of bitterness and fear. Please would you offer a special prayer for her. A fortnight ago she was finding the love of God, her family and friends, after months of struggling. She loved the beauty of your Church and a few weeks ago you spoke to her after a Healing Service, which comforted her, as she felt you were her loving friend. I have found a new faith of love and peace since coming to your Church and if I had known and understood years ago, this dreadful illness would never have happened."

The following witness has been contributed by Dorothy's former Matron, who knew her well, loved her dearly and worked with her closely:

THE MINISTERING DOROTHY: THE GRACE OF GOD WAS IN DOROTHY

"Dorothy entered a sick room only if asked to do so. In her heart she said 'I am only a little piece of pipeline.' A humble phrase. A dynamic statement. But her step across the threshold was a transforming moment.

"Dorothy sat by the bedside of a depressed woman. The sad face was covered with unsightly abrasions. Between them lay a jigsaw puzzle. The patient saw broken pieces of wood. Dorothy saw a broken life. One hand moved wood. One heart moved in prayer. The puzzle was completed. The face was healed."

"BEHOLD, I MAKE ALL THINGS NEW"

" 'No one can take this sorrow from my heart,' sobbed a heart-broken Mother. Here was a story of human error ending in tragedy beyond recall. The Faith and mental discipline needed to surmount the memory was not known to this woman. She sobbed for ten days.

"Bowed with grief she met Dorothy. Within a matter of minutes an upright, composed old lady left Dorothy's study. Dorothy had looked on her and loved her. In the Greater Love, the memory of the tragedy burnt up."

CHAPTER 20

Dorothy's Staff

THIS chapter attempts to portray Dorothy's rewarding relationship with her Staff: her beloved and trusted friends, her spiritual family without whose devoted co-operation, as she has herself frequently testified, it would not have been possible for her to have fulfilled the great mission entrusted to her by our Lord Jesus Christ at the time of her miraculous healing in 1912. In a physical sense they were the pillars upon which rested the enduring spiritual edifice built up by her over the years.

We have seen in the preceding chapter how numerous are the tributes paid to the wonderful love and kindness of the Staff which makes of Burrswood "a real Home of Healing – an abode of peace and joy".

Had Dorothy not succeeded in inculcating in her workers, by her daily example and through years of close association with her, this spirit of selfless service inspired by love and understanding, disaster inevitably must have overtaken Burrswood when, suddenly, the place was bereft of the mainspring of its life: its guide, its captain, its never-failing inspiration.

Many of the older members of Dorothy's Staff had first come to her as patients and had received our Lord's Living Touch through the channel of her healing ministry. They remained to help in her divinely ordained work as an expression of their thanksgiving for God's gift to them of wholeness of spirit, mind and body. They had come from different walks in life, from varying backgrounds of interests and training, but one common factor united them solidly: a sense of vocation, of dedication, and a whole-hearted acceptance of the necessity of obedience to God's will as it was revealed to them through His humble servant.

Dorothy held before her Staff a clear picture, from which she never deviated, of what she conceived to be the obligation of souls called by God to serve Him and His suffering children: they must with unceasing effort try to empty themselves of 'self' in order that their emptiness could be filled with the Power of His Love, His Healing and His Peace.

No small ideal to live up to, but it was the constant aim of her own endeavour – in her case triumphantly achieved – and they were inspired by her example to follow her lead, stumbling in her wake, but ever striving to mould themselves to the pattern of perfection she set before them, each to the measure of his or her ability. This high standard of excellence obtained throughout the ranks of all who were privileged to work at Burrswood in the days of Dorothy's stewardship, from its saintly Head down to the last recruit, whether domestic helper, nurse or a member of the outdoor staff.

At the Chapter Meetings held during the year, Dorothy never failed to stress the importance of each member of her staff, bearing constantly in mind that they were living cells in a Mystical Body united in Christ. "Christ in us, we in Christ" could be said to be the motto she inscribed upon the Burrswood banner, and how truly and well she built on this foundation is proved by the fact that visitors to the Home after her death have all voiced their gratitude and astonishment that it remains filled with the same atmosphere of love and peace that had distinguished it in her life-time.

The paragraphs that follow are taken from the Minutes of these Chapter Meetings. They are here quoted because nobody can express better than Dorothy herself the conception she had of the part to be played by each member of the Burrswood Family.

"All the Staff, whether they be nurses or part of the house or outdoor staff, many of whom are voluntary workers, are one body and family called into the service of our Lord. There is no difference in degree or standing among any of the Staff – whether their work be sweeping the floor or dressing the Altar. The nurses happen to wear a uniform, but that does not mean they are any different to the house staff. They are wearing that uniform because they are tending the sick and it gives the sick patients a feeling of security, but they are just as much the family of Burrswood as the house staff. This is my conception of the picture and always has been. If the house staff are pressed, then surely the nurses will gladly lend them a hand, and if in their turn they are pressed, the house staff will gladly go to their assistance. We have got to be one family in Christ, doing our utmost in love whatever we may be called upon to do, not standing on our dignity and thinking this or that is not our job. It is our job to do anything that falls to our notice.

"I have spoken to you very frankly from my heart because I regard myself as God's steward here, and I have watched His work grow up over the years, and it is up to every one of you to do your part towards the fruiting of it. I consider it does not matter whether it is an M.A. sweeping the floor, or an S.R.N. cutting bread and butter, or Dorothy Kerin cleaning out a gutter. I want you to know that every word of this has come from my heart and under the guidance of our Lord whom we all want to serve."

It was inevitable that from time to time an atmosphere of tension should prevail, misunderstandings occur, resulting in emotions being stirred and perspective becoming blurred. These upsets happen in all communities – whether these consist of men or women – where life is lived at close quarters and where the members are subjected to the stresses and strains of constant pressures.

How fortunate is the community whose Head is blessed with spiritual vision and filled with wisdom that is watered by grace, strengthened by charity, and that has flowered through discipline; a Head whose life, deeply embedded in the Eternal Life, is lived in the world but is not of it and, because it is so near to God, is near to souls. Such a Head was Dorothy Kerin, called by Christ to heal. If ever the need arose, a touch of her guiding hand was sufficient to right the vessel and set it once more on an even course.

"The few words I want to address to you this morning, I do not want to address to you as my staff, but my intimate, trusted and beloved friends.

"I want to take you all back to the past for a few moments. This work was originally started in faith and trust and over the years God has, in a wonderful way, abundantly blessed the work that has been carried on at Chapel House, Ealing, and now in Burrswood, and today Burrswood has become a focal point, not only to us but to the world, where people are looking for the manifestation of our Lord's Living Touch. They look to Burrswood for love and health and peace. That is a great responsibility that God has laid upon each one of us.

"All of you are in agreement that you have been called into this work by God. Our Lord has called you to serve here in the Ministry of Healing. It is a great privilege but it is also a great responsibility. He has called each one to work in the existing conditions at Burrswood. He neither promised you an easy time nor that He would enable you to adapt Burrswood to your conditions. All here are called to a life of love – of glorious and joyous sacrifice. I recall to you the words of our new

Archbishop* when he said he had been called to follow a Crucified Lord, and to follow Him into His glorious Resurrection Life.

"All through the years, from the very beginning of this work, it has been built up and maintained through faith and obedience. There have been times in the past when we have been called upon to face great difficulties, some privations, and great financial problems, and those who were with me at the beginning of the work know to what I am referring. These difficulties have been overcome, and we have much to thank God for, living in this beautiful Home which He has filled with His Holy Spirit. Of all this we are so conscious. People say the Staff is so loving and giving, and that Burrswood is full of peace, and this, I thank God, is true, but in the last few weeks I have felt a foreign element was creeping into the very heart of the work. At first I did not know what it was, but I frequently saw tears in the nurses' eyes and harassed looks on the faces of the domestic staff, and I could not understand it. I prayed about it and waited, and I promised the Lord I would tarry His leisure until I heard and saw for myself.

"I think it is because the human heart in us has failed in love that all this grief and unhappiness has come about in Burrswood. We could spend a great deal of time in listening to all the injustices, mistakes and misunderstandings that have arisen among us, but I believe that the only way to peace is for everyone of us to go to our Lord in humble penitence, asking for forgiveness for our failure in love, with the fervent prayer to re-dedicate our lives to His Service, praying for the gift of God's grace to overcome that which is destroying in part the lovely atmosphere of His Home.

"I believe that you have all been called by our Lord to serve Him here in this Home, but in great humility may I just add that it does not necessarily follow that you will all be permitted to run the course to the end. Of one thing we can be sure, and that is that our Lord never makes a mistake, neither can He go back upon His word in calling us to serve Him, but it is more than possible that we may fail to measure up to the standard required by Him. I beg of you therefore to forbear with each other and try to see the good there is in each one of you. Let us look constantly at our Lord's Life, and try to copy in our humble way His glorious pattern of a perfect Life. We have His own promise, 'My grace is sufficient for you.' When troubles arise, when you are misjudged, whenever you are misunderstood and are unhappy and bewildered, instead of running to each other, go straight to our Lord and unburden

* Rt. Hon. and Most Reverend Michael Ramsay.

yourself to Him, because that is where you will find guidance and peace and the answer to all those problems and difficulties. And now let us unitedly ask Him to accept the re-dedication of our lives, and let us take for our slogan: LEAVE IT TO HIM."

Dorothy was no 'plaster' saint, but a very real, loving and warm-hearted human being. She would sometimes humbly refer to what she called her "feet of clay", but her virtues, easily discernible, far outnumbered what few defects she may have believed herself to have possessed. Among these she would have included a fiery Irish temperament, whose emotions quickly flared and as swiftly subsided. Her grief when a flash struck some defaulting member of her immediate entourage was something to treasure in memory, for her humility was a very real characteristic of her nature. The heated reproach spoken, the unhappy recipient would hastily remove herself; scarcely had the door closed upon her than it was again opened, and on its threshold would stand Dorothy expressing her regret in terms that immediately annihilated all feelings of resentment, if any such had arisen. The incident may have been trivial, but it invariably called forth her great magnanimity of soul, which was of a quality and degree that only Saints possess.

To have incurred Dorothy's righteous wrath, however, was quite another matter, and no one unfortunate enough to have called it forth is ever likely to forget the searing experience. Self-revelation is seldom palatable, however salutary, and the disclosure of how deeply the offending culprit had failed our Lord was often the turning-point on the stony path to sanctification.

Some members of Dorothy's Staff have kindly given their witness to the influence she had in transforming their lives. Each one found in her the physician they needed for their spiritual ills, as well as receiving through the channel of her great charismatic gift healing for physical sickness. Much of this transformation was achieved through intercessory prayer and the influence of daily contact. Dorothy rarely taught through the medium of words. The power of her 'teaching' resided in example. She set herself a high and exacting standard of efficiency in work, which she expected her staff to follow: they rarely disappointed her. 'Being' was a science she had mastered, and the spiritual emanations that flowed from this mastery were far more effective in creating the climate of gradual transmutation than any number of eloquent discourses.

The first witness comes from the pen of Gladys Modin, of whom mention has several times been made as being a loved and trusted senior member to whom Dorothy confided the task of directing the household staff, and overseeing the upkeep of the Nursing Home. To her tribute she has given the title:

WHAT DOROTHY DID FOR ME

"In a moment of blind obedience to a known call of God to do something for someone in great need, I met Dorothy Kerin. As I stood and watched her come into the room, I knew that my quest was ended, for here stood before me one who KNEW, one who could reveal all I had clung to and believed, one who measured up to all I knew must exist somewhere in a living person with a living faith, if God and His word be true. Do not ask how I knew – I do not know, but I knew . . . and I wanted to go out and shout from the housetops 'I told you so!'

"Not long after, I was invited to spend the day at Ealing, and early in the day she said to me, 'Before you go, we must have a little bit in Chapel.' The time sped by, and she was called away continually, and not many moments were left to me to catch my train when she came back at last. 'Is there time?' I asked. 'Come on,' she said and we sped up the stairs and into her own little private Oratory. What passed in the next few moments is written in the annals of Heaven, but when she rose to her feet and faced me, the human eyes had vanished in two blazing lamps of pure white light which looked one through and through, and for the first time in my life I knew I was looking into the eyes of a Seer. Then suddenly she said, 'Bless you!' and was gone. How I caught my train I do not remember. My feet had wings, but not for the train, and again I wanted to shout aloud, 'I told you so!'

"That would have been no isolated, epoch-making event for her, as it was for me. Scores, nay, hundreds of people would testify to some such similar experience as a result of her impact upon them. Why? Surely because she walked in the Spirit, and was so poised that she instantly responded to the Spirit blowing where it listeth with every breath she drew. That was the secret of her lightness of heart, and of her lightness of touch upon life. Complete freedom of Spirit because of complete abandonment to the Spirit, complete obedience to the Will of God, not for tomorrow, but for today, NOW AT THAT VERY MOMENT. 'We only want what He wants' would be her joyous cry when making some particular demand of any of us, and however hard, or seemingly impossible, or fantastic, it would be done. That too was the secret of her own way of life, of the quantity of work she piled into every day. Every moment had its job, begun, finished, dismissed – and on to the next.

"It was difficult at first to learn not to act on one's own initiative, not sometimes to 'know better', or 'improve' on her suggestions – for she never gave orders – but as time passed, each one of us would learn to pour our obedience, and our loyalty to her known wishes into the Crucible that was of her own planning, and out of that commingling came the Burrswood that was her creation, and by the grace of God will ever remain so.

"Dorothy rarely taught in the academic sense of the word and yet one was learning all the time. Of one who did not measure up to her hopes I heard her say, 'I can't understand how she can have been here for so long and absorbed so little!' It was just that to be with her, not necessarily in the flesh, but in spirit – for she always said smilingly 'propinquity does not matter' – was the very Life of God which she breathed, and expected us to breathe. 'Vast fields are opening before you,' she said to me in early days, and when I demurred, shrinking, 'and you can't go back', she shot at me with a challenging glance, and I knew I did not want to 'go back', whatever the future held.

"My memory of her is all joy – the gay adventure of serving such a Lord as she revealed to me. She could not bear gloomy Services. They had to be swift flowing, full of confidence, full of praise. Hymns to her were only Songs of Praise. 'Let's have a jolly one' she would say, and on occasions when we were up against difficulties or trials of faith, it had to be 'Onward, Christian soldiers' or 'He who would valiant be,' which she would lead with her singularly sweet voice, probably on her own as she walked into the Church. Who of us will forget her happy joyous 'Good morning, girls!' as she sped past the kitchen door on the way to the Study; or her cheerful, confident 'Hallo! what's the best news?' when called to the telephone, or her resourcefulness in turning an awkward situation at the psychological moment by a joke, a burst of song, or a trilling laugh.

"We were never allowed to get away with second best. Here was not the egotistical pride of the perfectionist but the plain, simple belief that nothing but the BEST could be offered to our Lord. On one occasion there was a room to be got ready, turned round, and new curtains put up in a great hurry for an incoming guest. All was ready on time, and she came in to put flowers and to give the finishing touch, as she always loved to do, but one knew that there was just one weak spot: the curtain frill was badly made. Her eye travelled quickly around, and inevitably up the curtain and rested on the frill! There was dead silence, and then her eye travelled in the direction of the culprit, who, of course, promptly began to make excuses. She listened quietly, and then as if struck with a brilliant idea said 'Let's ask our Lady what she thinks of it!' And silently with downcast eyes and clasped hands, two figures stood. After a moment that seemed like Eternity the culprit shyly glanced up, to see a face appearing above two hands, with well-feigned horror (but an unmistakable twitch at the corner of her mouth), looking across to her and saying in a whisper, 'She says she does not think much of it!' And of course the frill came down, was put right and put up properly, surely to the satisfaction of our Lady and all concerned. That was the way in which she taught us, and trained us – like her Lord, by parable rather than precept, and the parable drove it home, and the lesson was never forgotten, in its widest magnitude.

"What then did Dorothy do for me? She taught me of holy things; she showed me the Service of our Lord which is perfect freedom. She led me out into those wide, wide fields from which there is no going back, and set me free to wander on and on."

Kathleen Nest, loved by Burrswood's guests because of her cheerful disposition and readiness at all times to give the maximum amount of help to those in need, has called her witness:

WHAT DOROTHY MEANT TO ME

"I came to Dorothy in a very wonderful way. After seventeen years spent in nursing my mother through an increasingly difficult and sad illness, and many family troubles and sorrows, I arrived at Chapel House, Speldhurst, soon after my mother's death in a state of complete exhaustion and collapse. For five months I remained there as a patient, the most wonderful five months of my life during which I climbed slowly back to life while learning through Dorothy how to use the health and wholeness so miraculously being restored to me. Our Lord was working within me, and Dorothy was always there understanding exactly what He was doing, and interpreting to me all that puzzled and bewildered me. The high lights of this period are many. I arrived in Holy Week in glorious Spring weather and experienced the joy of being out-of-doors resting in the sunshine, after so many sad months in my mother's sick-room. Down in the garden at Chapel House, and sometimes at Burrswood, I spent many hours of stillness and silence listening to the song of the birds, of cuckoos calling, drinking in the scent of the Spring flowers and the pungent smell of the azaleas.

"In these silent hours there was ample time to ponder upon my talks with Dorothy and to thank God for her deep understanding and compassion. I was not only sick in body but very sick in spirit for I had tried to bear the burden of the past years in my own strength. There had been growing resentment against God, a sense of unfair and unloving treatment from Him, and beyond all this, a deep heart-breaking misery over it all which threatened to drown me, so fast was I held in its depths, and I was full of fears and dread of the future. Very gently and steadily Dorothy presented to me the Lord Whom she loved and to Whom she had given her life. Gradually the misery receded, and I felt as if strong arms were lifting me from the terrifying depths into which I had fallen, into a new life of glorious possibilities ruled by a God Who was indeed a God of Love.

"There came the lovely Spring morning of the Feast of Corpus Christi when, in the little Chapel which is now the Staff-room, I received through Dorothy's ministry the Healing Touch of our Lord. This was followed a week later by a talk with Dorothy in which she pointed out the great Adventure of Life that lay ahead; of the wonderful things to be learned; of using this period of quiet to be still and tarry the Lord's leisure: a time in which to learn to be an empty channel – still, quiet, waiting to be filled. I remember the joy with which I heard her say, 'You see, if you give yourself, your will, utterly to Him you have nothing left to fear.' 'Perfect love casteth out fear.' 'When fear comes into contact with perfect Love it turns and flees, it cannot stand up to it, therefore you have nothing to fear.'

"In due course, she made me a permanent member of the Staff, and as the years passed I was to get to know her more and more intimately. Words cannot express all that this has meant to me or of how greatly I longed to have a deeper spiritual understanding in order to apprehend more fully her unique and saintly character. In reading the lives of S. Catherine of Siena and S. Teresa of Avila I have been forcibly struck by her likeness to both. May I try briefly to give the reader the likeness of Dorothy as I saw her. She was the first human being in my life who taught me what our Lord is really like, for through her selfless love shone His Love, His passion for souls, His humour and Divine Common-sense (both startling revelations to me). She was the greatest exemplar of true humility; no sense of self-importance ever obtruded in her relationship with people. She never spared herself and she never expected her Staff to spare themselves, a standard which I found both exhilarating and exciting. She taught us that after illness there always came a point in convalescence where human nature longed to prolong the ease and comfort, but our Lord expected us to return to work and to 'step out in faith,' and trust that we should receive wholeness and health. Her courage, too, was outstanding; courage in our Lord which carried her through deep sorrow and suffering for others; through her own physical sufferings; through the bitter hurts and disappointments to our Lord caused by the defection and failures of many she tried to help. Finally, one remembers the patient trust in which she went forward in the development of His work at Burrswood, and increasingly, out to the four corners of the earth, though sometimes overwhelmed by it all as her weary body longed for rest.

"It was always a revelation and a tonic to see how, even when seemingly overwhelmed, her whole being would suddenly be made new through her complete trust in her Master, and she would bubble over with joy, gratitude and fun. No wonder her staff, and all who knew and loved her, were proud to give all their loyalty and service to her in her work for God."

A vital part of Dorothy's healing ministry consisted in visits to the sick who were unable to come to Burrswood. No S.O.S. call was ever refused by her if it was humanly possible to answer it. Needless to say, no charge was ever made for these visits: they were purely a labour of love, done in her Master's Name and in obedience to His command. Many a grievously ill patient in some remote county had his or her last days on earth gladdened and enriched by the presence at their bedside of Christ's ministering messenger. Many miraculous recoveries resulted from these visits. It was Peggy Simpson's privilege to drive Dorothy on these errands of mercy, and she has recorded for us her memories of these unforgettable occasions.

" 'How beautiful upon the mountains are the feet of him
that bringeth good tidings, that publisheth peace.'

" 'Now we are off:' How often have I heard Dorothy say this, seated in the back of the car, as we set forth on some journey, either on a sick visit, or to hold a Healing Service in a church, or on a shopping expedition.

"For many years I had the joy and privilege of driving Dorothy: we must have covered thousands of miles together. I have been allowed in some small way to share her joys, and to see something of her sorrows and sufferings, and always her trust in God at all times. I know that she supported me with her prayers during all my driving hours, and especially so on very long journeys.

"To visit the sick and those in need, Dorothy travelled the length and breadth of the country. At first we made very early starts on long journeys, but eventually found that travelling through the night was more convenient, as Dorothy could sleep and rest in the car, and arrive, when possible, in time to go to early Mass in some church nearby and then have breakfast. Then she would make her visit and perhaps have a short rest and we would start our homeward journey, doing this in easy stages.

"We have watched the dawn come up over Dartmoor in company with wild ponies. We have crept through thick fog, snow, over icy roads and through floods, but have been rewarded countless number of times with glorious scenery, and above all with the joy and happiness and peace which Dorothy took to each patient and which showed so visibly in their faces. On these journeys Dorothy always had her time of prayer before we reached our destination, and on over-night journeys she kept always to her early morning prayer hour, when we would drive in silence broken only by her when she had finished. To Dorothy it was unthinkable that anything or any journey should break in upon this sacred hour.

"The longest journey we had was to Edinburgh some years ago where Dorothy was to visit a sick woman. This was in early December. The weather reports for the north of England were bad and the papers were full of stories of people buried in the snow, and ambulances working at full pressure rescuing people from cars. Miss Friend read them to Dorothy and did her best to prevent the journey, but Dorothy, knowing the dire need of her patient, was determined to go. Finally we left after evensong on a Sunday, taking Lady Ypres with us. It was an uneventful journey to Grantham, where we ran into freezing fog which was dense over the Yorkshire moors, but we followed the rear lights of a lorry until daylight. Even so, it was difficult right to the Scottish border where it turned to heavy rain all the way to Edinburgh, which we reached finally at 11.20 a.m., and pulled up at our destination on the dot some ten minutes later. The sick woman ministered to, greatly cheered and comforted by Dorothy's presence at her bedside, we had early lunch, a rest and then down to Princes Street for tea, and off home again at 5.30 p.m. We encountered the same kind of weather on the return journey, arriving at 8 a.m. at Baldock where even Dorothy enjoyed a breakfast of bacon and eggs! She then found the energy to shop on the way through London! It was a memorable journey, not because of the big mileage but because it made me realize how sustained I had been by Dorothy's prayers, and the giving to me of strength for what was necessary.

"Long journeys, short journeys, journeys abroad – there are many stories which would fill many pages: for me these sixteen years of driving Dorothy are rich in precious memories. To have seen the peace and joy of God in the eyes of the sick who were visited; to have heard the hush in Church and hall – wherever Dorothy has spoken, and seen those same places filled to capacity to the amazement of lay people and clergy alike has been an immense privilege for all who travelled with her. And at the end of each occasion, Dorothy's humility and thankfulness to God for using her for His glory in all her unworthiness. How receptive was Dorothy's heart to His Voice, for on every journey before a talk and a Healing Service she would say, 'I don't know what I am going to say – I haven't a thought in my head!' so that one knew she had indeed emptied herself of self – the better to hear His Voice and pass on His message.

"Nor must Dorothy the gardener be forgotten. Burrswood at the beginning was a wilderness, having been untouched for sixteen years, but Dorothy wasted no time in getting labour in the form of her head gardener from Ealing, and six German prisoners who gradually cut their way through the undergrowth. She herself with her children and some of us spent many happy hours clearing the parkland year by year until her own work claimed all her time. Dorothy loved every corner of her garden and would have it all full of colour, informal with no straight lines. To her, beauty in the garden was as much a part of God's healing work as were the lovely things she bought for the house. Even in these recent years, when the pressure of her work made it impossible for Dorothy to spend all but an occasional hour in her garden, she knew very well what was being done and what improvements needed to be made.

"To work for Dorothy was hard, but a joyous privilege. Her own capacity for work was tremendous, her energy unflagging, her joy inspiring, her enthusiasm unbounded, and her vision far-seeing; but it entailed sacrifices from her in many different forms. When we came to work for her – for Him as she would constantly repeat – she did not promise us a 'bed of roses', quite the contrary, but who else under the circumstances could have loved and encouraged us in spite of all our many failings? We thank God for being allowed to share Dorothy's life: for her great heart and love for all people; for her patience in all her many trials and sufferings, and above all for her constant example of His Love. One could learn so much from just being with her or seeing her: it required no word to understand her radiance in love and trust in God. May we who continue at Burrswood be ever conscious of her prayers and try to carry on her work as she would have it done, just as she taught us to do it. May we remember Dorothy's words, spoken so often in her thankfulness to God, 'More than we can ask or think', and may we echo and re-echo them in gratitude for the privilege of living and working with Dorothy."

Ruth Farr, known to hundreds of readers of the article "Miracle at Burrswood" which she wrote for the magazine *Church Illustrated*, under the pseudonym of Mary Powell, has kept a precious memory of:

AN ANSWER TO PRAYER

"My most vivid memories of Dorothy range between the two extremes – the comic, witty Dorothy who would suddenly reduce one to helpless laughter and the 'praying' Dorothy reaching to the Sublime, and shedding its radiance around her. One naturally lingered over this latter manifestation, therefore the memory is more detailed.

"There was a day when a particular problem sat so heavily upon me that I sent a message to Dorothy for her prayers at our next Communion Service. When that hour arrived, I was kneeling at the back of the church as Dorothy entered, and as she walked up the aisle she turned and looked directly at me and smiled. I knew this was her way of saying 'I will remember your request.'

"The Service started. There were not a great many people there that morning, but about five rows directly ahead of me, a friend of mine – another member of the staff – knelt in her usual place with her back towards me.

"The Service went on, and we had nearly reached the Consecration, when I became aware, as it were, of a wave of something quite ineffable, flowing towards me from the Sanctuary where Dorothy knelt. This was something so delectable that I hardly dared stir or breathe. It closed around me like an enchantment and I longed for it to last and last. Somewhere a part of my mind struggled very faintly to analyse its nature: was it Joy? Was it Peace? Was it God's Holy Spirit?

"It lasted for the remainder of the Service, and only afterwards did I probe the experience more concisely. I knew for instance that this had happened before when Dorothy prayed. I knew that her method of prayer was to hold the person she prayed for, by an act of the will and the imagination, in His Presence. I decided that if you were fortunate, and had the right make-up, you received in time not only God's answer to your particular problem, but for the duration of that prayer you might even share something of that mystical Presence. This was the only way I could explain it all to myself. But how very tangible it all was. I was to receive confirmation later that morning when I ran into the friend who had been at the Service at the same time as myself. We were alone together and she said, 'It was a particularly lovely Service this morning, wasn't it?' I agreed and then she said something that made me gasp.

" 'You know, just before the Consecration I felt the most wonderful wave of "something" coming towards me from the Sanctuary.'

"So she had felt it too! Needless to say that in time I had an answer to that prayer which was so satisfactory that the exact nature of the problem that oppressed me has long since been effaced from my memory."

A department of Burrswood's domestic activities that is unrivalled in its importance to the smooth running of the place and the well-being of its many guests is its Kitchen. It has been said that all roads lead to Rome. Equally can it be said that at Burrswood all paths converge upon the Kitchen. In this key position, Dorothy placed "Bocky" to rule over its destinies and those of the many assistants who give a helping hand to its hard-pressed cooks. Bocky, tested by years of faithful and ungrudging service, possessed Dorothy's complete love and trust. No greater tribute can be paid to the unstinted measure of of her fidelity to the work entrusted to her. Sometimes, when passing by the door leading to the kitchen premises, Dorothy would pause as peals of gay laughter issued from behind the baize door. "Listen! That's Bocky," she would say, and it was lovely to see the light of tender love and approval that lit her face as she said this. She knew she had in Bocky a disciple who had been imbued with all her own notions of obedience to God's Will and complete dedication to the work she was called by Him to do at Burrswood. Bocky has sketched a brief outline of what Dorothy's friendship and example meant to her over the many years she worked for and with her.

WHAT DOROTHY'S FRIENDSHIP AND EXAMPLE TAUGHT ME

"To her Staff, Dorothy was not only an example and inspiration, but a true and wonderful friend. She made us have a real desire to give only the best, and all we have, to our Lord.

"We all came to work here at different times, and for each of us there was a different reason, but through Dorothy we were all united in our work with one aim and object: to serve God. The secret of Dorothy's leadership lay in her unerring knowledge of the individual needs of each one of us. We were a mixed lot of people with backgrounds and personalities that did not always react harmoniously. Left to our own inclinations, we probably would never have freely commingled, but she led us in such fashion that she brought out the best in each one of us. Through the example of her own unfailing charity and patience, we learnt to be charitable and tolerant towards each other. There is no doubt she was an inspiration to every member of her Staff, and to her our love and loyalty were given wholeheartedly and unconditionally.

"Dorothy was so wonderfully human. She shared in our personal sorrows and troubles, and in our pleasures and joys. Her sense of humour was irrepressible and was one of her most lovable qualities. How she loved to come and join us at work, and laugh, and sing and play jokes until the house rocked with the laughter coming from 'BEHIND THE BAIZE DOOR'. Never was there a more lovable, unselfish, fun-loving, but at the same time inspiring person to work for than our much-loved Dorothy."

Marina Chavchavadze requires no introduction to members of the Fellowship or to the many friends of Burrswood who, over the years, have constantly found in her a kind and sympathetic friend, ever ready to help them. The oldest member of the Staff, with the exception of Miss Friend, she has written a powerful and moving account of the gradual transformation of her richly endowed but worldly personality into a dedicated servant of God called to sanctification through intercessory prayer and the costly travail wrought on her behalf within the heart of a saint.

THE CRUCIBLE

"I owe everything to Dorothy. My deepest bond with her was founded on my failures, and for this reason I write this account with some diffidence. The time has come for the truth about her to be made known, holding nothing back and thereby giving glory to God.

"When our paths crossed in 1936, I had never heard of Dorothy. I was in the throes of a breakdown and could no longer eat, sleep or dress properly. Like so many of the young, who are driven by a lack of security and love into irresponsibility and various excesses, I had lost my bearings and had shut myself in against a threatening world. 'Put an end to it all' was a recurring thought. When this kind of disintegration of the will sets in, only the perception of others can save us from destruction. Lorna was an elderly friend whom I did not know very well but who acted as my good Samaritan. She had recently been healed of a breakdown through Dorothy's prayers and knew what to do; she rang up Dorothy and hired a car. There remains only a hazy recollection of the drive to Chapel House, of meeting Miss Friend, and of going to bed wondering where I was.

"Dorothy did not come to see me until the evening. She had been told in prayer that my soul was laid upon her charge. As she sat beside my bed and we talked, my reserve in the presence of this stranger gradually vanished, and I confessed all that had accumulated over the years and was now crushing me. It was a clean sweep of my conscience, and I slept in peace for the first time for months.

"The next morning Sister Friend brought me Dorothy's book *The Living Touch* to read. It gripped me from the beginning, for this was a story of healing. As I read, it became a revelation. Christ was a person after all, He was so real that she had looked into His face and felt His touch, He had intervened between her and death and was now guiding her life. This changed everything for me: it meant that He also knew me and that He cared for all His children. After so much wandering, this then was the harbour for which I had been looking. Only those who have known shipwreck can realize what this means, or understand all that followed after.

"The next day, Dorothy took me into the Chapel and we knelt before the Altar. She prayed, presenting me before the mercy-seat of God and asking that I might be made whole. While she was speaking her prayer was answered and I was filled with a great sense of joy. This feeling cannot be described. All that was broken and dried up was now mended and brimming over with life. Nothing in the vast range of human joys can equal this experience. My sickness which should have taken months, if not years, to be clinically cured, was healed within three days, and it all happened in the stillness of the Chapel.

"That afternoon I went for a walk along the lane, discovering as I went a new creation within myself and in my surroundings; the houses, trees and people were translucent with light. This is an experience known to many who receive healing. Some believe, as I did, that this state is permanent and should be maintained at all costs, but changes on a deeper level have to follow, and changes meant growing pains. It was not long before I learned that this happiness was only a preface to many more chapters.

"I went back to work but shrank from re-entering the life of the world. Dorothy kept in close touch encouraging me to persevere. She knew better than I did how easily the tiny spark that had been lit could be extinguished; on the other hand, she also realized how much in the past I had been in love with the world, that its fruits were not only bitter but also very sweet, and above all memory was short.

"When my family left London, Dorothy offered me to come and live in the cottage at the gate of Chapel House, which I inhabited with two other homeless friends. There I made fresh spiritual discoveries. God's will unfolded as I grew to understand that I could no longer lay claim to my life which I had wrecked. I asked that God's will might be made clear and He showed me that I was to serve Him in Chapel House and, subsequently, in Burrswood. The seal was set when my spiritual director gave his blessing and approval.

"Dorothy accepted suffering as the gate of love because the Cross is the only approach to the Resurrection. But for me the first attempt to pass through that gate met with violent opposition, not from others, but from within myself. It was a surprise to discover that there is resistance in our physical nature to the admission of the Holy Spirit, stirring every kind of rebellion from bursts of temper to subtleties of self-deception, from escape-illnesses to sleepiness at prayer. I had reached that place where so many are called and so few are chosen, where we begin to learn discrimination and obedience, and so often turn back. Holy Scripture warns us of this tangled sphere and the danger of overlooking the little things that we pass by, the seeds of evil thinking, the little foxes that spoil the vine, the backward glance when the hand is on the plough. It was in these small desertions that I drifted imperceptibly to a final point of betrayal. I failed, not for lack of prayer but for lack of watchfulness.

"This time Dorothy had to do more than pray, if I was to be saved from the laws of retribution. I learned that she had consented to suffer vicariously for my release. These labours for the salvation of souls, wrestlings of the spirit with demonic forces and agonizing for those who have fallen by the wayside, are the experiences of many who are called to the prayer of intercession, but some of the saints knew even greater sacrifices when they followed their Lord to Golgotha or to Gethsemane.

"Her public life is known to many thousands, but her hidden life in Christ she kept from the world. Today this biography had to be written in order that her message and the source of her strength and gifts of the Spirit might be revealed. Laying sacred truths before the world is a grave undertaking, but with Dorothy it is the fulfilment of her calling. Her message is a challenge to all, a cause for scandal to some, a proof of God's love to others. To us, the weaker brethren, it brings a reminder of our responsibility for our sins, because God has called everyone of us to be saints. But whatever our calling, we learn through failure that we can claim Christ's promise that He will never forsake us, even unto the end of the world."

Mention must not be omitted of the remaining senior member, Lal Anson, whose great gifts of tact and peace-making are at the disposal of everyone. Joined to these precious qualities is a robust common-sense that makes of her an invaluable counsellor, as many have found to their strengthening and helping. She obtained freedom of spirit and release from her crippling physical handicap through an act of obedience. In a time of domestic crisis, Dorothy asked her to help in the kitchen. For most of her life, Lal has suffered from a serious weakness in her back that had threatened her with life-long invalidism, and she, therefore, shrank from the thought of lifting heavy pots and pans. Nevertheless she gave her services to the kitchen without hesitation. Soon after, the day came when, kneeling at the Altar-rail, she felt a comforting warmth tingle down her spine: this was the prelude to receiving through Dorothy's laying-on-of-hands the blessing of our Lord's Living Touch, and she was healed of her infirmity. Dorothy once said of her, "Lal, whose whole life is a prayer," and this is reflected in the peace and serenity that emanate from her.

Dorothy loved her garden: she had in her head gardener, Mr. Hammerton, a valued and trusted collaborator whose faithful and ungrudging services over the years she greatly esteemed. His prodigious capacity for work, joined to his unequalled knowledge of the requirements of gardens and his love for Burrswood and its Head, has been an invaluable factor in achieving the beautifying of its grounds.

We have had an opportunity of looking at Dorothy through the eyes of her Staff. A factor common to every tribute is the insistence upon her inspired leadership and her ability to call forth the best in each one of her workers, arousing in them the desire to give of their best to whatever section of God's work He has called them to do in His Burrswood.

This chapter fittingly closes with these words taken from an Address given by Burrswood's Bishop Visitor to the community shortly before the first Lent after Dorothy's death:

"I thank God that here in this lovely place some of you are at work in this thrilling, but terribly difficult adventure called PRAYER. It cannot fail to have marked effect. You are creating people of prayer, an atmosphere of prayer in this place. One feels it. You are bringing peace and health to tired, lonely and sick people. You are placing yourselves at God's disposal, and anybody who does that is helping God's mighty purposes to be achieved.

"Burrswood must always be a place where people focus upon prayer. Why? Because all around us in this busy world people are constrained, rushing around with false priorities. They are hard at work getting on, getting rich, getting a good time. And so are lost in the superficial. It is up to us in this place to live deeply: to live a life of prayer deep down in God, so that people coming here may immediately sense that peace, and become adjusted quietly, without too much tension. It's a bad change of gear that causes noise; it is a good change of gear when it happens quietly.

"As you know, when people used to come out of an interview with Dorothy Kerin they hardly knew what had happened. She hadn't talked much about sin, but she had so radiated the Love of God that she had made that person long for that Love, wanting it desperately, and she helped that person to enter into the Love of God, with the result that they became different. They found peace, and harmony and love. They had been born again, and in being born again they saw the need for a total readjustment, which included their sins, and their false values, and their wrong priorities. They were healed. They were made whole. They were put on the road to holiness. Why? Because of contact with the All Holy in the life of a holy person. But that happened only as a result of prayer: hours of prayer, a life of prayer."

CHAPTER 21

Missions Abroad

THE year 1959 marked yet another milestone in the life of the Foundress of Burrswood. It was in the spring of that year that Dorothy began her apostolic journeyings abroad to make known to peoples of other lands the redemptive message of Divine Healing our Lord had commissioned her to proclaim to the world, and which, in the hour of His own choosing, He led her forth to do. The years that followed were crowded with arduous and fruitful Missions to Sweden, France, Switzerland, Ireland and the United States of America. At the time of her death, she had received invitations to visit Canada, South Africa, Australia and New Zealand, and plans had been made for her return to the United States in the autumn of 1962.

Dorothy embarked upon these Missions abroad in a spirit of pure oecumenicity. A devoted and loyal daughter of the Anglican Church, deeply influenced by its Catholic tradition, her heart none the less was wide open to those of other denominations, whom she accepted as followers of her beloved Master, members all of the Mystical Body of the Church of Christ in its most comprehensive sense. She knew no spiritual barriers: these faded at her approach. In the warmth of her flaming love for souls, all who came in contact with her knew they were welcomed and cherished as fellow Christians, united in the Divine Heart of the Divine Shepherd of souls.

In January, 1959, Dorothy had a supernatural experience that was symbolic in its relation to the oecumenical nature of her Missions that were soon to follow. She found herself in a Banqueting Hall of vast dimensions in which preparations for a banquet had been made. There were flowers in profusion upon the banquet table, and seats for a large company of guests. Some distance away from the table stood those who apparently had not been invited, and among these there was one who had lately come to Burrswood to serve on its nursing Staff, and who was a Nonconformist. This nurse had been told by the Chaplain that he could not admit her to the Communion Table. At the time Dorothy had supported him in his decision.

In the great Banquet Hall where the guests had assembled, a silence fell upon the company as there entered ONE before Whom all prostrated themselves in loving adoration. When the assembly rose to their feet, our Lord went to Dorothy and took her by the hand, and led her to the place of honour at His right Hand. The other guests took their seats. Then it seemed to Dorothy that Jesus looked at her with what was almost reproach in His eyes, and told her none of His committed followers should be excluded from His Sacred Feast; His eyes seemed to rest upon the figure of the nurse standing aloof. Dorothy went to her, and taking her by the hand led her to a place some way down the great Table; she then returned to her seat by His side.

The meaning of this experience was very clear to Dorothy: no one has the right to exclude from our Lord's Table any who sincerely follow Him and believe in Him. She said she had been shown other things which she could not yet reveal, but which might have seen the light of day had she lived to write the book it was her intention to publish in the near future.

In the spring of 1959, Dorothy received her first invitation to visit Sweden. This came from a group of Swedish members of the Burrswood International Fellowship who used to meet together regularly in Stockholm as an Intercessory Prayer Group. This first Mission was confined to Stockholm: those that followed covered an extensive area between the port of Göteborg and the capital. Plans had been made for a fourth Mission to include a visit to Finland in 1963.

The question has sometimes been asked why Dorothy chose Sweden for her first mission field. Dorothy did not purposely do so: God in His divinely conceived pattern for her work gave to this country a prominent place in her apostolic activities.

Dorothy's Missions revealed an immense hunger for genuine religious experience: all the churches, and they were many, in which she spoke, whatever their denomination, were filled to capacity. The Swedes are an oecumenically minded people and they flocked in amazing numbers to hear and see Dorothy, whether the church was Lutheran (Established Church of Sweden), Methodist, Congregational, Free Lutheran or Baptist.

On May 2nd, Dorothy set sail for Stockholm for the first time, accompanied by her friends, Marina Chavchavadze and Violet, Dowager Countess of Ypres. Marina has recorded for us her impression of this initial impact of Dorothy's personality upon the Swedish people.

"The Rector of the uniquely beautiful Engelbrekts Church, John

Nilsson, had invited Dorothy to speak in his church, reputed to be one of the largest in Stockholm. The church itself is modern and very lovely, built in massive proportions with a pulpit placed high above the congregation. There had been no publicity beyond a notice in a daily newspaper, yet the church was filled with 1600 people. An impressive feature was that the congregation consisted of every Christian denomination. Dorothy had for her interpreter a Salvation Army Officer, and the sight of an Anglo-Catholic speaking from the pulpit of a Lutheran stronghold, interpreted by a member of the Salvation Army, was for many an inspiring event. This gathering left a luminous memory. When Dorothy Kerin rose to speak, she appeared as a very small and frail figure. Her opening words, 'Let the words of my mouth and the meditation of my heart be acceptable in Thy sight, O Lord, my strength and my redeemer,' were received with an intense silence. This silence grew and deepened, gathering power as she spoke, her faithful interpreter repeating sentence by sentence the message of *The Living Touch.* The translation flowed in perfect harmony and seemed to strengthen rather than weaken this inspiring story, for it gave the listeners time to absorb the full meaning of its purpose.

"During the Service, a spiritual experience was granted to two people present who did not know each other. This vision was a witness of God's Presence, true to the tradition of Scripture, and it came at the end of the Service, after Dorothy had finished speaking. Standing in the pulpit by the side of her interpreter, frail and small in her white veil, she spoke in a clear voice the words from Tagore:

" '*Have you not heard His silent steps?*
He comes, comes, ever comes.'

"In the silence that followed, a white cloud, lit with flakes of fire, filled the dome of the church and descended slowly into the nave, blotting out Dorothy and her companion. As it passed lower and enveloped the people, a voice spoke within the onlooker, 'I will enter into every heart that is willing to receive me.'

"It was a sight never to be forgotten, especially to those of us who were witnessing for the first time the Holy Spirit of God in action, through His servant, among great numbers. Since that night, there have been many testimonies of gratitude for moral and physical healings which took place in the course of that unforgettable Service."

The towns in which Dorothy held Healing Services during her subsequent Missions include Göteborg, Boras, Jönköping, Tranas,

Norrköping, Örebro, Uppsala, and again Stockholm. On each occasion the Swedish Salvation Army provided outstanding interpreters: Colonel Gertrude Mortimer and Colonel Judit Ordell. It is impossible in the space of a single chapter, in which mention must also be made of Missions in other lands, to do justice to the great work done by Dorothy in awakening the Swedish people to the need for a renewal of their spiritual life. At the time of her death Dorothy had a large following in Sweden. She had been asked to broadcast her message to the nation, and some of the national newspapers, as well as most of the religious periodicals, carried sympathetic articles about her work and the impact her personality had made upon all who came in contact with her. The Swedes are an amazingly kind and hospitable people, and they opened wide their hearts and homes to God's gentle and unassuming messenger. Her Missions were a personal triumph, however hard she strove to keep herself out of the limelight, continually reminding those who listened to her that she was but "a bit of empty pipe-line that our Lord in His goodness deigned to use".

A brief account, however, must be given of a few outstanding Services that will for long remain in the memory of those who were present: one at Stockholm in 1960, and at Norrköping and Göteborg in 1961. All the churches visited were of exceptional beauty, and immaculately kept. The Swedes believe that the House of God should be a place of beauty as well as worship.

The opening passage of Dorothy's Addresses, given always from the pulpit, lifted her congregation into the very Presence of the Living Lord she had known and loved and served all her life. The wording might subsequently vary, but the emphasis remained unchanged.

"We have all met together tonight with one purpose and desire in our hearts, and that is that we may enjoy the intimacy of our Lord's Presence. Let us pray that our hearts and minds may be alert to the sound of His Voice, because unless we can hear the sound of His Voice speaking to us, there is no purpose, no point in our being here."

This challenging statement invariably provoked a silence that was expressive of the heightened tension of spirit, of an expectancy of mind and heart on the part of those listening, that reached its climax with her closing words:

"I believe that some of you may be coming to receive the Laying-on-of-Hands. In so doing, let us be quite clear that we are obeying our

Lord's command, and unless you can come with faith believing you are going to touch the hem of His garment, do not come, because Dorothy Kerin has no gift to give you: she is only God's instrument. There is only one Healer, and that is our Lord Jesus Christ who uses human instruments to convey His gift. It is His Power, His Living Touch, otherwise it is no use at all.

During her second Mission, Dorothy was asked by Pastor David Sandberg to hold a Healing Service in the Methodist Church of the Holy Trinity, Stockholm. It was the occasion for an unforgettable downpouring of the Holy Spirit. No words can describe the atmosphere of that 'other-dimensional world' into which those present felt themselves lifted by the Power of the Spirit. Pastor Sandberg had for weeks prepared his flock for the coming of Christ's messenger, and it was in a spirit of at-one-ment in Christ Jesus our Redeemer that this Service was held. This Church is dedicated to the Holy Trinity and it was, appropriately, the scene of a remarkable manifestation of the Triune Power of Father, Son and Holy Spirit. Healing of soul, mind and body took place during the Service, and a number of conversions followed from its impact upon the lives, not only of those in the church at the time, but also on others who heard about it from relatives and friends.

Dorothy was invited during her 1961 Mission to address an important oecumenical meeting of priests and ministers in the crypt of the Methodist Emmanuel Church at Norrköping, an ancient sea-port on the Baltic coast. She was the only woman among the dark-coated clericals, and she presented a charming sight, becomingly dressed in the blue she loved to wear, seated at the head of the long table around which her interlocuters gathered. She began her talk by saying:

"My Reverend Brothers in God: it has been a wonderful experience this coming to your country again, and I humbly believe the Holy Spirit has blessed and used what we are trying to do in His Name. My heart has been so warmed and filled with the warmth of your welcome and obvious love, and the wealth of your prayers. As you know, I belong to the Anglican Communion, but what has impressed me most is the wonderful spirit of brotherhood and unity among all denominations of Christians here, and this is really what the Holy Spirit has laid upon my heart – this need for man-made barriers to be broken down, and that we may permit the Love of God to heal these wounds within His Church. You know much better than I do that Peace can never be in the world until we have peace and unity within the Church of Christ.

The breaches in England seem to me to be much wider than here in Sweden, because at all the Services I have been privileged to attend, there has been nothing but love and welcome, and one has been made so conscious of the family and brotherhood of Christians. I thank God for this, and that is the message that I shall take back with me to England. We have so much to learn from you. May we be humble enough to learn it."

At the close of this meeting, an incident occurred that was significant because it held the promise that the purpose for which our Lord sent Dorothy to Sweden was being accomplished. One of the priests, belonging to the State Lutheran Church, offered up in the name of all the clergy present a beautiful prayer, in which he asked for God's forgiveness for them all for their neglect of His gift of Divine Healing.

From the Baltic to the North Sea, from Norrköping to Göteborg, is a long drive from one side of Sweden to the other. Dorothy was to hold a Healing Service in the Church of St. James in Göteborg at 3 o'clock on the afternoon of May 10th; at 7 in the evening of the same day she was to board the boat for her return journey to England. Dorothy and her travelling companions had become accustomed to the large and attentive congregations that had filled every church in which she had spoken. Nothing however, had prepared them for the colossal gathering that awaited them at Göteborg. They entered the church punctually to find the nave packed with people, every available seat being occupied. The gallery was filled; the walls of the nave were lined with men and women of all ages, prepared to stand patiently throughout the long Service; the side halls, in which loud speakers had been installed, were crammed with late-comers; the porch was crowded, as were the steps leading to it, and people had gathered in the street in the vain hope of being allowed to enter the church. Between four to five hundred people came to the Altar-rail to receive the Laying-on-of-Hands. They came in a seemingly never-ending flow: quietly, reverently, deeply moved, they knelt to receive through His servant the blessing of our Lord's Living Touch.

In the course of her three Missions to Sweden, which were organized with great efficiency and skill by Pastor Thunstrom of the Methodist Church, Dorothy must have given her message to 20,000 people, and in addition ministered to close on 2,000. No mention has been made of her many interviews with those seeking her guidance and spiritual help, nor of the number of sick ministered to by her in hospitals and private homes in the various towns she visited. Dorothy spent herself without stint in her Master's service, and to many despairing souls she opened new doors of hope. The bond that bound Dorothy to Sweden was the strongest and deepest that can exist, for it had been forged by the Love and Power of the Holy Spirit, and was full of promise for the future.

Sandwiched between Dorothy's second and third Missions to Sweden was a short Mission held in Geneva at the invitation of two Swiss ministers, Pastor Bernard Martin and Pastor Hubert Grivel.

The two churches of the Swiss Reformed Church, in which she spoke, were filled to their utmost capacity. After the meeting held in the Temple des Eaux Vives, where she had been asked to address clergy and doctors, but from which it had not been possible to exclude the public, who insisted upon their right to attend a gathering held in a church, Pastor Martin introduced Dorothy to some of the many people anxious to put to her their personal problems, or to be allowed to touch her garment and kiss her hand, as an expression of their love and gratitude. It was a touching sight to see the eagerness and warmth with which the practical, level-headed Swiss took Dorothy to their hearts.

The Service of Divine Healing held the next day in the Temple de Montbrillant, of which Pastor Grivel has charge, was greatly blessed, and a number of healings resulted from it. This church, whose architecture is ultra-modern, was filled with people who had come great distances, many of them from France, to hear God's messenger give her ever-new, ever-inspired and inspiring message of the Living Christ Who moves among us today, just as He did two thousand years ago, to heal and make whole the diseased in body, mind and soul. Pastor Martin gave a masterly translation of Dorothy's Address, and conveyed the very essence of her life-renewing gospel of good tidings. During the Laying-on-of-Hands that followed, the two Pastors took it in turn to say the Prayer, as Dorothy moved up and down the constantly changing rows of men, women and children (many of them very ill), who came with touching faith to seek the whole-making Power of the Divine Physician.

After the First World War, Geneva was selected to be the home of the League of Nations; at the close of the Second World War, when the League became the United Nations with its centre in New York, the city continued to harbour some of the subsidiary world-organizations belonging to the parent body. In consequence, Geneva has acquired a large cosmopolitan population in which the British and American elements predominate. This foreign population is increased during the periods when Geneva becomes the scene of the great international conferences.

Dorothy was also asked to speak in the English Church of the Holy Trinity and in the Emmanuel Episcopalian Church. In both these churches she addressed large international congregations.

On the last day of her mission she was the guest at a lunch given in the dining-hall of the United Nations Building by the heads of some of the world-wide Christian organizations that have their headquarters in Geneva. These men and women, who labour ceaselessly to bring about better religious and social understanding between the nations of the world, unanimously expressed their appreciation of the opportunity to talk with one whose message was universal in its appeal. "Her luminous presence", one Leader said, "has made a lasting impression, and we would like to know more of her life and work."

It was the fervent hope of those who had worked hard to make this Mission the undoubted success it was that Christ's messenger would return in the near future to water the seed she had so promisingly sown in His Name and for His glory.

During the many years of her ministry, Dorothy acquired a number of influential French friends. Some of these were members of the Fellowship, others were linked to her by personal ties that dated back to the early Ealing days. From time to time suggestions had been made that she should visit Paris, but nothing had come of these discussions. In 1961, at the instigation of a group of her Protestant friends, she received an invitation from Pastor Charles Westphal to deliver her message in the French capital under the auspices of the French Reformed Church, of which he is the revered head. She was also asked to speak in the church attached to the English Embassy.

It was a Mission rich in spiritual experiences. Contrary to popular notion, the French are not a sentimental race. Their processes of thought, logical in the extreme, make them quick to detect pseudo claims, whether in the field of religion, the sciences or the arts. The French have been the creative thinkers of Europe during centuries of her civilization, and they are proud of their Greco-Roman heritage. The average Frenchman has no use for thought that is not clear and logical in expression, and he attaches great importance to all that is genuine and true in the domain of the intellect. Was it not Pascal who said, "Man is a thinking reed"? They have a word that expresses their approval of ideas and persons that measure up to their standard of values. This word is '*authentique*', and its meaning has a far wider significance than its English equivalent 'genuine' by which it is usually translated. A phrase constantly heard in reference to Dorothy during her French Mission was: "*Elle est authentique.*"

It was late in May when Dorothy went to Paris, and the chestnut trees were still in bloom in the Champs Elysées. The weather was kind, and the capital looked gay and beautiful under a blue sky. Its atmosphere has a tonic effect on most people, and Dorothy was captivated by its charm, and delighted with the reception she received during her short stay.

She had been asked to hold two Services on two consecutive days in the Church of the Holy Spirit in the rue Roquepine. This church was built by the Empress Eugenie in the time of the Second Empire. It is a vast and depressing mausoleum-like building in which it is difficult to "mount on eagles' wings of prayer", and yet this soaring spiritual flight was accomplished by a large congregation, among whom were Jews, Orthodox and Roman Catholics. She was introduced at the first Service by Dr. Westphal, and after his talk she mounted the pulpit and gave an inspired Address. The Service on the evening of the next day began with prayers and hymns, and Dorothy again gave an Address, translated by the Pastor Grosjean. This Address was followed by a Communion Service which was a real 'breaking of Bread at the Lord's Supper Table'. After the Communion Service, Dorothy gave the Laying-on-of-Hands. She had been warned by the promoters of the Mission that it was unlikely the church would be more than a quarter full. What happened has been told in an article entitled *Miracle at Pentecost** which appeared in a French Protestant weekly, and it describes vividly what took place in the Church of the Holy Spirit.

"Nobody seemed to know where the crowds came from that filled the great Church of the Holy Spirit in the rue Roquepine, on Saturday and Sunday. With the exception of a brief notice appearing in two religious periodicals, there had been no publicity in regard to these two Services.

"A woman was present in our midst, known to many as Dorothy Kerin. This woman, of whom above all we remember the tender smile so revealing of her immense love steeped in joy, is neither a 'faith' healer nor a pseudo-visionary, nor the follower of some obscure sect. She is a living member of the Anglican Church, who was instantaneously healed in her girlhood of an incurable disease by our Lord Jesus Christ,

* Published in the Protestant weekly *Reforme*.

from Whom she received a mission to bring back to His Church the exercise of her forgotten ministry of Divine Healing. She underwent many years of preparation and waiting upon God before she exercised her ministry, which she has always refused to do outside the Church, or to limit it to one religious system or group. Without equivocation or ambiguity, she has everywhere proclaimed that the only Healer is our Lord Jesus Christ, the same yesterday, today and forever.

"On Sunday, at a Service commemorating the Last Supper, with Pastor Grosjean standing at her side to say the Prayer, she made a moving appeal to the sick present to come with living faith to receive the Laying-on-of-Hands, so that through the Power of the Holy Spirit they might be healed of their physical, mental and spiritual sicknesses. At that Service, when some 250 people came to receive the Laying-on-of-Hands, I knew many would be healed and many were, and I had a vision of the thronging crowds that moved our Lord to compassion. I felt shaken by the unbelievable dryness of our Protestant Services, by their deadness and their inability to reach man in his hidden depths and so touch his life in its reality. In these days of Pentecost, I came to realize that the Church, so faithful in preaching the Word, and in ministering the Sacraments, has deprived herself with inexcusable timidity from exercising the fullness of the Power conferred upon her by Christ, and which she alone can offer to the hungry and shepherdless crowds. This is a question open to lengthy discussion, around which theological arguments can rage furiously, but any such would be meaningless, for they would neither add to nor subtract from the authenticity of the spiritual experience of the hundreds of people who at this Service saw with their own eyes our Lord Jesus Christ manifest astounding miracles in their midst through the channel of His humble servant Dorothy Kerin."

One of the astounding miracles referred to in this article happened in connection with a woman who went up to receive vicariously the Laying-on-of-Hands for a blind friend. She had gone to the Service with the intention of receiving this blessing for herself, but as she followed the long line of people moving towards where Dorothy stood, a strong urge came upon her to substitute for her own need, the greater need of her blind friend. She obeyed her guidance and thought no more about it, but the next day when she visited her friend to tell her about the Service she found to her amazement that this blind woman had recovered her sight. Her friend told her that at the very hour the Laying-on-of-Hands was being received vicariously on her behalf, she had felt a terrible burning pain shoot through her eyes. Nothing further happened, but the next day, when she awoke, she found she could see perfectly, and is now able to thread the finest needle.

Another remarkable healing was that of a woman who had lain on her back for six months, immobilized with cancer of the spine. She suffered from excruciating pain in her head. Nevertheless, she managed to attend the Service and to sit through the two-and-a-quarter hours that it lasted, in spite of her doctors having condemned her to lie immobile in her bed with her arms stretched at her side. The astonishment and thankfulness of her friends were beyond words when they saw how from one day to the next she was able to resume a normal life and busy herself again with the affairs of her school and to clear up matters that had remained in abeyance ever since she began her illness.

This short account of the Paris Mission closes with this tribute from a Roman Catholic who attended the Healing Service in the Embassy Church:

"I want to thank you for one of the greatest moments in my life. I have always believed living the way you do, walking about in such simplicity and goodness towards all who suffer was the reason for your being on this earth – and yesterday, in the British Church, I knew that LIFE had come through in your person, in front of me. I knew a better life could start in this world, and all my critical and sick mind opened to an illuminating love and understanding. I can never thank you enough for all this, and wished to tell you my love and gratitude for ever."

The Mission to America was Dorothy's greatest in regard to the extent of the territory covered, the churches visited, and the number of men, women and children to whom she ministered.

This Mission owes much to the dynamic planning of Mrs. Aymar Johnson, an American Member of the Fellowship, whose constant watchfulness over its progress, and alertness to forestall whatever difficulties might arise, did much to ensure its success. In New York, Dorothy was the guest of Mrs. Walter Hoving at the beautiful Riverside Club, which overlooks the waters of the East River and presents its visitors with an unrivalled view of the famous skyscrapers of the city.

Dorothy and her travelling companion sailed from Southampton on September 28th on board the *Queen Elizabeth*. The spacious cabin they they shared was filled with flowers. For some time after the ship had left port, these continued to be brought in, until every corner was gay with colourful blossoms, whose beauty was a reminder of the volume of love and prayer with which the Fellowship was to sustain Dorothy throughout her strenuous Mission.

The warmth of her reception by the great-hearted American public had never been in doubt: nevertheless it exceeded every expectation. No picture can adequately convey the wealth of love with which she was everywhere received, and the generous hospitality lavished upon her and her companion in every town which they visited.

The Mission began on the evening of October 4th in the famous Marble Collegiate Church in which Dorothy had been invited to speak by Dr. Norman Vincent Peale. It was a thrilling moment on entering that vast building – in which the most famous religious leaders of the Old and New Worlds have given their message – to find it filled with a sympathetic, expectant congregation, who had come to hear their frail-looking visitor from England bear witness to the most spectacular healing in our time. She stood on the chancel step in her becoming blue ensemble, looking very small between the two big men, Dr. Peale and Dr. Blackburn, while they presented her for the first time to the American public.

Dr. Laurence Blackburn had led a delegation of Americans on a Spiritual Healing Pilgrimage to England and the Continent in the early part of 1961, and in the summer, accompanied by his charming wife, had visited Burrswood. From the first moment of their meeting, a spiritual bond was forged between Dr. Blackburn and Dorothy Kerin. In his introduction, after remarking it was most unusual for two people to introduce a speaker, he paid this arresting tribute to Dorothy:

" 'Ever and anon from the hid battlements of eternity, a trumpet sounds.' This striking quotation might be interpreted to say, in terms of the experience we are to have tonight, from time to time there walk among men those who clearly reveal the Power of God and who by their testimony call us to a positive faith.

"In almost the same breath, Jesus uttered the promise, 'Ye shall receive power,' and gave the command, 'Ye shall be my witnesses.' That promise and that command were not only to that day but also to ours.

"Our primary witness is to what we have let God do for us. In a nation and a world surfeited with power, the people cry aloud for the conviction of a God Who is real, Who is near, Who cares. The world will never believe that God can mend our broken world until it sees that God can make whole a person in body, mind and spirit.

"The one who comes to us tonight has achieved that power. Her life is a wonderful witness of gratitude in loving action. Great crowds have felt the impact of her spiritual power in Europe and in England.

"I have heard her speak. I have visited her beautiful Burrswood. I have witnessed a Service of Divine Healing in her exquisite Church of Christ the Healer. I have felt the upsurge of power as she placed her hands on my head with prayer.

"Have you ever seen a miracle? There is one among us tonight – walking, talking, witnessing. She is a living testimony to a living Christ, a gracious gentlewoman of England whom it is a privilege to introduce to America."

Dorothy then gave from the pulpit her eagerly awaited Address. This moved to their depths the hearts of those who listened to her, and awoke in many a hunger and a longing to know Jesus and walk with Him, for here was one who had both known and seen Jesus, and was therefore able to share with them the spiritual fragrance and reality of her experience of the living Christ.

From New York, Dorothy travelled to Philadelphia, Washington, Richmond, Norfolk, Baltimore, Boston, Providence, Newport, East Islip, West Orange and back to New York, where she held the last Healing Service of her American Mission in the Church of St. Bartholomew before sailing for England on November 1st.

It is not possible to contain within the limits of a few pages anything like an adequate account of the happenings of this immensely blessed Mission. A few of its highlights are here recorded, although their choice is arbitrary, for every stage of the Mission had its special facet and held its unforgettable spiritual experiences.

Washington is perhaps the world's most beautiful capital. Its wide avenues lined with trees, its gracious houses of a past era, its lovely vistas that converge upon the Capitol, its noble monuments, give to this unique metropolis an air of dignity and space denied to the crowded capitals of the Old World. During Dorothy's stay in Washington, she was the guest of Dr. and Mrs. Vereide at Fellowship House in Massachusetts Avenue.

Dorothy held five Healing Services in Washington's famous St. John's Church. This church is known as the Church of the Presidents. It stands opposite the White House, and whenever there is a crisis in the affairs of the nation, the President of the time* steps across to seek in prayer God's guidance for the momentous decisions he may be called upon to make. The Rector of St. John, his assistant Rector, and their Curates, were all present at the Services. They told her how greatly they valued and appreciated what our Lord had wrought through her during the whole of her Mission to them, and that it was their fervent hope that she would return to water the seed planted during her stay. From St. John's Church came the following appreciative letter:

"In thanking you for your Mission at our Church, I know I am voicing the enthusiasm, hopes and thanks of all those who came to hear you. The joyous faces of the people coming out after each Service told their own story. You will long be remembered for the good work our Lord accomplished through such a precious channel as you are."

The two travellers noticed a difference in atmosphere and climate as they journeyed further south. The tempo of living slowed down considerably. There is a marked prevalence of English and Scottish names, and people seem proud of their British ancestry. Their voices are softer, their manners more leisurely. The 'cousinship', so often stressed in public utterances on both sides of the Atlantic, here seems a reality. The architecture too is different. The old colonial style has been preserved, and many of the houses date back to colonial times. Another factor that differentiates the southern from the northern States is the prevalence of coloured folk. They are to be met with everywhere. Dorothy loved them. A great number presented themselves to receive our Lord's Living Touch in all the churches she visited, and their rapt faces were a testimony to their spiritual receptiveness. Dorothy laid her hands on their woolly heads with a special love and tenderness.

Norfolk in Virginia was among the highlights of the American Mission. The travellers arrived in the city in the late afternoon. In the evening Dorothy gave an Address followed by the Laying-on-of-Hands in the Church of the Epiphany. She had been on the move ever since early morning and had ministered to a sick child on the way. Nevertheless, all appearance of fatigue dropped off her from the moment of her meeting with Father Joseph Buchanan in the lobby of the Golden Triangle Hotel where she stayed. "The Spirit bloweth where it listeth" and takes no account of man-made edifices! It was evident that the Holy Spirit of God took over from the moment their paths converged. Father Buchanan and his prayer group had for many weeks

* Except when, as in the case of President Kennedy, he was an R.C.

prayed that our Lord would mightily use His messenger during her stay with them. Their prayers were answered "more than they could ask or think". Two-thirds of those present in the church on the night of that first Service came to the Altar-rail, and many testified that they had felt the 'draught' of the Holy Spirit pass over them as they knelt to receive, through Christ's humble channel, the blessing He knew they were most in need of. Father Buchanan's letter is a glowing tribute to the sanctified days spent in Norfolk:

"You cannot know except through the Spirit how deeply moved and changed we are by the Power of Jesus through Miss Kerin. He reached so many people. The level at which He reached them was deeper than has ever been done before. The Peace of our Lord still lingers. How many have spoken of His Peace! We are grateful indeed for His mighty servant Dorothy Kerin. Please convey our deep gratitude to her for the powerful Love of Jesus we all experienced."

It is a long drive from Norfolk to Baltimore. The Episcopalian Church of Christ is situated in the centre of the town in what was in bygone days a residential quarter, but has now become a busy business section. Mrs. Requard, the leader of the local prayer group, who first suggested that Dorothy should come to Baltimore, warned her, when she came to the hotel to fetch her, that a large number of people were not expected to attend the Service, because the church had ceased to be a parish church. Mrs. Requard shared Dorothy's astonishment on entering the church to find it filled with one of the largest congregations of the entire Mission. A great many coloured people were to be seen scattered among the crowd. Dorothy's time in Baltimore was all too short. The soil was so ready to be ploughed; the sheep so hungry for what our Lord, through His servant, so abundantly gave them that night. It is never easy to judge numbers, but not far short of 450 must have gone to the Altar-rail: there were as many men as women, and also coloured folk of all ages and sizes. Many of these knew that they had been taken into the very Presence of their Lord and Saviour by one who both knew and served Him: the tears were running down their faces as they reluctantly moved to make way for others.

The Boston members of the Order of St. Luke were commemorating their "St. Luke Day" at a great festival in Emmanuel Church on the day after Dorothy's arrival. She was asked to give the Address at this Service. The next day, she again gave her message to a full church. This was followed by the Laying-on-of-Hands, when she ministered to over 300 people. The following morning she spoke at length to a big gathering of members of the Boston prayer group, which, under the inspired leadership of Mrs. Franklin Day, has become a powerful channel for intercessory prayer in Massachusetts and bordering States. In the course of her talk, Dorothy told of God's gift to Burrswood of a brilliant young doctor, who, in obedience to what he believed to be God's call, had abandoned a large and lucrative practice in order to become the resident doctor in her Home of Healing. This doctor is now the Warden of Burrswood, designated by Dorothy to be her successor.

For many days Dorothy had been spending herself, giving her all to her Master's work without counting the cost. The calls made upon her had been incessant, and she had responded to them with her habitual selflessness. The strain of constant travel, and meeting with and ministering to enormous numbers of people, had exacted from her a heavy price. She had known little rest since the start of the Mission. Thanks to the kind hospitality of Dr. and Mrs. Blackburn, she was able, after holding a Service in Providence, to enjoy some days of quiet at Miramar in Newport. It was during the drive from Providence to Newport that Dorothy and her companion encountered the full glory of an American Fall. The colours have to be seen to be believed: russet and gold and flaming red with the sunlight dancing on branches and leaves, giving at times the impression of molten gold so fantastically beautiful as to be unreal, not of this world. Miramar had once been the palatial summer home of a wealthy New York family, who handed it over to the Episcopalian Church after the Second World War to be used as a centre where church conventions and conferences could be held in lovely surroundings. The house stands at the edge of the Atlantic, and here, for a few all too short days, Dorothy rested and slept to the sound of ocean waves breaking against the rocks beneath her windows. Even in this quiet rest centre, however, her work intruded itself. At Dr. Blackburn's request, she addressed forty-five Naval Chaplains who had assembled in conference in Miramar's big hall. They belonged to every denomination, and many of them had recently been recalled to active duty with the American Navy. These fine young men were deeply moved by her talk, and when it was over they gathered around her and eagerly plied her with questions.

The last Service of the Mission was held in St. Bartholomew's Church, one of the largest, most beautiful and most fashionable churches in New York. This was the last time Dorothy was to have an opportunity of speaking to the American public. There was about this final

Address some extra quality of 'other world' love, beauty and power, that drew a tremendous response from her congregation. Rarely had such unity of spirit been manifested, such sense of one-ness in Christ achieved, as at this last Healing Service. It was as though Jesus was Himself present to seal with the crown of His divine blessing the work done in His Name by His faithful servant. He alone knows how many souls, during this strenuous Mission, were given new hope by being brought to knowledge of His Love through her love, and were enabled, because of her burning faith, to experience the reality of the Presence of the Living Christ. It was this transcendent experience that evoked the universal comment, "We have had nothing like this before," and "Life will never be the same again" – a spontaneous witness to the revelation they had been given of the Love and Power of God.

CHAPTER 22

Last Days

ON November 6th, Dorothy arrived back in Burrswood after her successful visit to America. Her physical energies were seriously depleted, for the demands made upon them had been incessant ever since she disembarked from the *Queen Elizabeth* on October 3rd. It was fortunate that the return journey was made by sea and not by air, as this gave her a few days in which to rest before becoming immersed in the many commitments awaiting her at home. She at once busied herself with making the final arrangements for the great annual Thanksgiving Service which was to be held for the first time in London's historic Cathedral of St. Paul on November 8th. A colossal correspondence had piled up in her absence, and for some time her nights were given to answering the letters that required her personal attention. In reality, Dorothy never quite recovered from the effects of her American Mission. Her health, undermined by the years of exacting work and constant fatigue to which it had been mercilessly subjected, was further weakened by the recent drain made upon it. A year of complete rest away from the scene of her work might have halted the deterioration in her heart condition that began to show itself to the concern of her immediate entourage. But there was nobody with sufficient authority to insist upon her doing this, and Dorothy's sensitive conscience would have rejected any such suggestion had it been made by those around her. She appeared to be in the grip of a driving urge to give every minute of the day, and not infrequently of the night as well, to the furtherance of the work her Master had entrusted to her. This insistence upon overtaxing her strength may have been due to a premonition that her days were numbered and that the sands of time were swiftly running out.

Members of the Fellowship gathered in their numbers to attend the Thanksgiving Service in St. Paul's. They travelled to London in spite of the season's threat of dense fog, from remote parts of the country to join in a paean of thanksgiving to God for the safe return of their beloved Foundress. In her Christmas News Letter, Dorothy wrote, "Those who were there will never forget the glory and wonder of that great Service." It was an impressive moment when the Dean welcomed to his Cathedral Christ's faithful servant, sitting inconspicuously among the vast congregation of her friends, followers and supporters, almost everyone of whom had been helped by her personally at some crucial period of crisis in their lives.

"BELOVED in Christ, we welcome you to St. Paul's Cathedral. We are met here to give thanks to Almighty God for the revival within our Church of the ministry of healing; in particular for the miraculous healing of Dorothy Kerin nearly fifty years ago, when she was at the point to die; for His employment of her to bring healing to the sick, comfort to the sorrowful and faith to the faithless, in our own and other lands."

Dorothy's engagements that autumn were exceptionally heavy. She received many requests from churches of all denominations to hold Healing Services and to give them her message. Some of these visits necessitated long night journeys by car. Two outstanding events were Dorothy's appearance in the great Free Trade Hall at Manchester, and her visit to Eton College. She took her seat on the platform of the Free Trade Hall at the side of such notable figures as Dr. Leslie Weatherhead and other shining lights of the Nonconformist religious world. Her Address was unanimously acclaimed as the highlight of the great Methodist Conference. She much enjoyed her visit to Eton College. She had been asked to give a talk to a gathering of the boys, and felt very nervous at the prospect of facing a crowd of critical youngsters. She had no cause to be anxious, for she held their attention throughout the duration of her Address, and the ovation that followed was a sure indication of the extent to which she captured their young hearts.

The year 1962 held prospects of a fourth Mission to Sweden, a visit to Ireland to attend a Healing Conference in Dublin, at which she was to be the chief speaker, and a second mission to America. None of these events were destined to take place. It was becoming increasingly evident that the condition of Dorothy's heart was rapidly worsening.

The doctor earlier referred to as having given up his large and flourishing practice in order to devote his life to God's work at Burrswood was now firmly established there. His presence was a source of great happiness and comfort to Dorothy, who knew she had in him a 'spiritual son' on whom she could rely, in whom she could confide, and to whom she could safely entrust the stewardship of Burrswood, when the time came for her to relinquish her Master's work. She first met Dr. Edward Aubert in 1957. At that time there seemed no likelihood that he could ever leave his practice and bring his family to live in England. The story of how, through a series of circumstances, God released him from his commitments in a way that aroused no resentment in his partners – he was the senior member of a partnership of doctors on the island of Guernsey – is in itself a remarkable story, showing that where God guides, no obstacles can stay the fulfilment of His purposes. There had been an immediate recognition on the part of Dorothy that Edward Aubert belonged to her work in a very special sense, and at the time she said to a friend, "When I go, he will be my successor." Never was choice more wisely inspired. Today, as the head of Burrswood, he is carrying on his shoulders a heavy responsibility with a serenity and a poise that are a sure indication that the Holy Spirit of God works through him.

Dr. Aubert shared the concern of those around Dorothy that she was overtaxing her strength. This letter that he wrote to her shows he tried his best to persuade her to relax and take the rest which she so urgently needed:

"As your physician with responsibility before God for your precious health, I have watched with concern the return of signs of fatigue in your heart, and of strain on your physical resources. I believe the long trips to Cheltenham and to Leamington, and the extra exertion associated with preparing for Christmas, are responsible. I have not said anything before, partly because I knew how difficult it was for you to stop your activities prior to Christmas, and partly because you had given me your word that you would let me know whenever you felt your heart might be showing signs of strain under its heavy programme. I suggest that your tremendous sense of duty – which I greatly admire, even though it not infrequently militates against the extra rest I would like to see you taking – is urging you on. I find it hard to believe that it is His will that you should drive yourself to this extent, and I therefore beg of you to take a day in bed at the first opportunity."

1962 was also the year of the Golden Jubilee of Dorothy's miraculous healing. A Thanksgiving Service was held in St. Martin-in-the-Fields to commemorate this event on Sunday, February 18th. No one who was present at this Service is likely to forget the poignant experience. Long before the hour at which the Service was to begin, the Church commenced to fill, so that by 2.30 not a seat was vacant. Down the centre and side aisles chairs had been hurriedly placed by the vergers and were immediately occupied by those fortunate enough to obtain them. The atmosphere pulsated with the tremendous volume of love that converged from all parts of the church upon the small radiant figure, dressed in soft grey, when she rose from her seat in the stalls and asked the congregation to join with her in praising and thanking God for all the blessings vouchsafed her ministry over the years. This was to be the last occasion when Dorothy would address the Fellowship who had so faithfully supported her work and had given her their utmost trust and unbounded love.

There was a surprise in store for the congregation. Before the pronouncement of the Blessing by the Bishop of Coventry, the choir sang these beautiful words set to music by Handel:

> "*Let the bright Seraphim in burning row, their loud uplifted trumpets blow.*
> *Let the Cherubic host, in tuneful choirs, touch their immortal harps with golden wires.*"

The surprise lay in the accompaniment to the music by the famous trumpeter, David Mason, whose incomparable mastery over his instrument made its silvery notes soar heavenwards in a rendering of unsurpassed perfection. Its effect was to make those listening feel around them the heavenly choirs rejoicing and giving thanks to Almighty God, together with the 2000 souls assembled in the church, for that miraculous healing of fifty years ago, and for the glorious fruitful ministry that had resulted from it. As the congregation moved from the 'other-worldly' atmosphere of this Service to the noisy streets of the great city outside, love, joy and thanksgiving filled every heart for the privilege of having been present in St. Martin-in-the-Fields on this occasion of the Golden Jubilee Thanksgiving.

Much against her own inclination, Dorothy went on a short holiday to Italy in May. She was not in a fit condition to go abroad, and should have spent the time resting quietly at home, enjoying the beauty of her lovely garden, and surrounded with the care she needed. But a life-long habit of thought for others prevented her from voicing her disinclination to travel. She had arranged to go with three friends, and it was her fear of their disappointment that made her put aside her own wishes. The holiday was a nightmare for all concerned. Hardly a day passed without Dorothy suffering from a painful heart attack. Each time these became progressively more acute, until, towards the end, it seemed problematical whether she could be got back to England. Mercifully, this was achieved, though at great physical cost to herself, and for three weeks she rested on the strict orders of her doctor. It was during this period that there took place a supernatural happening that deeply influenced the entire community and reassured them as to the likelihood of her recovery.

Dorothy asked to be anointed with the Holy Oils. Burrswood's Chaplain was away at the time, but, staying in Chapel House together with his wife, was a saintly old priest, who was so emptied of selfhood that he had become a pure channel for God's sanctifying grace. It was at the hour of Compline that the administration to Dorothy of the Holy Oils took place in her own private Oratory. There were present Father Browning and his wife, and the three permanent members of the household. Dorothy was the last to enter the Oratory, and she knelt close to the altar by the statue of our Lady of Sorrows. Father Browning said the prayers appropriate to the occasion, and then anointed Dorothy, after which he left the Oratory. The rest of the little group remained on their knees to supplicate the Divine Physician to grant healing to His servant to whom long ago He had said, "I will love thee with an everlasting love, and I will never leave thee."

The minutes slipped by and the silence deepened as each prayed for the beloved disciple, who had served her Master so well and given Him all she had; who loved Him and dwelt in Him wholly, and whom Jesus had called to the Way of the Cross which she had trodden uncomplainingly in the blind obedience of uttermost love.

Quite suddenly, the atmosphere became charged with supernatural Power. Dorothy rose to her feet and stretched out her arms towards the Crucifix on the altar. Her face, which had looked so drawn, became transfigured with a light not of this world. Her eyes were fixed on SOMEONE who was visible to her, but remained invisible to those kneeling. Then Dorothy spoke in a voice that was hers, and yet in some strange way not hers, "He says, '*I will make unto thee a new heart*'." She then withdrew to her bedroom, and the awestruck but comforted little group quietly dispersed to their rooms.

The News Letter of July, 1962, contains this expression of Dorothy's belief that she was on the high road to recovery:

"I want to take this opportunity of thanking you all for the help of your prayers during my recent illness – a heart attack the doctors say brought on by overwork and lack of rest. It was such an enormous help and comfort to know that I was being upheld by your prayers and love, and, of course, through it all I had that wonderful promise from our Lord made at the time of my Anointing: 'I will make unto thee a new heart.' This promise has been abundantly fulfilled, and, thanks be to God, I am completely restored."

The question is sometimes asked why this promise was not honoured, for God does not mock his children with false pledges. But our Lord did not say He would make Dorothy a new heart for what remained to her of life on earth; we must not forget that she was verging on 73, and that her body, not only her heart, was spent with a life-time of toil in her Master's vineyard. This "new heart" awaited her on the other side of the veil, now wearing so thin. Since Dorothy's death a number of explanations have been put forward, but surely the simplest and most likely is to be found in our Lord's use of the little pronoun "thee". Our Lord clearly stated the "new heart" was to be given to Dorothy, not to any other person or group of individuals. So Christ the Healer is still continuing His gracious ministry among us, and we are in no doubt that the prayers of the saints are being effectually used – not least those of our beloved Dorothy – in this His healing Ministry. We can rejoice that in the communion of Saints, she now offers to our Lord the powers of this glorified and renewed heart, with all the immensity of love and compassion.

It was, however, very natural that the 'wishful thinking' of the community should converge upon the hope of recovery that the message seemed to hold, and the improvement in Dorothy's health which followed for a time bore this out. She took an active part in the dedication of St. Luke, the resident doctor's house, when Bishop Grey of Connecticut visited Burrswood to perform this ceremony on June 7th. She wrote in her News Letter, "the Russell Brothers with their usual ability and skill have built a house of grace and beauty which we hope will be a very happy home for our beloved Physician. It is impossible to assess how great a blessing he has already become. We do indeed thank God for His good gift."

Far from curtailing her activities, Dorothy added to them by increasing the number of Healing Services held in the week from two to three. For those who could not come on week-days, she established a

Service on Sunday afternoon at 3.30 with the approval and blessing of her Diocesan Bishop and her Bishop Visitor.

Summer gave place to autumn with no perceptible improvement in Dorothy's health. From time to time she had heart attacks, and she looked increasingly frail. It was noticeable how quickly she tired, but she did not seem able to limit her activities to the immediate needs of her work at Burrswood, and continued to do her utmost to meet the calls that came to her from all parts of the country.

Owing to a series of unpredictable circumstances which had their origin in the United States, it had been decided to postpone the second Mission to America, much to her regret. This was a merciful dispensation of Providence, because Dorothy could not have coped with the tremendous demands this Mission must have made upon her fast dwindling strength. Her great, courageous heart, so utterly selfless where her Master's work was concerned, grieved nevertheless at this postponement of the opportunity to consolidate the work so successfully begun the previous year in Christ's Name and for His glory.

A new interest gladdened these last months of Dorothy's life. Gladys Modin had acquired a charming little cottage at Fairlight near Hastings; it was to be used as a holiday resort. It stands on the edge of a cliff overlooking a wide expanse of sea, and is a perfect retreat in which to obtain the conditions essential for creative writing. Gladys and her friend occupied the upper part of the house, and she decided to let the lower rooms to a suitable tenant. She mentioned her intention to Dorothy, who, to Gladys's joyous surprise, in her usual humble way, asked if she might be considered a 'suitable' tenant, and the matter was quickly settled between them.

Dorothy got immense pleasure and real refreshment out of furnishing her rooms in the "ARK", as she christened the little house in memory of a cottage she had owned in bygone years. Readers will recall that it was at this previous ARK that she had had the remarkable vision of the Cross and the Dove. Dorothy intended to retire for some weeks to the ARK in the spring of 1963 in order to write the book which for many months she had been feeling a strong urge to embark upon. Twice she had seen an Angel with a golden pen in his hand pointed towards her: this she had taken to be an indication that it was in God's pattern for her to write this book. It was to be called *Out of an Acorn, an Oak*, and in her mind she had already conceived the form it was to take and decided upon the contents of its chapters. The first chapter was to open with this question addressed to the reader, "What is the earliest thing you can remember?", and she intended to follow this up by relating her own earliest memory when, as a small child, she saw our Lord coming towards her, holding in the palm of His outstretched Hand a tiny brown object. "Tend this with obedience," He had said to her, "and I will water it with the dew of my love, and one day you shall behold a mighty oak."

It is much to be regretted that this book was never written. It would have contained the cream of Dorothy's life experiences; it would have been the means of disclosing to the world some of the revelations which, from time to time, Jesus had unveiled to His disciple on those occasions when He had 'walked and talked with her in the garden of her soul'.

Early in December, Dorothy asked the Bishop of Rochester, her Diocesan Bishop, the Bishop of Coventry, Bishop Visitor of the Burrswood Fellowship, and the Suffragan Bishop of Tonbridge, under whose immediate care Burrswood is, to come to Chapel House in order to discuss with her the formation of a Trust. After dinner, they all adjourned to the drawing-room to examine more closely this problem that was of such supreme importance for the future of Burrswood. Each Bishop in turn expressed his opinion that it was very necessary to establish such a Trust so that, when the time came for its Foundress to lay down her charge, Burrswood could continue to be a focal point for the Church's Ministry of Divine Healing. Dorothy then expressed her willingness to do everything possible to expedite the formation of a Trust, and she asked each Bishop if he would be willing to become a member of it, and each one gave his consent.

This important matter of the formation of a Trust had for long been in Dorothy's mind. Two years before she had instructed her solicitor to draw up a draft setting out the objects for which the Trust was to be established, but the project had remained in abeyance. Dorothy's answer to those who questioned her in their anxiety to see Burrswood safeguarded never varied: "I have received no guidance in the matter." In every important development of her work throughout the years of its expansion, she had always received her directive from the Master she loved, served and obeyed. Can it be wondered at that she hesitated to submit His work to any limitation, until she received from Him the clear guidance which had never hitherto failed her?

For some weeks prior to Christmas, Dorothy shopped in London, whenever she could spare the time, to purchase presents for her children and friends, as well as for all who would be spending the

Festival at Burrswood: patients, guests and the members of her Staff. As she had always done, ever since she opened her first Home of Healing at Ealing fifty years before, she selected each gift and wrapped it herself, enclosing her own personal message of love and good wishes to each individual. On Christmas Eve, she placed her last gift on the last trayload of presents to be added to the piles on the big round table in St. Michael's Hall, ready for distribution after the midnight Mass. Shortly before midnight she prepared to go over to the church. As she was slowly descending the stairs, it was noticeable how pale and drawn she looked. At the bottom of the stairs she paused and said with a little sob in her voice, "I can't go on." She turned to go up the stairs again to her room, but halfway up she collapsed, unable to move. The two doctors, Dr. Elliott and Dr. Aubert, were quickly on the scene and carried her to her bed. She revived sufficiently to insist that everyone should go to the midnight Service, except her personal attendant and devoted friend, Kathleen Burke-Collis, whom she kept with her.

Thereafter, except for two days at the beginning of January, Dorothy never left her room again. There came the unforgettable night when a heart attack of exceptional violence threatened to end her life. Dr. Aubert waged a grim battle with death, and not until the early hours of the morning did he pronounce her to be out of immediate danger. Several attacks occurred during the nights that followed, and Dorothy suffered much pain. In those last days, Edward Aubert, so soon to succeed her in the stewardship of Burrswood, drew very close to Dorothy in love and spiritual understanding. All that medical skill and devoted care could do he lavished upon her. A few of those closest to her were allowed to see her, but for the most part every effort was made to keep her as quiet as possible. Jummie, her faithful old friend of thirty-five years, was constantly at her side, and Dorothy clung to her. "Give me those dear hands of yours, Jummie, that have worked so hard for me," she said, two days before her release, and for a long while she held them pressed in hers. Francis, her eldest son, was the only one of her nine adopted children who was with her that Christmas, and her joy in his presence and loving attentions was touching to see.

Burrswood was deep in snow, as was the whole of England, and a great stillness enveloped the place. It was very cold, but Dorothy liked to have her windows wide open at night, and seemed to crave for air. She complained a good deal of thirst, and Kathleen, who slept in her room at night, would bring her frequent cups of tea. Never once was she heard to protest against her cruel suffering. When, after an attack of pain had subsided, she could say with a wan smile, "It's better now", one knew she was happy at being able to give this comfort to those around her.

The Bishop of Coventry had written to ask if he could spend the night of January 22nd at Burrswood, as he was to speak at Tonbridge. His visit was an immense joy to Dorothy, and it was arranged that he should anoint her before going to his engagement, and give her Holy Communion from her Oratory on the following morning. The Staff assisted at what was to be the last time they would share our Lord's Supper Table with their beloved friend and head. For many nights they had kept vigil in the church, relieving each other at intervals, and during those silent watches of the night, as they prayed our Lord to restore Dorothy to them, they forged a common soul that was to stand them in good stead during the first months of the shock of their bereavement.

Late on the night of the 25th, a heart specialist came from London to give Dorothy a thorough examination. It was decided she would be taken on Sunday to the Cardiac Department at Brompton Hospital to receive there the treatment he told her would hasten the recovery he considered she had a good chance of making. After he left the room, she settled herself to sleep with her customary prayer:

> And now I will lay me down in peace, and take my rest, for it is Thou, Lord, only that makest me to dwell in safety. In peace in the selfsame, I will sleep and I will rest, for Thou, O Lord, hast settled me in hope. Thanks be to God. Amen.

After a short pause she added: I LOVE HIM . . . I LOVE HIM . . . I LOVE HIM. No words can convey the limitless extent of the love contained in this expression of her uttermost devotion to Him in whom she had dwelt all her life.

On Saturday morning, January 26th, while Dr. Aubert was sitting by her bed, discussing with her plans for the future, she suddenly gave a little sigh and fell forward. All efforts to restore life by artificial respiration were of no avail. He summoned the stunned community to meet him that afternoon in the Church, where he read the following statement to them:

"At 11.15 this morning, while talking quietly to me about the present and the future, our dear Dorothy suddenly slipped from us. There was no warning, no premonition, no apprehension, no distress; just a little sigh and her spirit was away.

"This is not what we wanted. This is not what we expected. I must tell you that a heart specialist saw her last night. I had asked Dorothy several times since Christmas to let me bring one to see her, for I wanted her to have the best possible advice obtainable. Each time she had said, 'I do not want to see any other doctor at this moment, but if at any time I do, I will tell you.' On Thursday, she told me the time had come when she would like to hear the advice of a heart specialist. So, last night the senior cardiologist from the Brompton Hospital came to see her. He at once gained her confidence. He told her she had been critically ill with her heart, and that few people would have survived what she had been through. But she was now beginning to improve. He felt that her convalescence would be speeded up and made safer if she would come into hospital for special forms of treatment which could only be given in hospital. He thought she would be well enough to be driven up to London by Sunday or Monday and we were making plans to do this.

"This is not the moment to go into details about the future. Suffice it to say that I know it was her wish that Burrswood should continue. In fact she had told me more than once that she *saw* it continuing. So let us all – those who, to use her phrase, have borne the heat and burden of the day, as well as those who have only recently thrown in their lot with her – close our ranks and do our duty, for her, and for her Master."

Dorothy looked very beautiful as she lay on her bed in the still majesty of death. All trace of suffering had gone from her face: it was translucent and ethereal, shedding a radiance from those heavenly places to which she had gone, and there was around her an exquisite scent of flowers. Our Lord had called his disciple home to Him in the 'twinkling of an eye,' and the PEACE that surpasses our understanding held her in its embrace. She wore the expression of one who is listening, listening . . . surely it was to the Voice she knew so well, welcoming His faithful and obedient servant into citizenship of the Eternal City of God.

There can be no better ending with which to close this unique story of a disciple called by Christ to heal than these majestic words spoken at Dorothy's Funeral Service by the Bishop of Rochester from the chancel step of her beautiful Church of Christ the Healer, as her earthly vesture was about to be taken to its last resting place in the village churchyard at Groombridge:

Go forth upon thy journey from this world, O Christian Soul.
In the Peace of Him in Whom thou hast believed.
In the Name of God the Father Who created thee.
In the Name of Jesus Christ Who suffered for thee.
In the Name of the Holy Ghost who strengtheneth thee.
In Communion with the blessed Saints and aided by Angels and Archangels, and all the armies of the heavenly host.
May thy portion this day be in peace, and thy dwelling in the Heavenly Jerusalem.
Go forth upon thy journey, O Christian soul.

WHITSUN, 17th May, 1964
Burrswood, Groombridge,
Kent.

Index